MARGOT FONTEYN

'This is a most un-ballerinaish autobiography in that Fonteyn makes minimal reference to her roles, her triumphs and, mercifully, there is not a single quote from any adulatory criticism. What is so refreshing is that it is all about a woman and although she never in one sentence gives the slightest intimation of it, she emerges as a woman great as the sublime artist acclaimed throughout the world.'

Dance and Dancers

'It is an extraordinary life-story to set beside those other extraordinary lives of Taglioni, Elssler, Pavlova and Karsavina.'

Books and Bookmen

MARGOT FONTEYN

Autobiography

A STAR BOOK
published by
WYNDHAM PUBLICATIONS

ACKNOWLEDGMENTS

My deepest thanks to Robin Duff, Chairman of Scottish Ballet, for scrutinizing with such kindness, patience and humour the text of this book. Also to David Scrase for research, and to Carole McPhee for deciphering my longhand manuscripts.

Further, my warmest appreciation of the sympathetic help given by my English editor, David Hately, and by Robert Gottlieb of Alfred A. Knopf, Inc.

PROLOGUE

On 8 June 1900, an English boy aged eleven set sail from Southampton with his parents and his sister, three years younger than himself. They were bound for Brazil. His father's family had been mainly literary and musical, and his mother's family included a minor composer. Several of his uncles were active musicians or teachers of music. His father had broken with family tradition by going into engineering, and it was in this capacity that he had agreed to go to Brazil to take over management of the tiny railway line running from the mines up in the hills of Santa Catarina State down to the sea at Imbituba, south of Santos. The little family set off with household and medical supplies for five years, because they could expect to find few amenities in the tiny coastal village, which lacked representatives of either the law, the church, medicine or education.

In the end they stayed only two years, during which time the boy and his sister ran happily about the beach in absolute freedom. They learned Portuguese and ate Brazilian feijoada – black bean stew. The father of the family took home some Brazilian woods when they returned to England, from which he made tables of his own design in his basement workshop. Later, his grandchildren loved to visit his workshop, because of the scent of freshly cut wood shavings, and because, in his old age, he was such a very sweet old man, never saying a reproving word. He used to write charming verses for his granddaughter about obscure animals, such as the cacomistle.

The little boy was my father; and he chose as his wife a black-eyed beauty, the daughter of an Irish mother and a Brazilian father.

My parents called their two children Felix and Margaret, after my father and his sister, the little boy and girl who had lived so freely in the sun of Imbituba for two years. Somehow or other the second little Margaret became 'Margot Fonteyn'. Exactly how or why this happened is a considerable mystery to me.

There are some clues in the musicians on my father's side; in the Brazilian love of dancing on my mother's; and in the early travels of my father's adventurous family. Thereafter I think one must look at the myriad tiny pieces of experience encountered in life. They build up slowly like coral, in haphazard formations, until one day one considers the result, and says – 'How odd! That is me.'

ONE

Trying to remember myself as a child, I see something like an outline drawing of the adult that I am now – fundamentally the same person, but nothing filled in. I had the same character and temperament, and the same brain, though the problems that confronted me, however baffling they seemed at the time, were tiny by comparison with the complexities of my subsequent life. I see myself then as a simple, logical person proceeding on a direct course, unaware of alternative paths and therefore – mercifully – ignorant of the strain of making decisions.

I can find no characteristics in myself, or at least no good ones, that do not obviously come from my parents. My mother has a tremendous love of life. She can be caught up in a sudden enthusiasm for some new project, but has little will to persevere if it cannot be accomplished fairly easily. Perhaps she could have been a pianist, given the opportunity and more patience. She has a sensitive response to rhythm and music, and more particularly to movement, such as the wind blowing on a field of wheat, or a beautiful horse show-jumping. Most of all she appreciates grace and line in dancing. She is impulsive, and not much given to any strict or monotonous way of living or routine. My father, on the other hand, is a perfectionist in everything he undertakes. He will happily spend hours, days, weeks solving a problem of engineering or mathematics or whatever it may be. He likes everything neatly organized and working efficiently. By a happy mixture of these qualities I find that I myself have no interest in, or patience for, anything I'm unlikely to do fairly well, but have a bulldog tenacity to complete successfully anything on which I have once embarked.

My father gets on well with anyone; he is even-tempered,

tolerant and makes the best of whatever surroundings he may find himself in. He likes the tropics, but could be happy on a mountaintop. Although my mother inspires affection in all who know her, she is basically shy and able to be fond of very few people. She does not suffer fools gladly, but she has a quick instinct for the people and places she likes. Warm-hearted people and cheerful, light surroundings are essential to her.

I have something from each parent: I am sometimes desperately shy, and sometimes quite at ease with strangers. Just occasionally I take a violent dislike to someone I hardly know. More usually I think everyone has a beautiful character until I learn otherwise.

Comparing the outline drawing of that small child with the person I am now, only the ability to laugh at myself was then completely missing. Luckily my father's favourite pastime was to tease me. He would tell me all kinds of ridiculous things as though they were true, and laugh at me if I didn't see the catch in them. I soon learned that it was wisest to join in the joke even though it was at my own expense.

For many years the demands of my career carried me far away from my true self as though in a great arc, which has become clearly visible only now that I am well advanced on the return curve. The surprise is to find how little the adult has changed from the child I can remember, starting from about 1922, in which year, on 18 May, I was three.

We lived in a small house in the London suburb of Ealing. The rooms were light, giving on to a small garden in front and a larger one at the back, where there was an interesting wooden summer house, or perhaps it was just a garden shed.

To one so tiny the staircase was always an area of adventure. It was while playing about the stairs that I one day succeeded in flying. Whether I fell or slid or what happened I'll never know, but for a brief moment I

14

achieved the glorious sensation of flying freely through the air like a fairy and landing without a bump, four steps farther down. It was an experience never to be forgotten, and never to be repeated either, even though I tried and tried again.

About this time I awoke one day to find it was seemingly night. Everyone else disregarded this fact and continued to behave as though it was day. I asked repeatedly whether we should not go to bed as it was so dark, but they brushed it all aside and their explanation that it was called 'fog' did nothing to help me comprehend why they insisted on pretending we were in daytime. The whole matter perplexed me deeply. Needless to say, it was one of the old-time fogs, known as 'pea soupers', that have been obsolete for many a year now.

Another morning I was not allowed to climb into my parents' bed as usual because we had to set off early on some strange thing called a journey. This one, the first of hundreds, took us to the coast – and so a new element of great importance entered my young life: the sea. For it has most often been in moments on the sea, or by the sea, with the sun blazing and the breeze blowing in my face, that I have experienced the sense of total freedom and happiness. At sea, too, I first suffered the pain of separation and the bittersweet of nostalgia.

Minor things can become moments of great revelation when encountered for the very first time. One summer day, at our garden gate, I made the fascinating discovery that by holding my ankles and putting my head between my feet I could look through and survey upside down the whole world – which at that time consisted only of our quiet street. It was like Alice stepping through the looking-glass, a fantastic magic revelation. I remained there a while, lost in this wonder. Just then a maiden aunt came out of the house and said, 'Don't do that; it's a most unbecoming position.' Picqued by this reproof I went to the end of the back garden feeling very sorry for myself. A neighbour whose garden looked on to ours happened to be working on his herbaceous border. He looked over the fence and seeing my misery gave me a bunch of snap-dragons, showing me how to press the sides of the flowers together so that their jaws would open and close. All elated I rushed back to show my mother, but the instincts of Eve had been aroused and the next day I lingered as though casually by the fence. When I took the second bunch of snapdragons to my mother she told me that it was not polite to ask for presents. 'I didn't ask for them, Mummy, I just said I liked the flowers he gave me yester-day.' It was my first attempt at coquetry.

It must have been quite a while later, about two years at least, that I was suddenly and overwhelmingly struck with the greatest revelation of all: that I was an individual person different from anyone else. There was only one me in the whole of the world. It happened quite un-accountably in mid-afternoon, and I stood stockstill for several minutes, just where I was at the foot of the stairs, pondering on this strange new idea. That moment I count as the start of my conscious life.

My brother Felix, three years older than me, was always my hero. He had my unfailing devotion and respect from the very beginning, excepting only the day he threw the worm at me in the garden. It was alive, of course, and hit me just at the side of my mouth. I didn't like Felix at all that day.

Other children didn't attract me much, and when they did I was too shy to speak to them. Dolls didn't interest me and neither did children's parties. I dreaded the blancmange, and the noise of bursting balloons. The only good part was dressing up in the costumes made by my mother from the patterns in *Weldon's Book of Fancy Dress Costumes for Parties*. How I loved to pore over the designs until I knew them all by heart – the Mephisto-pheles, with pointed toes and forked tail, the Domino, the Penguin, the Gypsy and a host of others. Children's party games frightened me, except for musical chairs and sardines.

My mother was very insistent upon good manners. She could not abide spoilt children. Her best weapon for discipline was 'the look'. It was quite remarkable in its intensity, her black eyes fixing directly on Felix or me as she said very definitely, 'That's enough!' 'Be quiet!' We knew immediately that discretion was the better part of valour, and slunk off docilely to some innocent occupation in another part of the house. I could never stand being scolded; the sense of having done wrong upset me so terribly that I generally tried to be obedient and do all that was expected of me. At the same time, I had a stubborn rebellious streak that manifested itself most strongly on the question of food. Here I had certain eccentric preferences, and very strong dislikes, which nothing in the world could force me to overcome. As the dislikes included meat, fish, vegetables, eggs and milk, my mother was extremely concerned about me until the family doctor observed, 'She looks healthy enough, so let her be.'

Thereafter she stopped worrying as she left me in the charge of a waitress at Paul's Tea Shop in Ealing Broadway while she went shopping; and there I would eat my way methodically through as many doughnuts as I could manage in her absence, usually at least six, always biting carefully round the jammy centre and saving it till last. I sat alone at a table near the Art Nouveau fireplace, gazing at a large china cat with a very elongated neck and getting my fingers incredibly sticky. I never uttered a word except to say, 'Yes please,' when the waitress offered more doughnuts.

Sometimes at home there would be a head-on collision with my mother over some carefully prepared new dish. 'I don't like it,' I said as it was placed before me on the table. 'How do you know you don't like it if you haven't tasted it?' she asked, reasonably enough. 'I know I don't like it,' I replied stubbornly. 'Oh, don't be so obstinate,' said my mother, beginning to get cross. But it was useless.

Once my mother blindfolded me and told me I was going to get a favourite dish, and that I must guess what it was. This ruse aroused my suspicions at once, so I refused it, adamantly. Sure enough it was the hated egg – scrambled – that she was hoping to trick me into accepting. On another occasion she sent me upstairs to bed for refusing to taste roast lamb, but I won that day, too, by raising a temperature and having to be nursed for three days.

I never resented my mother's attempts to make me eat what she considered good for me. I just thought grown-ups extremely dense. The curious thing is that my instincts were not purely capricious, for many of the foods I declined as a child still do not suit me. I suppose I will end up as I started, living on bread and butter, potatoes, cheese and baked beans.

My mother showed a lot of imagination in her attempts to keep me from getting bored and so annoying her. One simple trick, which worked well until I was about six years old, was the cushion, the pin and the lump of sugar. It involved first sending me to fetch a pin, which she then put on the floor under a cushion. If I sat on the cushion for long enough without speaking, the fairies would trans-form the pin into a lump of sugar. If I looked at the pin myself the fairies wouldn't come near. If I spoke, the transformation would take longer. From time to time my mother would come into the room and look under the cushion. 'Oh dear,' she would say, 'it's still a pin. I'll come back in a minute to see if they've changed it.' Then she went off and finished baking the cake, or whatever she was occupied with, and when it was done she looked under the cushion again and exclaimed, 'Look now! There's the lump of sugar; the fairies have changed it at last.'

My father bought a Stoneleigh car in which we were supposed to go for country drives on Sundays. The picnic would be prepared, my mother would have us ready to leave – and my father would be found underneath the car or with his head inside the bonnet repairing the engine, or more likely making an improvement, as he was inge-nious and inventive. The sun would go behind the clouds and my mother would get furious. Then, all in his own time, my father finished the job, wiped the oil off his hands and climbed into the driving seat. Off we went, Felix and I counting cows or policemen or devising some

18

other game for the day's outing. Sometimes my father exclaimed, 'Look up there, over on the right! There's an aeroplane.' We didn't see one every week. I would gaze at it solemnly, imagining what it must be like to climb up that long high ladder to get aboard. A year or so passed before he said one Sunday, 'Do you see over there? That's an aerodrome where the aeroplanes land and take off.' I found it quite an extraordinary idea that planes should come down to the ground, but I was also rather relieved to know that I would never have to climb the precarious ladder swaying in the wind.

Soon we moved to a larger house in Elm Grove Road. It had a marvellous billiard room, perfectly suited to all kinds of games, such as careering around the polished floor on cushions taken from the raised spectators' seating. At this point I suddenly became obsessed with the prospect of being able to read. I took great pride in learning the alphabet, and I seem to have learned it remarkably quickly as I skipped along beside my father across Ealing Common on the way to my first school lessons with a governess at the house of some friends. Books soon became a top priority in my life, and reading aloud from *Winnie-the-Pooh* was my favourite way of showing off to admiring relatives.

Aunt Margaret came to stay and was taken ill with pneumonia. It was a most dramatic and exciting time for Felix and me. The doctor called three times a day, cylinders of oxygen were delivered, and, when she became delirious and saw snakes under a glass cake cover in her bedroom, there were day and night nurses. A telegram, which was an exceptional event in itself, had to be carefully worded to summon my grandparents from Devonshire without causing them excessive alarm. After three desperate days the moment of crisis was safely passed, to the slight disappointment of Felix and myself, although we adored Aunt Margaret. Excitement was restored when the doctor ordered champagne for her convalescence, and a lot of mirth issued from the sick-room, which we were at last allowed to visit. A conviction that champagne is good for the health must date from that time; after all, it was prescribed by the doctor for someone who had very nearly died.

My seafaring started with a cross-channel trip for a holiday at Ambleteuse. It was here that Felix showed early signs of his analytical mind when he observed, apropos of the traffic driving on the right side of the road instead of the left as in England, 'Careless people, the French.' In the realm of ballet, I have many a time had reason to remember his words.

Our next voyage was to the tiny island of Lundy. It was an unforgettably rough crossing that had the whole family dreadfully seasick. Lundy at that time still had the distinction of minting its own money. The currency was in puffins, named after a local sea bird.

There were besides all manner of exciting events, such as the eclipse of the sun in 1927, with my father carefully smoking pieces of glass for us to look through, and the general strike of 1926, when my father, along with other businessmen normally bound to office life, was enabled to indulge his love of steam locomotives (with which he was very familiar from his childhood years in Brazil) by acting as a volunteer driver. We went down to Ealing Broadway station to see him on the footplate of the West Country 'Express', taking with us lovingly prepared picnic baskets, warm mufflers and other such comforts for the brave.

I had often heard grow-ups talking about 'going to the pictures'. Since the only pictures I saw when we went shopping were those of birthdays and weddings in a big glass frame outside the photographer's studio, I imagined that one of the strange practices of adults seeking amusement was to go down at night to the Broadway and stare into all these windows. It sounded awfully boring. Enlightenment came with Charlie Chaplin in *The Gold Rush*. What an ideal introduction to the cinema that was!

So it was really all there by the time I was six. I had won a pink sash for dancing the best polka in my class. I had encountered the sea and travel. I loved to laugh and dress up, and I knew devotion as well as the rudiments of flirting. I believe too that from the age of six I sensed the existence of just such a person as my husband. Had we met then, a silent, black-eyed little boy, and a round-faced, solemn little girl, we would have had a wordless understanding as deep as the deep blue sea.

My childhood was carefree. Dancing had crept into it early as a natural part of life. Then, as now, it was some-thing to be taken very seriously when engaged in and otherwise put out of mind. It is generally believed that my father suggested I should have lessons in deportment, heaven knows why, and that my mother accordingly took me to the local dancing teacher. But the circumstances of my initial attendance at Miss Bosustow's Academy are too indistinct in the minds of those concerned for anyone to be really sure.

Miss Grace Bosustow lived in a pretty little house just around the corner at the end of our street, about three minutes' walk I should think. One passed through a gar-den gate and almost immediately up two front steps, and rang the doorbell. Inside, the house seemed very quiet when one attended for private lessons. The rooms had delicate furniture, small knickknacks on the tables and white lace mats and antimacassars. No children seemed ever to have lived there, but it was a happy house to go to because of Miss Bosustow herself. She had the ideal per-sonality for teaching infants, always cheerful and en-couraging and completely absorbed in what we were doing. Her degree of concentration held ours, so she rarely had inattentive pupils.

The room to the right of the front door had almost no furniture. On the wall opposite the window was a barre for ballet exercises, and there was a large mirror near the fireplace. The most particular feature in my memory is the linoleum – deep green with a bluish tinge like the colour I was to see again so often in the wake of big ocean liners. I remember the floor so well probably because my eye level was quite near to it. A frame on the wall showed photographs of Dame Adeline Genée demonstrating the five positions of the arms in ballet.

When I was still only four years old I made my stage debut. I was a 'Wind' in the babies' ballet that opened the programme, and I also appeared later in the proceedings. But it was Felix who, according to the programme, was featured as a principal dancer, though none of us, not even my mother, can remember the event. It was definitely not his world, what with all the fussing over offspring in pink tulle, pastel georgette and rosebuds.

Luckily my mother was sensible and practical. While concealing her satisfaction as she watched my progress, she became useful at the school – learning how to make ballet skirts, elves' costumes, Irish peasant dress, crino-lines and the like for school displays. She did not push her child or demand solo dances or give what Miss Bosustow called 'mother trouble'. As a reward she was able to in-dulge in a little pride as I passed my first Association of Operatic Dancing examination with honours and 85 marks. The certificate was framed for my bedroom wall, and the occasion merited a visit in full regalia to the photographer. 'Week', my soft toy rabbit, had to be taken along to divert my attention when I got bored with posing before the mysterious contraption manipulated by a man who kept hiding behind it under a black cloth.

In those days I never heard the word 'ballet'. People talked of dancing and of dancers. Anna Pavlova was the magic name. One day, trotting along holding my mother's hand as we went shopping, we stopped at the hairdressing salon. Hanging on a card in the shop was a photograph of a dancer in costume. It was a playbill advertising forth-coming performances in London. It seems that I asked my mother, 'Who is that lady?' 'That is Anna Pavlova, darling, the greatest dancer in the world.' I gave this a moment or two of reflection and said, 'Then I'll be the second greatest!' Modesty had evidently not yet entered my soul. My mother forthwith arranged for us to see Pavlova at the Palace Theatre but, unfortunately, I cannot say that this experience was the inspiration of my dancing life, nor even that I was transported into an unimagined fairy-tale world. Nowadays, when loving mothers assure me that their little daughters will be for ever enriched, inspired or whatever else, by my performance, I am more than dubious, remembering that had my mother not drawn attention to the way in which Pavlova was performing her *retirés* I might have no memory at all of that genius of the dance. My mother's comment clearly implied that my own *retirés* could stand some improvement, but, with a dozen or so lessons behind me, I did not agree at all and found her suggestion deeply wounding. The affront to my vanity acted as a fixative to some faint visual memory of that performance. Alas, I never saw Pavlova again. There was more than vanity involved in the incident, however. Perhaps I should say that it was the early stirrings of professional pride, for undoubtedly I tried harder at the next lesson to satisfy my mother's criticism. I think that the driving force throughout my career has been this compulsion to fulfil the expectations of others. As a child I invariably ran a temperature three days before my dancing examinations, causing terrible anxiety and much telephoning between my teacher and mother. 'Will she be well enough to enter?' 'I don't know. Her temperature is still a hundred.' 'We must see how she is tomorrow.' And so on, until the last moment. Somehow I always recovered just in time and passed the exam to everyone's satisfaction. I was quite unconscious then of my fear of letting them down.

In school displays I was so intent on doing all I had been told that an earnest expression would settle on my face, and during the more difficult steps my tongue would appear out of the corner of my mouth – a trick that helped me to concentrate. It was usual for my mother to stand in the wings and whisper, 'Put your tongue in. Smile.' This was not so necessary in character dances, which I found easy and could perform with a happy grin that at times lacked one or two milk teeth. Certainly, from this time on I was aware that the stage has its own laws. Something has to be created beyond the mere repetition of movements learnt in rehearsal. My attitude has never changed. I cannot imagine feeling lackadaisical about a performance. I treat each encounter as a matter of life and death. The one important thing I have learnt over the years is the difference between taking one's work seriously and taking oneself seriously. The first is imperative and the second disastrous.

TWO

Devotion to my brother dominated the years in Ealing. I was eight when heartbreak came. My father was offered the position of Chief Engineer of the British Cigarette Company in Shanghai, a subsidiary of the British-American Tobacco Company, where he subsequently became Chief Engineer and Director. He would get home leave only every four years, and was advised that Felix, now eleven, should not accompany the rest of us to Shanghai, since boys of his age were usually sent back from the Far East to public school in England. Felix was therefore settled at Ripley and later at Cheltenham College, where he must have spent miserable cold months interspersed with rather lonely holidays at our grandparents' home in Devon. It was decided, however, that my mother and I should return to see him every second year to break up the long separations.

Perhaps Felix and I got on so well because I never questioned male superiority. It suited me perfectly to have an older brother and to do his bidding – to fetch and carry his bicycle repair kit, or to stay at home when he went off on adventures with his school friends. Sometimes I was allowed to join them and would run behind as fast as I could across the nearby housing site, which was still half muddy fields littered with planks and piles of bricks. Best of all was to swoop about Ealing Common on our bicycles, and then spend our pocket money in the little sweet shop on the corner. Now this happy life was coming to an end.

A minor Sino-Japanese conflict made it inadvisable for us to proceed directly to China, and so it was arranged that we should go via the United States and stay there until the trouble had blown over. The Ealing house was sold and on the eve of departure the whole family gathered for dinner at the St Pancras Hotel, where we were to spend the night before embarking. Although the rest of the family was resigned to my unusual diet, my grandmother didn't believe in giving way to children. She positively insisted that I eat some oxtail soup, which allowed me the triumph of being as sick as a dog in bed at three in the morning, causing quite a furor. I left England rather pale, but happy to have scored off Grandma so successfully.

We set sail on 5 November 1927. Suddenly the parting from Felix had become a fact, and in the succeeding days of the voyage I learned that one can look down at the deep, green-grey sea and feel an unbearable melancholy and longing for the companion left each day farther and farther behind. Although I was diverted by the strangeness of life on board, the immense ocean stretching empty to the horizon constantly renewed this unfamiliar sensation of heartache with remembrance that two years must pass before I would see Felix again. There were other children aboard, including golden-haired girl triplets, who were kept in a rarefied atmosphere, well-groomed and unapproachable at all times, as they were on their way to Hollywood and stardom. I once thought I saw them in a Paul Whiteman movie a few years later. There was also a brash little boy who didn't turn out to be at all companionable. He liked to report what he had managed to see by peeping through stateroom windows at the hour when grown-ups were dressing for dinner.

The Atlantic crossing took ten days. Then followed the Statue of Liberty in the morning mist, the busy tugs nuzzling our ship into the quayside, my mother packing the last suitcase and my father going to the purser to change pounds for dollars. Eventually, everyone's passport was stamped by Immigration and we were in the big customs shed, with wardrobe trunks and steamer trunks being opened up all around. We were on American soil for the first time, feeling rather wobbly until we lost our sea legs. Porters deftly managed the mountains of luggage.

We were in New York only two or three days. Our destination was Louisville, Kentucky, where we would wait until conditions were favourable for us to proceed to Shanghai. First, however, we went to Richmond, Virginia, and I was amazed at our train's very un-English behaviour on arrival there, for it ran through the streets, a big bell clanging on its engine, and set us down next to the William Byrd Hotel. Here we encountered the southern accents, the crisp early winter days, the quick squirrels shinning trees in the park, and halting abruptly in their scampering over the grass to observe us with a shining morning eye.

I became my mother's companion, exploring new shops and sightseeing while my father was discovering the tobacco business. I was very aware of the strangeness of the place, of the light, the gardens without fences, the drugstores and hotel coffee shop. My parents liked new places, new people, new foods; the idea of sausage meat covered in syrup on pancakes startled them both, but my father pronounced it a delicious mixture – perhaps the southern corn dishes reminded him of his two years in Brazil as a boy. Warm-hearted black maids and waiters spoiled me. I was quite small, with a very round face, and my hair cut square across my forehead and just above the lobes of my ears.

Our train to Louisville passed through Covington, Virginia, where my father's old friend and schoolmate Dennis Whittle was the Episcopalian minister. We stopped over for a day to visit him, but the Whittles invited me to stay on while my parents went ahead to find a flat. I found everything so strange in this American home, especially the religious emphasis, for which I was unprepared. My mother believed in letting children take to God of their own free will as and when they wished. She had been forced to attend church three times on Sundays as a child, so never went again except for weddings. Consequently, I never went either and knew nothing about the services.

The Whittles had a daughter called Wendy, three years younger than me. We took an immediate and violent dislike to each other. I had always been shy and easily aware of my shortcomings. Wendy soon realized that I was terrified of the telephone and of the toilet flush, that I did not know most of the prayers and couldn't sing carols, that I wouldn't eat eggs or drink milk and that I was generally an inferior being. The final humiliation was having to eat meals with her at a low kiddies' table. For as long as I could remember I had sat at the dining table with the grown-ups. It did not occur to me that my presence might have made her feel equally inferior and put her nose out of joint.

A family friend asked me for my impression of America. I had pictured in my mind an endless wooded landscape peopled by redskins, and I replied cautiously, 'Well, it is not as wild as I had expected.' This caused a lot of merriment, and I vowed to myself that when I grew up I would never laugh at the things children say. In the light of their limited knowledge children are usually absolutely logical. I now try always to take them very seriously.

My parents returned within two weeks, in time for Christmas, which was cold but still crisp and sunny, so unlike the drizzly English climate. A huge fiery cross burned at night on a mountainside. My parents were fascinated to know that it was the work of the Ku Klux Klan, that ominous hooded sect whose dress was quite familiar to me, having been one of my favourites in *Weldon's Book of Fancy Dress Costumes for Parties*. After the strain of trying to fit into American family life, I was happy at being restored to my parents and we moved on to Louisville, where I was entered at the co-educational public

l. This was a long step from a governess in Ealing, at the late age of eight, school was an unknown quantity. Left at the entrance by my mother, I was taken to the classroom and singled out by the mistress for a short preliminary test. The alphabet was my pride. I could rattle it off at great speed and came cleanly through to the end, X, Y, Zed. 'X, Y, *Zee*,' corrected the teacher. 'X, Y, Zed,' I repeated, not knowing what she meant. 'X, Y, *Zee*,' she insisted. 'Zed,' I said stubbornly, and we remained deadlocked. Arithmetic had come easily to me, too, so I had no worry until the teacher reversed the process for subtraction and asked, 'What do you add to two to make four?' Flexibility was not in my nature. I found it impossible to subtract two from four by means of addition. The upshot was another deadlock. After that, I only excelled in things like making a model of George Washington's log cabin, complete with cherry tree. The self-assured children in class did not appeal to me at all. Only one little boy, very clean with fair hair and too shy to speak, reminded me of England. We had a silent friendship, which the others sensed and teased us for, so that I blushed for shame.

School did not provide me with any friends, and the little boy living in the flat above who sought my company to play was considered obnoxious by my whole family. So my mother looked for a dancing school. She found only one in the telephone directory. At the first class, which of course she watched, the combination of some very imperfect ballet movements, with a few high kicks and splits, so appalled her that she said firmly, 'I don't think you will go again; it is better to wait till we find a good teacher like Miss Bosustow.' So that was the end of dancing for the time being. I did not mind at all. There were plenty of diversions, including a visit to the Mammoth Caves in Kentucky, a fairy-tale labyrinth to thrill any child. The three-day train journey to Seattle was full of new experiences, like the big baked potatoes the size of my shoe, which I ate filled with butter for every meal except break-fast, when I ate griddle-cakes.

In Seattle we joined the S.S. *President Jackson*, bound for the Far East. By now a seasoned traveller, I was at home on board ship as soon as we sailed, and again I would spend hours leaning over the rail, gazing at the bottomless ocean. As the days got warmer the sea changed to that deep blue-green colour, like engine oil or Miss Bosustow's linoleum. I missed Felix terribly as the ship cut through the swelling sea farther and farther away from England. I could never have guessed then how much of my life would be spent in separations from the people I love. Travelling carries with it the curse of being at home everywhere and yet nowhere, for wherever one is some part of oneself remains on another continent.

THREE

In spring 1928 the S.S. *President Jackson* sailed into Yoko-hama port, giving us just time enough for visiting the great Buddha of Kamakura and for sending picture post-cards to loved ones far away. Touching land brought home to me a clearer realization of distance: we had arrived at the other side of the world – to go forward or back meant six weeks in either case. The pain of separa-tion was thus fixed in a way that the jet age, with its possi-bilities of reunion in a matter of hours, has happily alleviated for ever.

We steamed through the Inland Sea as voyagers filled with wonder and, a day or two later, awoke in the cool misty morning to see, at last, the coast of China. Excite-ment mounted as we reached the great Yangtze Kiang River, then the Whang Po, and finally dropped anchor off Shanghai on 12 April. There was the famous Bund lying a few hundred yards in front of us. As I looked at this waterfront of sedate banks and turn-of-the-century commercial buildings, I suddenly felt a comfortable sense of familiarity. 'But China looks much more like England than America did!' I said.

The Astor House Hotel was a landmark of the white man in the Far East, like Raffles Hotel in Singapore. At first we were put in the oldest part of the building, known as the barracks because of its high-ceilinged, echoing rooms and corridors. Our rooms were big, sparsely furnished with old-fashioned wardrobes and dressing tables and only a small rug or two on the cool stone floors. Even the bathrooms were vast empty spaces. Each bed had its mosquito net, knotted up like a canopy during the day and tucked under the mattress all around at night. The nets had a curious musty smell and never looked quite clean, nor were they completely effective. My father maintained that he saw the mother mosquitoes pushing their young through the mesh while they were still small enough to get through so that they could grow up inside to torment him. For some reason they never bothered me.

The hotel lobby was furnished with those heavy mahogany chairs and coffee tables considered essential at that period. The Chinese 'boys' who served teas and drinks wore white robes, black cotton trousers and black cloth shoes, and always had a fly swat to hand. The place was crowded with jovial Europeans talking loudly and calling 'Boy! – Bring another round.'

Outside, the busy streets were thronged with rickshaws. I suppose one took taxis for longer journeys, but the rickshaw was the common means of transport. Little shops crowded each other, filled with strange foods, medicines and every kind of merchandise. At night in the 'barracks' bedroom I was frightened by the thought that little men from the noisy street below might climb in through the window, but otherwise I quickly felt at home in Shanghai.

The city really sweltered in summer. One took several cold baths a day to little avail, and it was generally believed that anyone who didn't wear a sun topee, or pith helmet, would get sunstroke. New arrivals from Europe were also told never to drink water that had not first been boiled, to avoid fresh fruits and salads and always to wash with nasty-smelling carbolic soap. Dysentery and cholera were much feared, along with lesser diseases and infections to which we were supposed to be an easy prey. In any case, most infections were a serious matter before the discovery of antibiotics.

My father was made a member of the Shanghai Club, renowned for having the longest bar in the world. It was here that an old resident advised him, 'Hookham, old chap, if you just remember always to keep about two inches of whisky in the bottom of your stomach you will never have any trouble.' Of course he welcomed this agreeable tip and, so far as I know, he was never ill in the twenty years he lived in China.

My mother's experiences in Chinese housekeeping started in the north, in Tientsin, where we settled at the end of May in a house belonging to my father's firm. Tientsin, like Shanghai, was divided into Concessions: French, British, International and so on. Our home was in the Russian Concession, which was a pleasantly old-fashioned sector across the river from the main part of the town. My father's cigarette factory was in that area too. With the company house came a boy, a cook, a coolie, an amah and several relatives, smiling people who, in the case of the boy from north China and the cook from Canton, communicated with each other in pidgin English much of the time, finding it easier than understanding their disparate dialects.

My mother had always enjoyed cooking but, with so many servants, she would have 'lost face' had she lifted a finger to do anything herself in the house. So, with time on her hands, she would take me down to the ferry which crossed the river to town. There we would sometimes find a French or German military parade taking place in the main street, but how proud I felt when it was the Scots Guards with full military band swinging along the road so splendidly in their immaculate uniforms, faultless in every detail. The Drum Major out in front twisting and throwing the mace with perfect aplomb completed this magnificent display. No wonder the British sometimes felt superior.

We would make our way in rickshaws to the German cake shop, Kiesling and Bader, where my mother usually had a rendezvous for morning coffee with some friends. If she went only to buy some pâtisserie and cakes from their incredibly delicious assortment, I was happy when she had to wait a long time to be served. The shop permitted customers to taste free any of the petits fours and biscuits on display in open square glass sections of the counter. I knew exactly where to find the cheese straws and would go straight there and start eating steadily, concentrating on this one favourite variety.

Over coffee, the conversation of my mother and her friends centred for some weeks on the very handsome, popular Dr Colbert. All were agreed that he had a charming bedside manner, but he had been arrested and charged with attempting to poison his second wife. However, the lady recovered sufficiently to defend him in court so he was acquitted, which made everyone much happier. Sitting silently over my huge glass of iced chocolate topped with cream and ice-cream, I listened entranced to the saga of the glamorous Dr Colbert and his wives.

Now that we were settled in a new city my mother looked for a dancing teacher and found an elderly Russian lady, Mme Tarakanova. Her classes were not much in the style of Miss Bosustow, but my mother liked the teacher, and I suspect that she was starting to get bored with so little to do all day. Not only did I begin dancing classes, but I also began to invent my own dances at home. We had a portable gramophone, so small that it had to be rewound after every five minutes of play. Undaunted by this, however, we would spend a long time in the record shops choosing tuneful pieces and then going home to choreograph them. That is to say, I arranged the steps while my mother offered helpful suggestions or criticism. She would then design and make the costumes, accepting in turn my ideas or criticism. Was it Mme Tarakanova who taught me the tambourine dance that provoked my first press review, or did I arrange it myself?

> Miss Peggy Hookham was easily the hit of the performance with her clever dancing, the little girl's footwork being especially striking in the dance of a Turkish slave girl where she jangled her tambourine and flung herself into the dance with a gay abandon rare in such a young dancer.
>
> Tientsin, 1929

I believe it was my own composition – whoever heard of a Neapolitan tambourine being used in a Turkish dance!

Copies of the *Dancing Times* were ordered from London so that we could keep ourselves informed, two or three months later, of the Sunshine Dancing Competitions and more professional events. My mother studied the information about teachers and schools in London very carefully.

In September I entered the Tientsin Grammar School, leaving my mother even more time on her own. She made an effort with the afternoon bridge and mahjong parties, but they did not in any way fill her life. She preferred the jostling mob of benign-faced, cotton-clad Chinese shoppers to the inhuman snap of cards and cool clink of ivory pieces on a green baize table. She needed real life and movement around her. In the evil-smelling little pet shops her heart went out to the exquisite birds in tiny cages, waiting for a purchaser who would then wager the song of his thrush against that of another belonging to a friend. 'It's so cruel to confine them like that. I can't bear it,' she would say as she bought lots of birds and let them fly free in an unused bedroom. She saw youths selling day-old chicks and ducklings in the street on a hot afternoon. 'Poor darlings, they're half-dead with exhaustion; why don't you give them some water?' she said angrily as she bought the whole boxful and tried to revive them at home with brandy from an eyedropper. Unfortunately they never lived more than a couple of days. Next it was rabbits. Officially they lived in a cage in the garden, though they spent a great deal of time loping about our living-room floor. When I wanted to practise a dance the rabbits had to be put back in the garden.

When winter came I tried skating on the pond in the near-by park. It was a hopeless failure. I always over-balanced and fell, my knees together and feet out sideways like wings. My father meanwhile tried to learn Chinese from a little professor who spoke no English, and so acted out the words and sentences, giving my father a lot of amusement as he chuff-chuffed round the room to illustrate a steam train. My father didn't learn much Chinese, but he was very happy with the new job and the new people – and his car, which was his hobby as animals were my mother's. On some Saturday mornings he would drive me to the factory, and this was my greatest treat. The big bales of tobacco leaf have to be kept in a humid atmosphere, which creates a rich and haunting smell. After passing through this agreeable area he would show me the big cigarette machines. These absolutely fascinated me. Once he started one up so that I could watch the ribbon of white paper unroll and move along to the gadget that dropped an amount of shredded tobacco on to it, which then vanished into a tunnel and emerged, almost completely rolled, to be glued and pressed down. Finally a guillotine device chopped the long white tube into neat cigarette lengths, which were collected up automatically in tens for packaging. At the end came the best part of all. My father would give me a handful of cigarette cards. These would show a series of Chinese actors or flowers or temples in beautiful colours, so different from the sets of aeroplane and railway engine cards that Felix collected in England. I sent him a lot from China, but never heard if they were appreciated at Cheltenham. Probably not.

With the coming of spring I had only one interest and ambition in life. I wanted to ride a horse. For months on end, how I pestered my parents! Each time we drove out to the Country Club past the paddy fields and water buffalo, the shallow creeks and bamboo clumps, I would set up a refrain, 'I want to ride a horse.' 'When can I learn to ride?' 'Please let me learn to ride.' It proved difficult in Tientsin, but eventually, when we were living in Shanghai, I got my way – only to fall off at the sixth lesson and lose my enthusiasm. I suppose it is the first stirring of romantic feeling that makes so many little girls of ten begin to picture themselves galloping across the countryside in glorious freedom, their hair flying in the breeze.

The time came for my mother and myself to return to England to see Felix. By the Trans-Siberian Railway we could be home in a mere fourteen days – which was unbelievably quick compared to the long sea voyage. We had been in Tientsin one year and some days when we set off in June 1929, going first to Mukden and thence to Chang Chun, where we left the Chinese coaches and boarded the wide-gauge Russian train which stopped at Harbin before reaching the frontier at Manchouli. It was spacious and comfortable, the roomy carriage converting into a sleeping compartment at night. I didn't much care for the restaurant car cuisine, but of course my mother had brought lots of tins of sardines and Heinz baked beans, still favourite foods today. Heaven knows why, when I can tour the world these days with four pieces of luggage, we then had fourteen pieces to contend with.

The fascinating journey was broken by stops at little village stations where peasants brought incredibly delicious farm butter and hot fresh bread for the passengers to buy. Also roast chickens and wild flowers, of which the plum-red lilies-of-the-valley made an unforgettable impression, their smell so sweet and strong, redolent of the pure air and clean earth in which they grew. It came as a surprise one morning to draw the blinds and look out on to the clear vista of Lake Baikal after travelling through the endless miles of forest. Our train skirted the lake all day, and no doubt at stations the peasants brought smoked fish, but I only liked tinned sardines, so I don't remember.

Not everyone travelled that line as comfortably as we did; there were coaches of what was called 'hard class' accommodation, consisting of bare wooden shelves, lower and upper level, on which soldiers and peasants sat for days at a time, cushioning the unfriendly surfaces with their thick clothing and what bundles they carried with them.

At one of the stations there was a lot of shouting and excitement at the discovery of a stowaway clinging to some underpart of the carriage between the wheels. He was a sad, pale youth who had travelled a couple of hundred miles undetected.

The Russian phrase books were brought out in readiness for a four-hour stop in Moscow, where everyone except me was anticipating the luxury of a bath in the hotel. Once arrived, I was much more interested in the enormous stuffed black bear that reared up in a corner of the hotel lobby, and I didn't care at all that no baths were available – whether for lack of hot water or bathrooms I don't know. Disgruntled and scruffy, the passengers climbed back into the train with nothing but a sight of Red Square and the Kremlin to show for the much looked-for stop in the capital. There had been a big red-tape fuss about passports, and the delicious meal some passengers had counted on did not compare to the standards of cuisine set by many *émigré* restaurants in the Far East. We heard a lot of gourmet grumbling as we reboarded for the last leg of the long journey.

My mother and I stopped in Berlin and there arranged for what turned out to be an enchanting boat trip along the Rhine from Mainz to Coblenz, seeing the Lorelei rock and those unbelievable turreted castles perched precariously on mountain tops which anticipated my long life in the shadow of Prince Siegfried's castle in *Swan Lake*. I think that brief excursion strongly influenced, albeit unconsciously, my sensibility to the mood and atmosphere of the ballet.

I became almost sick with excitement as the reunion with my brother grew nearer, and to this day Victoria Station, with its musty smell and clanging of iron and banging of carriage doors, gives me a little jolt of nostalgia. As it turned out, Felix and I actually found little to say to one another on meeting.

It seems that my mother and I stayed ten months in England, and my father came on long home leave in the middle of that time. I was put into a local school for two terms and attended various dancing classes. I coached with Miss Bosustow for a ballet exam, but had more fun doing my own character creations in the Sunshine Dancing Competitions – my Turkish Dance was good, though unaccountably to music called 'Ballets Egyptiens'. (On our next home leave I choreographed a French sailor kissing a girl in a bar and getting his face slapped – a piece inspired by our ship putting into port at Marseilles.) When I met Sammy Davis, Jr, not long ago, he enjoyed hearing of these early episodes in my career and was absolutely delighted to hear about a number called 'Pickin' Cotton', which I danced in a line of children at the Albert Hall, wearing a turquoise velvet tunic with gold ribbon round the upright collar and turquoise bows on my tap shoes. I think the story humanized Sammy's view of ballerinas.

Returning by the sea route to Hong Kong, we travelled on a German liner. I was practically the ship's mascot, running all over the place and playing endless deck quoits and endearing myself to the Chief Officers (whose photographs I still have). One of my few childhood friends, Elvi Koenig, was on that trip. I had another friend in Tientsin and a few at school in Shanghai, but that was all. I spent most of my time in the company of grown-ups and had little in common with other children.

The following summer that I spent on the beach in Hong Kong was the most important of my childhood because I literally lived in the sea from morning till night, swimming and diving until water was the most natural element for me to inhabit. A tall Norwegian, who had spent several years as a diplomat in Russia before the Revolution, was my great friend. He was a handsome man, big-boned but lean and well-preserved with the blue eyes of a sailor, and he loved dancing. At every tea dance in the Repulse Bay Hotel we waltzed and foxtrotted and danced the *paso doble*, he so tall and me a little shrimp of eleven years, but in perfect harmony. I could say it was my first dancing partnership. He had loved the ballet in St Petersburg and Moscow, knew about all the ballerinas and talked to me for hours on the beach about Tamara Karsavina in *Sleeping Beauty*. My uninformed mind could not visualize the delights he was describing, as I did not know at that time what a big ballet company was. Many years later I danced in Oslo, where I got a letter that said: 'I wonder can the famous Margot Fonteyn be the little Peggy I used to know in Hong Kong?' Enclosed was a snapshot of us sitting together on the beach, and written across the back were the words, *This is Peggy, she swims like a fish and dances like a ballerina*. It was dated *Summer, 1930*.

After he left Repulse Bay I played on the beach with a very quiet boy a bit younger than myself. My father had made a sort of flat-topped canoe on which we could paddle to little coves in the bay while his amah waited patiently for him on the beach. She chuckled a lot as she said to me, 'Michael not boy, Michael girl, ha-ha, yes, girl,' and explained in pidgin English that he had been registered as 'sex uncertain' at birth and would be re-registered decisively when he was fourteen. Such matters seemed unimportant to me and I was far more interested to learn, from talking to the room boy, that my unusually large ear lobes were a sign that I would have a very lucky life.

My mother and I crossed on the Star Ferry to Kowloon, which was absolutely deserted in the hot afternoon sun. We were in search of a dancing school, but the only one given in the telephone directory proved to have closed down, so I went happily back to the beach. No school and no dancing all that long summer – heaven!

When we moved to Shanghai, however, we found a

good deal of artistic activity: there were several dancing schools, amateur dramatic societies and occasional visiting artists. It must have been the best time for my parents. My father's work called for resource, ingenuity and leadership, while my mother could do all the things she enjoyed – buying birds and animals, watching my lessons, making costumes for the performances and mooching about the shops with me. They could dine together at excellent Russian restaurants, and Shanghai was famous for its night life. There, too, I attended school fairly steadily for the first time in my life. It lasted from early 1931 to the end of 1933, with an eight-month interruption while we took the sea route to England and back. It is hard to know how I learned anything at all with such a scant education.

During the last eighteen months in Shanghai my mother began to take my dancing more seriously, and this was a good deal due to June and Mrs Brae. My mother heard that a Russian teacher, George Gontcharov, had started to give lessons. She found him in the Brae family's front room instructing June and an American girl, Virginia, while Mrs Brae gave accompaniment on a somewhat wheezy piano. Here was a far more professional atmosphere than in the children's dancing schools, for George Gontcharov had trained and danced at the famous Bolshoi Theatre in Moscow. He was an *émigré* who found that the only outlet for his art in the Far East was in night clubs. He had joined forces with two other young Russians, George Toropov from Moscow and Vera Volkova from Leningrad, and had formed a trio. They danced the more spectacular passages from classical ballets and choreographed artistic numbers to make a suitable repertoire. Vera Volkova, a perfectly trained product of the finest school in the world, found the work incredibly taxing in the poor conditions and humid climate. Gontcharov supplemented his income, and perhaps his interest, by teaching.

Our lessons took place after school hours, and one day a tall, slender young woman entered through the wide double doors and into the front room / ballet studio where

39

Gontcharov was setting the ronde-de-jambes exercise. Gontcharov, I thought, blushed slightly with pleasure at seeing her, and her presence brought an aura to which the little room was quite unaccustomed. In those days one would have said she looked Parisian, thus paying the highest compliment to her style of dress and her deportment. It was an extremely hot afternoon and she wore a very simple dress of printed silk with a flared skirt. Her face was not conventionally beautiful but attracted one with its oval shape, delicate nose and large eyes. The picture was rounded off by a wide-brimmed black straw hat. The hat made such an impression on me that I was to be strongly influenced by it all my adult years, and even now have three or four like it stored away – they are the most impractical objects when travelling. The vision she presented gave me my first inkling of what a ballerina should be. It was, of course, Vera Volkova and she was to become a renowned teacher.

We had another teacher besides Gontcharov, a bizarre Russian Jew called Edouard Elirov, about whom there were insubstantial rumours and innuendos, whether for bad debts or for being some sort of secret agent I never found out. A man of expansive personality, he was rather fat and heavily built, and a receding hairline gave him a high forehead. His wife was a dancer at the Folies Bergère in Paris. He taught dancing with an artistic flair backed by a minimum of knowledge, and for this the conservative Gontcharov detested him and even suspected him of intentionally loosing a dog on stage during my performance of a beautiful dance choreographed to the song called 'Trees'.

Elirov's mysterious enemies pulled a coup of Chinese simplicity and ingenuity at a benefit he had organized in aid of himself. They threw large quantities of pepper into the auditorium from the upper tiers, disrupting the evening most successfully.

At about this time my confirmation in the Shanghai Cathedral provoked a brief bout of religious mania. It coincided with an even briefer enthusiasm for knitting, which led my mother to observe, as she saw me sitting up late to finish a sweater in time for Sunday morning, that she hoped I was not going to develop into one of those smugly regular church-goers who thought more about their clothes when they got there than about God.

June Brae was an unusually expressive dancer, and she involved herself deeply and seriously in the ballet classes which, up till this time, I had found boring and dry. Fired by her example, I strove hard to assimilate Gontcharov's instruction, for it stung my pride not to be unquestionably the best pupil in the room.

My mother and I talked rather expansively about our sojourns in London, the ballets we had seen, and about classes at the studio of Nicholas Legat, who had partnered Anna Pavlova in his youth in St Petersburg. Many of his pupils were professional dancers. This sort of talk fired June and her mother to make a decision: they would leave for London in four weeks' time. This left me and my mother standing! The sense of competition had taken hold of us all, and it was not long after June's departure that I said good-bye to the headmistress of my school and told her that, now I was fourteen, my mother was taking me to England to dance. She warned me that in later life I would regret abandoning my education so young. 'You will feel yourself an ignoramus among other people,' she said, and advised me to read extensively, concentrating on the classics. She was right in everything. But my mother was right, too, for if I was going to get on in the ballet world I could not afford to lose a moment longer.

FOUR

Back in England we found June and her mother already settled. June was at Nicholas Legat's school, and I thought I would join her there. However, I decided that his Class of Perfection, as it was called, was too advanced for me. My mother's research in the dance magazines led her to the teacher responsible for training Alicia Markova. At the age of fourteen Markova had gone straight from Princess Serafine Astafieva's Academy to the great Diaghilev Ballet, so it was reasonable to suppose that the Princess would be a good teacher.

Accordingly we went to her studio at The Pheasantry in King's Road, Chelsea. We climbed a little twisted staircase and came to tall double doors that opened into a beautifully proportioned studio with long eighteenth-century windows looking on to the little forecourt and elaborate gateway that is still the entrance to this unique house. There was little traffic along the King's Road at that time, and the whole area was like an out-of-the-way village, getting shabbier as one went west towards the pub called World's End. (There was an excellent fish-and-chip shop near by.)

Princess Astafieva was tallish, aged about sixty, worldly and elegant with slender legs and an indefinable mixture of the stylish with the slightly grubby that only such an aristocratic personality from Czarist Russia could hope to carry off successfully. She always wore a scarf tied turban-wise round her head, and carried a long cigarette holder. She smoked Balkan Sobranies. When she was teaching she wore white cotton stockings and her black pleated skirt, normally knee length, was tucked into black silk bloomers. She had an aquiline nose and a fine mouth. Her expression was often sad but lit up quickly with an encouraging smile as she became interested in the class.

The first meeting was not easy. We arrived, apparently, on a day when she was sitting in her dark inner room in a Russian gloom, both physical and moral. She did not want to accept any more pupils. All her old pupils were ungrateful and neglectful. She was too old to teach any more. 'But,' my mother said, 'you are the teacher of Markova and Anton Dolin; you are the greatest teacher in London.' 'I never see them,' she replied, although she knew it wasn't true. 'I am too old. I won't take pupils more.' In desperation my mother said, 'You must accept my daughter. I have brought her six thousand miles all the way from China to study with you.' This argument must have amused or intrigued the Princess, and it was agreed that I should go either to a class or a private lesson each day.

Until this time I had found ballet dancing rigid and restraining, at least in classes – on stage I felt freer. Astafieva had a knack of knowing exactly on which single point to concentrate in order to facilitate a difficult movement. 'Take force from your left arm,' she said, and I sailed round on a pirouette; or, 'Let your breath out before you bend back,' and suddenly it was easy. Apparent ease was one of the outstanding qualities of Markova's dancing; one never saw a trace of effort in her feather-light movements, and doubtless she would acknowledge a debt of gratitude for this to Astafieva.

With the sun pouring through the long studio windows, Astafieva would recall steps from the old St Petersburg ballets, from *Sleeping Beauty*, *Paquita* and *Corsaire*; I hopped on one toe, pirouetted and *jetéd* about the room, with no time to think about which were the difficult steps. At last serious ballet dancing became a joy.

On Wednesdays Astafieva had a sparkle about her. A handsome young man called Nigel, also a pupil, was a rich and impassioned dilettante who had probably taken up ballet after he left university. Despite his genuine enthusiasm he occasionally missed a lesson, I imagine on account of a late night, but every Wednesday without fail he called to take Madame out to dinner *à deux*. No doubt she was a fascinating companion, having lived quite a life in the last days of Imperial Russia. She was very beautiful, and Diaghilev had created ballets specially for her. She must have had many a marvellous tale to tell her young escort over dinner. These evenings, I feel, were among the few happinesses of her last sad years.

Keith Lester was a favourite ex-pupil. He happened to come in during one of my lessons, and Madame took the opportunity to ask him to partner me in some turns and lifts. What an extraordinary sensation it was, the first time I found myself held high in the air, rather like being caught up in a tree by the shirttails! Madame explained that I should take a deep breath as I left the floor and hold it while lifted, also to hold my back very straight. The next attempt was more successful. I could see in the big mirror that I looked more like a dancer and less like a sack of potatoes. This impromptu lesson stood me in good stead after I joined the ballet and sometimes danced with boys as new to partnering as I was.

Working happily with Astafieva, I was quite upset when my mother said she wanted to take me also to the school of the Old Vic and Sadler's Wells Theatres. 'But I am not nearly ready yet,' I protested. 'Never mind,' she insisted, 'I think you should go there to find out if you have any future in ballet. If you really have talent they will know what to do with it.' Needless to say, I was much too engrossed in myself to consider my mother's natural concern to determine her own future. It was not easy for her to leave my father in Shanghai, but she wanted to give me the opportunity to dance if I could make a success of it. I can see now how intelligently she went about it. In fact, taking me to the Vic-Wells School was another sacrifice for her, because very soon I worked with the professional dancers and she could no longer watch the lessons that she had always enjoyed so much.

So the day came when we took the bus up Rosebery Avenue to our appointment at Sadler's Wells Theatre. I was still mulishly protesting that my dancing was insufficiently advanced. Being ignorant of what would happen at an audition we did not take practise clothes or ballet shoes. 'Never mind,' said Ursula Moreton. 'Take off your shoes and stockings and stand at the barre in first position.' So the audition took place with me barefoot and wearing my petticoat. I was enrolled in the school and shown where I should dress with the other students in the Dress Circle Ladies' Cloakroom.

There were only about eighteen girls in the entire school, and they were derisively referred to as 'the bombs' by the ballet company, whose members looked down their noses at us and rarely deigned to converse. This was hardly like the happy hours I spent with Astafieva, whom I still sneaked off to see in the afternoons, although forbidden by the school to attend an outside teacher.

I had been there about a week when I nearly banged right into the already legendary Lillian Baylis as I ran up the stairs to class. 'Oh, excuse me, Miss Baylis,' I mumbled. She stopped me. 'Who are you, dear?' she asked. 'I'm the new student, Miss Baylis.' 'Oh – do you believe in God, dear?' 'Yes, Miss Baylis.' And she let me go without further comment.

Miss Baylis was old, almost dumpy, dressed in black, with glasses and untidy wisps of hair. There was an unmistakably Victorian air about her, though she was not in the least strait-laced. Her moral standards derived from her upbringing. She was very active, never thinking of herself, only concerned with bringing art to people living in the poor areas where her two theatres were situated. Stories of her unusual methods of getting the greatest actors and singers to work for her on a shoestring are part of English theatre lore. 'Please, God, send me a good tenor,' she would pray on her knees in her office. 'And let him be cheap,' she added. 'You are asking for more money? Just a minute, dear, I will have to ask God.' The unfortunate applicant stood there while she went down on her knees. 'I'm sorry, dear, God says "No"' was the inevitable verdict. Undoubtedly, God had listened when

45

she decided that her operas needed a small group of dancers to perform the ballet scenes, for He had sent her Ninette de Valois. The result was a totally unexpected burgeoning of British ballet, which is perhaps the richest of Lillian Baylis's artistic legacies.

Next day, as we were doing class in the Wells Room (which served as the Coffee Bar during performances), Ninette de Valois came in and sat beside Ursula Moreton, who was giving directions and beating time with a stick. 'Who is the little Chinese girl in the corner?' asked de Valois. 'Three and four and – she's not Chinese,' in a whisper, '– and seven and eight.' 'Where does she come from?' 'Shanghai. Right leg, four *grands battements en croix*.' 'There you are! I told you she was Chinese!' said de Valois triumphantly, and indeed with my dark hair and suntan and my round face I did look oriental. My eyes, too, had acquired the suggestion of a slope.

Miss de Valois decided that I had talent, but that 'we are just in time to save her feet'. She did not at all approve of Astafieva's disregard for such details as the perfectly worked foot muscle. I was still rather small for my age, and somewhat like a colt so far as control over my limbs was concerned. She now set about correcting my every fault, and I came in for a good deal of shouting. It was quite beyond my power to change quickly from the instructions Astafieva had given to the almost contrary instructions of de Valois. '*Will* you do as I tell you!' she said. I tried the step again. 'No! No!' she shouted, banging a stick on the floor and stopping the class. 'Go back and do it again as I want it.' I tried again. 'No! that's *still* wrong, don't be so obstinate.' By now she was absolutely furious. She grabbed up a sweater lying near by and slammed it down on the floor in rage. My mother, privileged that day to watch the students' class, nearly jumped out of her skin in fright. Two or three minutes later it was all forgotten by de Valois, but I was shattered for hours.

I was considered stubborn and a 'little devil'. After I had been at the school a while, however, I noticed that

46

new arrivals fell into one of two categories as far as Miss de Valois was cocerned. 'She's a nice child,' or, 'She's an absolute devil, but very talented.' It was the latter group that always seemed to get on. I tried to be a nice child, although I realized that it was a compliment to be shouted at all day long. The trouble was that one never knew what would provoke the next outburst of anger. Trying my hardest to correct the left foot as directed yesterday, it would all come down on me suddenly for something else. 'Your arm is too high again, I've told you before to keep it below shoulder level; pay attention *please*.' A detail like the colour of one's socks could equally well cause a violent storm. Arriving late was a catastrophe. One tried to peer through the little square of glass in the door to see if class had begun. If so, the best thing was to vanish quickly and hope she would not notice one's absence – a vain hope anyway. Unfortunately she sat right opposite the door and had eyes like a hawk. 'Come in at once,' she would shout imperiously. One crept in nervously. 'I won't have people coming in late, if you can't get here on time you can't do class, get out!' So one was no sooner in than one was thrown out again in disgrace. Since class was not exactly fun under the circumstances, I rather wondered why it should be a penalty to be expelled. It was sometimes more like a reprieve.

The company numbered only thirty-six dancers in all, so the students appeared in the bigger ballets like *Coppelia* and *Giselle*. Consequently, quite soon after joining the school, I found myself being taught the part of the third snowflake of the second group on the left in preparation for a performance of *The Nutcracker* two days later. The others all knew the ballet well, and such an insignificant role as mine did not merit much rehearsal, so I was utterly confused by the time I got on stage. For one thing I had not asked which direction was the front and somehow I expected the audience to be elsewhere. Luckily the girls near by kindly whispered: 'Now right'; 'Forward'; 'Turn'; 'Follow me'; and so on, all through the scene. Still it was something of a nightmare until we reached the point near the end where we all knelt in a group waving our snowflake wands while paper snow rained about our heads. At this moment the opera chorus was singing, Tchaikovsky's inspired music had reached its most beguiling climax, the lights were dimmed to a soft blue and the curtains swung gently together, muffling the applause on the other side. I felt an incredible elation; this was theatre, this was the real thing. All discouraging self-criticism was forgotten. From this moment on there could be no turning back.

My debut as a snowflake came about at the end of the season. During the summer the Vic-Wells Ballet was engaged to perform in the International Opera Season at Covent Garden. I was called to rehearsal at the Chenies Street Drill Hall, there to fall among the ballet company with all its wicked sophistication. To say that I was timid would be an understatement. I was also naïve to a degree, and quite confused by the 'worldly' social attitudes I encountered. I had thought 'nice' was the ideal to which everyone aspired the world over, only to find here it was more a term of disparagement, while 'brilliant', 'witty', 'eccentric', 'glamorous' or, at the very least, 'amusing' were the only desirable attributes. I noticed that the wit and amusement came mostly at other people's expense, but Robert Helpmann in particular was so funny with his sharp observations and fiendish comments that everyone laughed despite their better natures.

I joined in the mirth even when I didn't understand the point, while wondering what was said about me when my back was turned. Happily, three of the younger girls, led by Jill Gregory, said: 'I think we ought to look after that new child standing over there in the corner.' They took me with them to lunch at an ABC and showed me where to buy greasepaint: Leichner sticks numbers five and nine, and hot-black to bead my eyelashes. As false lashes were then unobtainable, one melted the black wax in a spoon over a candle and applied it carefully with a hairpin, building big blobs at the end of each lash (they sometimes fell into one's eye during the ballet). We occasionally used soap to block out eyebrows, but that also could run into the eye and sting as only soap can. Thick black lines edging the eye and extending out to the sides were known as 'tramlines'. A touch of red at the corner of each eye was said to give sparkle. Miss de Valois favoured the cupid's bow mouth, two rounds of red on the upper lip and one below, but the company thought it old-fashioned. It was all the rage to apply rouge with a genuine hare's foot. I had no sense of makeup and plastered my face so inexpertly that a lady in the audience was once overheard to say, 'Fifteen, indeed! She looks more like fifty!'

The Company thought the opera ballets something of a joke, but I was too new to take that attitude. I tried conscientiously to dance with abandon in *Schwanda the Bagpiper*, and to stagger convincingly under the supposed weight of a gigantic gold nugget in *Das Rheingold* while dressed as an old gnome complete with long grey beard and wig. The fun came during *Turandot* and *Die Meistersinger*, where Markova's sister, Bunny, and I were cast as children and set loose to roam about in the crowd scenes. We even dared to sing in the louder choruses. We were the two smallest and newest students, so we became great friends. Bunny was surrounded with an aura of glamour, being so close to the idol, but she remained completely unspoilt, revering her sister as much as I did.

Felix and I were still very close. For the summer recess we thought it a marvellous idea to buy tents and holiday under canvas in the fields of Devon and Cornwall. It rained a good deal and our poor mother had no alternative but to bear the ordeal bravely. For us, however, to wake up on a fine summer morning and feel ourselves in perfect harmony with the earth and the sky was a rare Utopian experience, and to wander barefoot across the sand dunes, once coming upon a tiny, abandoned church half-buried in wild grass, was the epitome of romantic

49

feeling for innocent teenagers.

Ever since I was quite young, certain combinations of landscape have aroused a curious sensation in my soul. It is somehow a sensual desire to unite with the sun-dappled countryside and at the same time an overwhelming nostalgia, as though I had once inhabited those very places in centuries long past. Occasionally, too, I have felt those brief flashes of understanding that Wordsworth described as intimations of immortality. These elusive experiences are always associated for me with the sun, which has an extraordinary importance in my life.

In September I reported again at Sadler's Wells Theatre for the new season. I still felt quite an outsider, so I was awed to see my name listed on the rehearsal board for the role of the Young Tregennis in a favourite ballet called *The Haunted Ballroom*. It was a gothic story, superbly choreographed by Ninette de Valois, concerning the Master of Tregennis, who is drawn to his death in a mysterious ballroom where the head of each successive generation of his family has died, and where his young son is fated to die in turn. My part as the little boy, in a Lord Fauntleroy velvet suit, consisted only of mime and was quite brief. But I had the responsibility of opening and closing the ballet alone on stage.

The role had come to me because the girl who created it had left the company, and I was the smallest one around, but the effect of this solo part so soon after entering the ballet school was to make me feel in some way different from the other students. I started to dream of becoming a ballerina.

An assessment of my attributes quickly discouraged me. I had black hair, which was no drawback, but it grew low on my forehead and destroyed the necessary perfect oval face. Anyway, the oval was further marred by my rather wide jaw, which produced more of a triangular effect. A long neck and high instep were also indispensable, but while I thought I could stretch my head up a bit there was nothing to be done about the foot. On the dancing side, my elevation was very poor, my pirouettes likewise and my arabesque low. So when I considered the matter realistically I could see there was little hope of succeeding.

Nevertheless, I was pushed into every ballet, feeling extraordinarily lucky to be one of the anonymous peasants or sylphs in the make-believe world which seemed to me so completely real. At all times on the stage I lived the story through from beginning to end, crying over Giselle's death, feeling the moonlight touch me in a wooded glade and suffering inexpressible melancholy in the mists of a mountain lake. As I moved among the other dancers they assumed for me their stage characters, so that my fear of them vanished until they regained their real identities next morning at rehearsal. Then all my complexes would return, my shyness and my sense of inferiority; not so much among the group of little girls who helped me and were my friends, but among the principals. I was mortified to overhear one of them say, 'That horrid child is always showing off, practising arabesques in a corner.' Of course, I really needed to practise hard, but unluckily I entered the ballet during a period when it was absolutely unfashionable to take anything seriously. One of the girls was much admired for hiding behind the upright piano and doing *The Times* crossword puzzle right under de Valois's nose during class. I was amazed at her boldness in view of the scene that would follow if she were caught out, and I longed to be one of those goddesses who took it all so casually and were always laughing at jokes way above my head. As gradually my position in the ballet rose with the new solo roles that came my way, I remained in many ways apart from my sophisticated colleagues. I disdained money and jazz music – and thought it immoral to talk to critics!

'Insecurity' had not yet attained its 'vogue' as a common human condition; 'self-confidence' was then much vaunted, and of that I had none. On the rare occasions when I opened my mouth among the higher strata of the company, I always said something so stupid that I immediately suffered intense shame. This did not, however, prevent me from wanting to be on the edge of the group, laughing at their absurd or outrageous jokes. My own set of standards for living, then struggling to take shape, underwent endless revision until I was so confused that the dark despair of adolescence took hold. The black moments were so desperate that I now wonder how I survived them; but possibly they were more concerned with ego than with genuine feeling. Perhaps suffering comes only later in life when the emotions have some background of experience to give them depth. But I think not. I think the pain of youth is sometimes so intense that afterwards certain feelings are a little blunted for ever more.

My dancing life was ruled by Ninette de Valois, a marvellous and unpredictable woman. In those days she danced, and choreographed, and directed the company and school. No wonder her patience was short. After rehearsing us all day, and attending to business in her office next to the Wells Room, she changed into practice clothes and did her own barre work in readiness for a performance. She excelled in such roles as Swanilda in *Coppelia*, having a strong sense of characterization and humour. She had beautiful legs, and a beautiful head carried with great distinction. Her movements were quick, like her temper. She once told me she took two aspirins, a hot bath and a glass of sherry so as to relax before dancing. Even so, I can remember her on stage doing *brisés* which seemed faster than the speed of light, and faster than any conductor could catch or musicians play. Intelligent to a degree, and far-seeing, she made decisions that often appeared completely wrong at the time and yet turned out completely right in the long run. Had she not understood that the repertoire of a national ballet company such as she wished to create must be based on the classical tradition, it is possible that the great Petipa–Tchaikovsky ballets would have been lost to the Western world for several decades. After Diaghilev's massive failure with *Sleeping Beauty* in London in 1921 everyone thought the classics were dead. Diaghilev knew better.

He said: 'I am fifteen years too early with this production.' Even Serge Lifar, his protégé, made no attempt to revive it at the Paris Opéra, nor were the Petipa works included in the repertoires at Vienna or Berlin. Milan audiences abhorred Tchaikovsky, and Copenhagen preserved the earlier Bournonville tradition. In North America it was not until the 1960s that a major company presented the full versions of *Swan Lake* and *Sleeping Beauty*. So without the productions at Sadler's Wells they would have been virtually unseen for fifty years. The exception was *The Nutcracker*, which has today become a universal Christmas tradition for children, though, curiously, it was never a purely seasonal affair at Sadler's Wells. It was the first Petipa ballet presented by de Valois and took its place as a classic pillar in the regular mixed repertoire. She followed it with *Swan Lake*, and in 1939, heeding Diaghilev's prophetic words, she produced *Sleeping Beauty*.

Surveying de Valois's career, I can see how she gradually dropped those activities which could be undertaken by other people, preserving herself for the ever-magnifying task of direction, until at last she relinquished her whole lifework with the observation, 'Women are good for the pioneer work but when it has developed to a certain point the men must take it over.' She handed over the company to Frederick Ashton.

She gave up her dancing in the 1930s, leaving an indelible memory for all who saw her in *Douane*, *Coppelia*, *Barabau* and, her last creation, as Webster in *The Wedding Bouquet*. Next she stopped her work as a choreographer, and therewith her preferred form of creation. In fact she had made few ballets, but they were constructed, like good architecture, with a strong sense of form and style. Because they carried so personal a stamp, her major works remain masterpieces and the minor ones would be found delectable today by the vast new public fed on many an ill-concocted dish.

In 1934 I saw only the alarming aspect of Miss de Valois. Up till that time I had never encountered anyone so volatile. Miss Fleet, headmistress of my school in Shanghai, who struck terror in pupils, parents, teachers and governors alike, was a remote dragon lurking in her lair, whereas de Valois might at any time breathe fire and smoke upon one in the canteen, or the corridor, or the dressing room. On the other hand, she had an enormous sense of fun and was often in the best possible humour five minutes after blowing up like a volcano. My mother got the same treatment as everyone else but, holding the edge in years, she withstood it philosophically, saying, 'I just duck my head and wait till the storm has passed.'

It was traditional in those days for ballet masters to be severe. De Valois's own teachers would certainly have emphasized a caustic reprimand with the sharp whack of a light cane on flagging legs or drooping hand. Whether this was the result of dyspepsia or of faith in the maxim 'spare the rod and spoil the child', I don't know. Gontcharov used to say that Olga Preobrajenska terrified her pupils, who stood at the barre in first position trembling with fright even before she entered the room.

De Valois had a marvellously dotty knack of confusing people, names and places; she laughed as much as anyone when it was brought to her attention. Once, for example, the ballet company had been dancing in Dublin and, at the end of the week, she was profuse in her thanks to a gentleman for all his kindness during the engagement. Leslie Edwards asked her why she had been so excessively grateful. 'He's the manager of the theatre, didn't you meet him? Such a charming man,' she replied. 'But Miss de Valois, he's not the manager, he's Jack Healey, your wardrobe master from Sadler's Wells.' Of course, the fact that Jack was Irish had been enough for her to decide he belonged to the Dublin theatre. In time we came to know her idiosyncrasies so well that nobody bothered to correct her when she said something about going to Egypt. We all knew she meant Edinburgh.

De Valois ran the company almost single-handed, so her secretary, Miss Trickett, was in a constant state of confusion, typing letters and making headdresses at the same time. I remember her wandering into the Wells Room during a break and asking several dancers, 'Are you a rabbit, darling?' as she struggled to correct the programme proofs for a current children's ballet. Sometimes, through the closed office door, we heard de Valois's anger descending on poor Trickett's head, and those of us not needed in rehearsal would beat a retreat to the canteen. I marvelled at the fearlessness of Robert Helpmann, who could always find the right words to transmute de Valois's rage into laughter. He was also brilliant at reading upside down the papers that lay on her desk, while he submitted, apparently meekly, to a severe reprimand in her office. After only a few minutes he would emerge smiling and bearing a mass of exciting information on future casting and other matters which were supposed to be top secret.

Hearing so much shouting, I came to think there must be some virtue in it. 'Temperament' was supposed to be rather glamorous and often considered indispensable to great artists. I was normally mouselike, but one day I succeeded in losing my temper with a woman standing next to me in Woolworth's. I was astounded to find myself actually telling her off angrily, saying something like, 'I am certainly not trying to take that comb away from you – don't be so rude.' A glowing sense of achievement came upon me; perhaps I had a potential temper after all.

At fifteen and a half my romantic heart was as soft as butter. It was not long until I developed a crush on William Chappell, who was so much the kindest of the awe-inspiring adults around me and who had such blue eyes. He was gentle, he never shouted, and would reprove Helpmann for some of his biting observations with the words, 'Don't mock people, Bobby – it's wicked.' I don't expect he was aware of my feeling for him; I would have thought it shameful to let him see. Happily for me, the crush coincided with rehearsals of my first principal part, in a ballet called *Rio Grande – or a Day in a Southern Port*. Billie Chappell was a sailor and I the girl he picked up. Thus was I provided most opportunely with an excuse to regard him affectionately while acting my role.

Having recently begun to feel conscious and proud of my Brazilian heritage, I slipped effortlessly into the South American atmosphere of the ballet, with little concern for the subject matter of the plot. My mother kept to herself her doubts about the decency of my see-through skirt and the general tone of the work; indeed, she has always managed to be as broad-minded as one could possibly expect, but Lillian Baylis, being a generation older than my mother, felt impelled to have the designer paint over a nude statue on the backcloth. If she were alive today, I think she would take such things in her stride – up to a point, for no one could imagine her permitting the nude ballet that was recently danced at Sadler's Wells. The disapproving spirit of Lillian Baylis was definitely felt hovering about the theatre on that occasion.

Frederick Ashton had been away for several months, choreographing Gertrude Stein's *Four Saints in Three Acts* as a Broadway musical. After his return to London I would frequently hear Helpmann and Chappell saying things like: 'Freddie is absolutely extraordinary since he returned from New York'; or, 'Freddie was quite mad at the party last night. He danced for four hours without stopping'; and, 'I've never seen Fred so exhilarated. He did a hilarious pas de deux with a chair.'

Such remarks added to my feelings of apprehension when I was called to rehearsal for a new dance for four little girls that was to be added to Ashton's ballet *Les Rendezvous*.

I did not know how choreographers worked, as my experience was limited to my own childhood creations. So I did not know it was Ashton when he came into the Wells Room dressed in an ordinary suit with collar and tie. I had expected him to be in practice clothes. This person was of very light build and medium height. He had small feet and hands but a very impressive head, well shaped, with a long thin face and a long nose that I thought 'aristocratic' without quite knowing why. His manner was at first diffident. He began by looking a little nervous, and then saying with a quick half-smile, 'Now, what are we going to do?' He appeared very unsure as he placed us one in each corner of the room. Then he started.

There is almost no way of describing adequately the incredible zest of Ashton when he was choreographing. After listening to a few bars of music he would fling himself into some swoops and twists and dives, his movements just flowing out of the music, apparently spontaneously. Then he would stop and say, 'What did I do? Now you do it.' I was flabbergasted by these extraordinary inventions, which were only occasionally related to the common steps of our daily class. There was not a dancer in the company, except perhaps Helpmann, who had anything like the same supple flexibility. We four little girls tried to repeat what Ashton had shown us, but I could never manage without losing my balance and nearly toppling over. He corrected me again and again: 'No, no, bend more; bend right over this side, then right over that side. Move your body more; don't be so stiff.' It was useless; I either overbalanced or remained rigid. That evening I complained to my mother, 'Frederick Ashton is absolutely mad; his steps are impossible.' He in turn complained to de Valois about me, saying that I was very obstinate, a judgment that she shared – but she believed that I was very talented, nevertheless.

Gradually I accustomed myself to trying the impossible, and there can be no doubt that my happiest moments on stage have been in Ashton ballets. Few choreographers have surrendered themselves to dance with such total abandon. He was greatly influenced by Anna Pavlova, whose lightning speed and dramatic impact he was always trying to impress upon us. He impersonated her movement, expression, use of her eyes, her unorthodox freedom of gesture and above all her theatricality. 'She had such grace,' or, 'Such fire; her elegance was marvellous; if only you could see her run across the stage like a comet trailing everything behind her; Pavlova never did more than two pirouettes, but she turned with such rapidity it took your breath away; you cannot imagine the drama she could make out of an arabesque.'

It was not only Pavlova who was re-created before our eyes each day but Tamara Karsavina also, whom he adored as much or more. 'If you could see Karsavina's dignity, her command of the stage, her extraordinary eyes, how she used her eyes! Why can't you do that like Karsavina?' Another day we would have the pure line and perfect technique of Olga Spessivtzeva conjured up for our inspiration. Next it might by Lydia Lopokova. 'Her vitality was indescribable; it was like the cork bursting out of a bottle of champagne.' And so we lived in this world of past glories, which made our greatest efforts seem puerile by comparison but which also sometimes goaded us into achieving things normally beyond our power.

What a rich vein is the genius of Frederick Ashton, and what an abundance of dance creation he has produced over the years. No other choreographer has so completely merged himself with the music. He seems able to divine the composer's thoughts as he wrote, and to make these thoughts apparent in his ballets.

FIVE

The days of effort and exhaustion, hope and discouragement, were offset by the feverish excitement of first nights, with their telegrams, flowers, champagne. Then back to class the next morning! The point at which I ceased to be a student and became a member of the ballet was never clearly defined. In some ballets I retained a humble place in the corps de ballet, while in others I danced the principal role. It was not until after my first performance in *Les Sylphides* that Ninette de Valois said to me in the car, as my mother gave her a lift home, 'By the way, I forgot to tell you, you need not wear student's rehearsal dress any more – you are in the company, you can wear a black tunic.' It was now 1935, just about a year after my audition for the school.

Miss de Valois gave me some soloist roles, like Papillon in *Le Carnaval*, purely to speed up my footwork, and she rehearsed me herself but to little avail. The sparkle eluded my feet, and I danced so poorly that she had to release me after a few miserable performances. The more lyrical ballets, like *Les Sylphides*, I loved. Mostly I just danced and danced, leaving no time to analyse thoughts or feelings. Optimism and self-criticism chased each other by day, I ate heartily, and I slept like a log at night.

To the company at about this time came a handsome seventeen-year-old boy from the West country. He had a supercilious manner and an unusual ability to leap high in the air. De Valois said, 'Somes is very talented.' We quickly found that his habit of holding his head back and looking down his nose was not due to a sense of superiority, but merely shyness. He had a wry intelligence and worked very hard, not relaxing and laughing over foolish things with the rest of us at a time when 'These Foolish Things' was the current hit song. It was already clear that he would rise above most of the others in his career.

For me this was a vital year. Not only had Michael Somes arrived and I had met and worked with Frederick Ashton, but it was announced that Alicia Markova was leaving the Vic-Wells Ballet. Markova was far above and apart from the rest of us. She was a star. She was unique. Not only did she have the essential physical qualifications for a ballerina – black hair, an oval face, a long neck and beautiful feet – she also had the lightness of a bird and possessed a strong stage presence. I never took my eyes off her when she danced. She combined extraordinary speed and ease, and this she accomplished without ever being seen to attend a practice class. Somehow she just appeared on stage a few minutes before curtain time, pointed her toes once or twice, and then proceeded to dance in the most scintillating manner, making difficulties look utterly effortless. If one had occasion to touch her hands during a ballet, they were ice cold. It was as though none of the usual rules applied to Markova; other dancers were hot and out of breath, but she only became cool and light as the sylph she so often portrayed.

From the point of view of her career I can see why Markova decided to leave the Vic-Wells in 1935 and form her own company with Anton Dolin. She was too far ahead of our company, and she could not afford to wait for us. After the death of Diaghilev in 1929, followed by the instant collapse of his company, a ballet vacuum caught most of his dancers with nowhere to work. In England, Marie Rambert, the Camargo Society and Lillian Baylis furnished the only opportunities, but none of them could provide an adequate home for a full-fledged ballerina. It is one of my greatest pieces of good fortune that I was exactly of the right age to be able to develop coincidentally with the Vic-Wells Ballet. I was like a surfer riding a particularly long wave, and it was Markova's departure that launched me. But I knew none of this at the time.

The news of Markova's impending departure threw me into despair. 'Whatever will happen to us without Markova? We will all have to work very hard, but even hard work won't replace her.'

Many people thought, as I did, that the company was finished. Miss de Valois thought otherwise. She could see ten years ahead. She had Robert Helpmann, whom she knew to be another star, and she had Ashton as resident choreographer. She had the brilliant advice of Constant Lambert as musical director. Having no ballerina was more of a challenge than a setback. Part of her system, perhaps formulated at that moment, was to insist that the company had no stars while at the same time doing everything in her power to create and build them.

The exquisite Pearl Argyle joined us, bringing a quite different, more worldly glamour. She had great beauty of face, the equal of which I have never since seen. De Valois, always responsive to beauty, said wonderingly: 'Imagine what it must be like to wake up every morning and see that face in the mirror.' June Brae, my friend from childhood in China, also joined the company, bringing her individual and very beautiful style of dancing.

Thus de Valois threw whatever she had available into the gap left by Markova, using Pearl Argyle as the central attraction, and dividing the other roles among five of us: Mary Honer, Elizabeth Miller, Pamela May, June Brae and me. I was the first of this group to draw a big plum, when that autumn Ashton mounted Stravinsky's *Baiser de la Fée* and cast me as the Young Bride. I was to dance, with Harold Turner, the first of many haunting and sublime pas de deux that Ashton would create for me. It is the form of choreography in which Ashton excels beyond all others, pouring forth a wealth and variety of poetic invention. Rudolf Nureyev summed it up, thirty-five years later, while watching the shimmering *Thaïs* pas de deux for Antoinette Sibley and Anthony Dowell: 'The bastard, he's done it again!' he said in heartfelt admiration.

In 1935 *Swan Lake* was still an almost new production in the repertoire, but it was by far the most important ballet de Valois had yet mounted as part of a long-term policy by which the classic works were to be the mainstay that would support modern innovations. Lacking Markova, de Valois was without a ballerina for the arduous double role of Odette and Odile. For all the deficiencies of my technique, it was decided that I should take on Odette, the easier of the two parts, and that Mary Honer would dance Odile. (In fact, I shared the first performance with Ruth French.)

I used to pore over photographs of Karsavina and Pavlova, trying to learn from them what Ashton meant about the importance of eyes, and how characterization is embodied in the angle at which the head is held. But I was chiefly influenced by having worked in the theatre beside Markova, who also made very expressive use of her head.

Markova's ballet costumes were made by a Mme Manya, who had toured with Pavlova for many years and knew the secret cut of her tutus, or tarletan ballet skirts. I decided that I, too, must have my swan dress made by Manya! So my mother and I sallied forth to Maida Vale, where the old dressmaker lived in retirement, to ask her to grant me this privilege. She probably thought me something of an upstart, and she was reluctant at first. When she finally agreed it was none too graciously. Since we never liked to ask her again, my mother took care to take a pattern of the skirt. This has served, more or less, for all the hundreds of tutus I have worn through the years. The first dress cost £16. I have often wondered where my mother found so much money at that time.

The critics had by now come to know my dancing, and I was surprised to see 'Margot Fonteyn', my recently invented stage name, being mentioned as a possible future star.

Fonteyn was not the name I had wanted to adopt. I wanted to use my Brazilian family name of Fontes, but the English branch of the family shied off connections with the stage. Theatre people were then still thought to lead more wicked lives than others, or at least to have more opportunity to live wickedly, which may or may not have been true.

I subscribed to a press-cutting service and bought a simple, linen-covered book into which I proudly pasted my clippings. I began with the old review praising my 'spirited tambourine dance'. Then there was one in which Margot Fontes played Young Tregennis. Thereafter Margot Fonteyn was born, and was to live far beyond her expectations, as it turned out.

It was not long before one or two young men presented themselves at the stage door, wishing to congratulate Miss Fonteyn and invite her to dinner. I was enormously flattered to be so regarded as an adult. I also hoped that I might be swept up in a romantic passion and carried off by a rich handsome man to live happily ever after. The first dinner did not go too well, for when confronted by the restaurant menu I realized that I had never in my life tasted any of the dishes offered: Heinz baked beans on toast were not served at the Savoy Grill. Rather lamely, I said I would have the same as my host, and this turned out to be a sole meunière. Slicing recklessly into the unfamiliar object on my plate, I ended up with a mouthful of bones. The rather astonished young man found himself giving me a lesson on how to eat fish.

After that I abandoned my child's diet and gradually learned to eat most foods except the hated egg. It did not take me so long to acquire a taste for wines – particularly champagne, which has always put me in the happiest humour.

Young people usually pass through a period of extreme ideals, and I decided that only the live theatre, classical music and serious authors were worth attention. Since I disdained the movies, thus missing a lot of the best films ever made, I was not well informed on the mechanics of kissing. In fact, I had given the matter no thought at all until one day an escort suddenly kissed me on the mouth. It was a quite disagreeable shock, not related in any way to my unspecific dreams of love and happiness. In a quick reaction of fright at this unexpected happening, I slapped the boy's face. I never thought for a moment how odd it was that, in the ballet, I would not hesitate to embrace passionately whichever dancer represented my loved one. Real life seemed often so much more unreal than the stage; or maybe I should say that my identity was clear to me only when I assumed some make-believe character. For myself, I was influenced this way and that, thinking in turn that I should be sparkling, or tragic, or intellectual – depending on the person last described with approval in some overheard conversation. Needless to say, I was none of those things.

It was so easy for me to step out into the limelight through the plywood door of Giselle's cottage and suffer her shyness, ecstasy, deception and madness as if it was my own life catching me by surprise at each new turn. It was a fresh, living experience for me at every performance as the drama unfolded. But when I left the stage door and

63

sought my orientation among real people, I was in a wilderness of unpredictables in an unchoreographed world.

There was little my mother could do to help my adolescent confusion, except just to be there, and that I have learned is precisely the essential thing about mothers – one needs to know that they are there, particularly at that age when, paradoxically, one is trying so hard to break away from parental influence.

People often ask if the discipline of my career is not irksome. On the contrary, I have found it an extraordinary advantage to have a rigid timetable prescribed for almost every day of the year. The necessity of going to class is not only healthy in itself – for the amount of compulsory exercise is far more than anyone would do voluntarily, just to keep fit – it is also therapeutic in times of emotional stress. No matter how often one attends a ballet class, one must still maintain a particular degree of concentration, for each class is different from all others, and the concentrating for an hour or more on the manipulation of one's limbs relieves and refreshes a mind that may be over-engrossed in emotional problems.

During my unusually long career I must surely have attended more classes with more teachers than any other dancer in history. Even in the early years at Sadler's Wells we had several guest teachers. My favourite was Stanislav Idzikowski, affectionately known as Idzi, a brilliant dancer who had been with the Diaghilev Ballet. He was diminutive, dapper and precise, speaking rather good English with a clipped Polish accent. Severe but never unkind, he knew exactly what he expected of his pupils and explained clearly how to achieve it. He demonstrated all the steps himself, even in pas de deux class, and he could deftly swing one into a lift supported with only one arm. What incredible strength and knack to partner, so airily, lumpy teenagers taller than himself! Forty years later he is still as slim and precise as ever, his face scarcely changed at all. I do not remember ever seeing him without a waistcoat to his neat grey suit.

Another teacher was unusual insofar as she never even pretended that dancers were supposed to follow the music. She only cared that we should learn to jump high. 'Stand up in the air, turn round and then come down' was her preferred way of setting an exercise. Finding that, not unnaturally, we came down to the ground sooner than she wished, she would start to shout, 'Don't listen to the pianist; she is only there to play. Stand in the air. Don't listen to the music.' She brought a favourite pupil from her private school to show us how to jump, but the poor girl, overcome with embarrassment, landed badly and sprained her ankle. We never did suceed in standing in the air.

There was one teacher who made ballet so incredibly boring that I made every effort to do the opposite of what she told me. In the end, as an antidote, I began going secretly to take private lessons with Lydia Kyasht, who had been Karsavina's classmate and friend in the St Petersburg ballet school. Kyasht filled the room with movement and music and I was happy to find dancing once more a thing of grace.

Nicholas Sergeyev was by far the oldest and most demanding teacher. A wizened little man but quite erect, with upright grey hair, the ghost of a moustache and wearing thin-rimmed glasses, his well-kept clothes hung rather loosely about his body. He was reputed to have been a not very great dancer in the old Imperial Ballet of St Petersburg, where he recorded all the famous ballets in the Stepanov system of notation. When he left Russia in the Revolution he took his notebooks with him. He went to Paris, then he was invited to London by the Camargo Society to produce *Giselle*. De Valois snapped him up a year later for *The Nutcracker*, and subsequently for *Swan Lake* and *Sleeping Beauty*. His classes were in the very old tradition and quite killing, but his sharp eyes noticed any slackers and his little malacca cane would come down with a light whack on the calf, or jab at some muscle that was not working to his satisfaction. To gain a breather we would try to inveigle him into conversation, but his French and English – and some said his Russian – were very limited. Someone would ask, 'How did you like the new ballet last night, Mr Sergeyev?' He would reply, 'No good moderna ballett! Publica like classica ballett. Classica ballett good.' It did not matter what new ballet it was, they were all no good. The same went for what he thought of as the younger generation of ballerinas: 'Pavlova no good'; 'Tamara Karsavina no good'; and so on. Only his favourite, Loukom, who danced at the turn of the century, ever got a word of praise. Heaven knows what he must have thought of us! But he was oddly indulgent, and I was very fond of him; he brought so much atmosphere of the old-style ballet school to Sadler's Wells Theatre.

Whenever Sergeyev was rehearsing a production from his notebooks he insisted on bringing along his own pianist, Ippolit Motcholov, so that together they could sort out where his notation fitted the musical score. Ippolit was the most charming and gentle man imaginable, with faultless old-world manners and a dreamy look. He really belonged in a Turgenev novel. He wore morning dress with striped trousers and a stiff wing collar. In the inside pocket of his black coat he carried a photograph of the Czar, the Czarina and their daughters. He had at one time given piano lessons to the Princesses. His air of ineffable melancholy tore my heart. How sad it was to see him banished for the rest of his life from the country and people of his birth. Nowhere in England could he have found the pale silver birch forests and vast golden fields of his native landscape, nor the winter snows nor the summer 'white nights' of St Petersburg, nor the colour of the Baltic glinting in the northern sunshine. His face had the subdued expression of one who bears suffering with never a word of complaint.

1936 was a vintage year for Frederick Ashton, and consequently a great one for me. In February he produced

Apparitions and in November *Nocturne*, the two ballets which put me on the crest of the wave. The role in *Apparitions* demanded a woman of elegance and sophistication – hardly a role I could adequately fill at the age of sixteen – and yet it was made for and around me. The final rehearsal was chaotic, for the costumes were nowhere near completed and everyone was very tense. Afterwards I shared a taxi with Ashton to a photographer's studio. By this time, the crush I had developed for William Chappell had transferred itself to Ashton, so I was already emotional at being close to him in the taxi. Then he started to tell me everything that was missing from my interpretation of the woman in *Apparitions*. I knew then for certain that I was going to fail him and the ballet, de Valois, the company and everyone. I burst into tears and went home that night desperately afraid of the fiasco to come. It is strange how such moments help foment the artist lurking deep inside the adolescent. The next night, by some alchemy of despair, I had matured just enough to meet the demands of the ballet. So many hundreds of times since then have I dreaded that my performance would let the company down. On countless first nights of new ballets, of London seasons, in foreign capitals, on New York openings and many, many other occasions, the same terror has overtaken me. It can never be completely mastered because it comes from a sense of duty and obligation to the other dancers and to the public. Without it, I suppose, I would be no good.

Cecil Beaton had designed ravishing costumes for *Apparitions* and, rather reasonably, did not want them made by the Sadler's Wells wardrobe mistress, whose idea of correcting an ill-fitting dress was to say, 'It's you that's crooked, dear; I can't do anything about it.' So Mme Karinska, who made costumes so exquisitely for grander ballet companies than ours, was called upon to carry out Beaton's designs. She was a great creator in her own right, interpreting the sketches quite beautifully – but in her own Russian time, which was not at all the same as Ninette de Valois's time! While the opening ballet of the evening was being danced, taxis were rushing up to the stage door with great clumps of ball dresses in the arms of frantic seamstresses. They were sorted, distributed and given a few finishing touches during the intermission. Some were still lacking bits of decoration, though there were plenty of loose pins. But from the confusion emerged a ballet of intangible beauty, a melancholy, haunting, laudanum dream.

It was in *Apparitions* that the harmony of dancing with Robert Helpmann began taking hold. It was curious, for although I adored Ashton and Chappell, I had remained a little frightened of Helpmann. I discovered only later on that a surprisingly kind heart lives behind the caustic humour. As a man of the theatre he was the finest mentor imaginable. Helpmann had only to walk on stage to draw all eyes to himself, for he had a magnetic stage presence. His role as The Poet in *Apparitions* dominated the ballet. The rest of us were his opiate-induced visions, transfigured from scene to scene as his hallucinations deepened. It is hard for me to explain the intensity of our involvement in that magical process of 'theatre'. To be constantly sharing the stage with such a personality as Helpmann's is to learn in a hard school, which is the best school, for only by a superhuman effort can one hope to hold the public's attention oneself. And yet as a partner Helpmann was easy and considerate; he must have shown a good deal of patience with me, as I was so inexperienced and he hated spending time on unnecessary rehearsals. I had complete confidence dancing with him. For instance, the fact that after our first few performances together of *Swan Lake* we never again rehearsed the last act didn't worry me at all. The fourteen years of our felicitous partnership gave me time to develop, albeit unconsciously, my own presence and style.

All this is not to say that he spared me his tongue! Some months before *Apparitions* I had passed through a group of dancers inside the stage door, and before I was out of earshot down the corridor I heard Helpmann saying, 'Did you *hear* what she said to Cecil?' I also heard the laughter that followed. My heart stopped for a moment. Whatever could I have done this time? I tried to remember back to the social blunder. Yes. It had been after a performance. Ashton was with some people in evening dress and had said, 'Margot, this is Cecil Beaton.' I stood tongue-tied, wondering what would be the correct thing to say to such an eminent person, and having in the back of my mind something like, 'What an honour to meet you.' However, the sentence which eventually mumbled itself out of my mouth was 'Oh! I have heard of you.' Still remembering this gaffe, it had been rather alarming to face him at rehearsals and costume fittings, even though he was gentle and unassuming. When I had to go, very shyly, to his flat to be photographed, I was amazed at the artificial grass that covered his living-room floor. I was also quite deceived by his pretence of knowing nothing about cameras. I reported to my mother that he even had to ask his assistant at what stop to put the lens, and that he didn't do anything himself but press the button. My naïveté, in general, must have tried him quite a bit, for as he saw me emerge in my costume he remarked in a slightly disappointed tone, 'Oh dear! Couldn't we have something a little more glamorous in the way of eye makeup?'

At heart I was still very childish. Now that I was at the theatre all day, my mother once more had started buying animals, and a strange series of pets came and went from the attic of our mews house. A meal was always ready for me after the long bus journey home. How good it was on a dark winter afternoon to get in from the miserable rain and to toast crumpets before the fire; they came from the muffin-and-crumpet man, a street seller who carried them in a cloth on his head and rang a big hand bell to announce his presence in the neighbourhood.

My mother now thought it was time she should tell me the facts of life, but I was too embarrassed to want to listen. Felix had bought a car for £25, and I was happier going with him to a candlelit café, feeling tragic as only the young can feel tragic in the face of impending adult-hood, than I was spending the evening with one of my stage-door admirers. Only one admirer really touched my heart, and him I never met. He was Clem Sohn, the Bird Man. He had invented a bird suit in which he could fly to the ground from an aircraft. There was a lot of pub-licity about his arrival in England to give a demonstration of his flight. After our ballet performance one Saturday matinée I received a little bunch of flowers with a note saying, *I don't want to be a Bird Man any more, I wish I was a ballerina like you. Clem Sohn.* A week later he had flown to his death. I mourn him still and wish that I had had the chance to talk to him.

Nocturne was also a glorious ballet for me. How com-pletely I could lose myself in the heart of the poor Flower Seller, cast aside without thought by the Rich Young Man. I lived the story through anew at each performance. Ashton was never satisfied at rehearsals, always urging me on to an unattainable standard and complaining about my soft feet, which would not move with the required steely precision. 'Margot's pats of butter' he called them. De Valois, having said when I first joined the school, 'We are just in time to save her feet,' was for ever ordering me to 'snap those feet off the floor', but to no avail. My mother had a gentler approach. She said, 'Markova has exquisite feet; I love to watch the way she uses them like a bird taking off for flight, but I never watch Margot's feet.' She also repeated over and over to me that my dancing was beautiful but all on the same plane, lacking light and shade. 'You need much more attack in the fast passages; there is no snap to your movements; they are all the same speed. Can't you make contrast in your work? It is lovely but monotonous.' I struggled to do as they wanted but felt hopeless.

Sophie Fedorovitch designed *Nocturne*. She had already done several Ashton ballets, bringing to her work a cer-tain mystical, evocative quality that no other designer has

70

ever quite matched. Perhaps she was exactly in the right time, her life span coinciding with the era in which her art could best flourish. Over the years she influenced and guided Ashton as he passed from spontaneous youthful creation to mature genius. Small, ageless, she was self-effacing and dominant at the same time. Not domineering, but so much the perfectionist that after days spent on coming to a decision about the exact colour tone for some costume there was afterwards no question that it might be otherwise. She could be adamant, and yet she spoke so quietly it was hard to catch the whispered phrases whose words were selected as carefully as were her colours. Strangest of all was the quietness of her movements: she did not seem to enter a room, but simply materialized there and later vanished, like the Cheshire Cat.

As we neared the end of the 1936 season we made a short provincial tour, on which I discovered that well-known institution, the English theatrical 'digs', or lodgings. The landladies piled bread and jam and cheese and cold meats on the table for tea, and cooked enormous hot breakfasts and lunches. One could eat like a pig, all included with the lodging charge, for about £2 a week.

Just before this tour, de Valois dropped another of her bombshells. 'I'm going to give you Giselle next season; we'll start rehearsing it on the tour.' I could hardly speak, I was so upset. 'But I can't possibly dance Giselle. I'm not nearly ready.' 'That's for me to decide,' she replied, putting a firm stop to the conversation. At home I carried on for hours to my mother about how ridiculous it was to give me Giselle. De Valois must be mad, I was not a ballerina, I could not do the steps, I just could *not* do it, and so on. The ballet had naturally lapsed from the repertoire after Markova left, a state of affairs that de Valois did not like. At home in the attic I endlessly rehearsed the famous mad scene from Act I, and tried to master some of the difficult steps. All my complexes returned: my soft feet, my pudding face, my neck; everything was wrong and I could never be Giselle. So far from being ambitious I found myself pushed into the great classical ballets against my will,

71

certain that doom and disaster awaited me and the public. 'What a beautiful step! I shall never be able to dance it' could be my epitaph.

On the first night I was still too inexperienced to know how much time I needed to prepare, and I felt embarrassed to arrive at the theatre two hours before the performance. I was barely ready when the curtain rose. Among all the telegrams I opened (afterwards!) was one which read, *And some have greatness thrust upon them. Good luck. De Valois.* When I went to thank her, she asked if I knew the full quotation, and shamefacedly I had to say, 'No,' and let her tell me. 'Some are born great, some achieve greatness –'

Miss Fleet had predicted that I would find myself an ignoramus. How right she had been! Now I began reading madly, and at random, all the classics I could lay hands on. Admirers were regarded first and foremost as a source of literary or musical information, to the point where I liked most the young man who could lend me the best books and records. Among other more suitable works he lent me James Joyce's *Ulysses*, which was at that time banned in Britain. De Valois boarded my bus one day as I was reading it on the way up Rosebery Avenue to Sadler's Wells. 'What's that, dear?' she asked, peering over at the book. She practically had a heart attack when she saw what it was. 'For God's sake, child, don't read that in public, you could be arrested!'

Every year at this time, Colonel de Basil's Ballets Russes would sweep into London like a forest fire. It was a magnificent company from the point of view of personality and power. Giant stars burned up the air of the Covent Garden stage: Massine's intensity seemed to gather itself into his strangely secretive black eyes, which rarely smiled or gave out any warmth but resembled the 'black holes' in the universe whose density is so great that their existence is known even though they give no light. His inward force held the attention of every eye in the theatre even when he stood motionless and expressionless. In contrast, Danilova wielded her impudent, witty, compelling charm through the theatre like a flame-thrower; no one was untouched. Of the three famous 'baby ballerinas' who had been only fourteen or fifteen years old when they had first astounded London in 1933, Irina Baronova was the most complete artist. Her technical accomplishment was such that her intelligence and humour were allowed full play. Tamara Toumanova, incredibly beautiful, epitomized the public image of the ballerina, with sleek black hair and never a smile. I tried hard to imitate her, but cheerfulness would keep breaking through. Only in *Tricorne* do I remember Toumanova's beautiful smile, glowing like the sun. Tatiana Riabouchinska was fair and more fragile, her wistful air appealing for its almost childlike quality.

Looking back, I cannot say that Act II of *Swan Lake* was particularly well danced by de Basil's company. The corps de ballet could in no way be compared with the purity and perfection of the Kirov Company or Royal Ballet in Petipa's classics. It was the excitement and verve, the power and the magic of those performances that made them, for me, so momentous. It was the richness of colour and music and 'theatre' in their work that fired audiences. And there were stories of temperament backstage and of parties in Bloomsbury far into the night. Many a British heart was lost to this annual invasion, which came like a Tartar horde, proud and passionate, until the caravanserai moved on, leaving a trail of memories for those who had lived for a few weeks close to the sun.

Years later, the Royal Ballet was also to make its stunning impact on foreign cities, but at that time, in the 1930s, it is small wonder that the little company, living so frugally at Sadler's Wells Theatre, should have been overshadowed if not quite eclipsed. Only a perceptive few were aware that de Valois and Ashton would change the orientation of classical ballet in the twentieth century from Russia to the West.

*

I still had a great sense of inadequacy in the roles that were thrust upon me so early. As a counterbalance, I wanted to have a good time outside the theatre, to use up my high spirits at parties. The eve of my second *Giselle* performance coincided with the Annual Vic-Wells Ball held at the Royal Opera House, Covent Garden. The casts and staffs of the Old Vic and Sadler's Wells Theatres attended in elaborate fancy dress, and I certainly was not the type of ballerina who would want to miss such an evening! I was seldom off the ballroom floor until, towards two in the morning, older members of the ballet started to say, 'Good heavens! you are dancing Giselle today, Margot; you should have been in bed hours ago!' The performance next day did suffer somewhat from the ill effects of those revels, but an even worse lesson was in store for me in Brighton, where we gave a special matinée performance. Arriving at noon at the theatre, I dumped my makeup in the dressing room and joined a group, including de Valois, who were going to fill in time by having a drink. They ordered sherry, so I did the same – I had never tasted it before. They ordered a second sherry, so I had another. Eventually someone noticed me sitting there quietly and said, 'For heaven's sake, you are on in the first ballet, it starts in twenty minutes.' I found myself lurching into the dressing room, lightheaded and irresponsible. The other girls looked up disapprovingly. 'There you are at last! Hurry up, they've called the quarter-hour.' Head swimming, and with a scarcely controlled desire to giggle, I somehow made up and manoeuvred myself into my costume and sailed down to the stage with bravado. There followed a nightmare I have never forgotten. My brain desperately commanded limbs that felt like lead and seemed to move so slowly that I thought they arrived in position five minutes after the music. One or two jumps left me panting for breath, and at any moment I felt sure I would sink to the floor and stay there, helpless and hopeless. An eternity passed before it was all over, including bows to an understandably unenthusiastic audience.

Never again would I risk a drink on a performance day.

It was at least thirty years until I found the courage to take so much as an aspirin before dancing to calm the pain of a badly strained muscle.

SIX

In ancient times the English people went 'a-maying' as summer approached. They danced in the sunshine, wove maypole ribbons, gathered flowers in the fields and surely enjoyed a good deal of flirting. Something similar used to happen to the Vic-Wells Ballet each year from 1936 until World War II came upon us in 1939. We went to dance in Cambridge in late May, just before the Long Vacation, when the undergraduates were supposed to be studying their hardest before taking their tripos examinations. With fortitude and gallantry, the undergraduates entertained the dancers in a sort of permanent, floating party that, breaking out afresh in different locations, never quite died down during the entire week. Groups formed and re-formed, sometimes splitting into three or four parties in various colleges at the same time. At the appointed hour, the ballet would gather in the theatre to dance with perhaps more enthusiasm than accuracy. Meanwhile, the undergraduates seemed to accomplish their set tasks, absenting themselves from the fun for just long enough to do what was academically necessary.

At first I was gauche, not knowing what to say to anyone. By the second summer I had some friends among the ballet company, notably Pamela May. Wanting to look grown-up, I had made an effort to smoke as nonchalantly as some of the other girls, although I didn't enjoy it at all. Frederick Ashton saw me one day and roughly pushed the cigarette from my hand, saying, 'Ballerinas *never* smoke!' It was the greatest favour he could have done me, for it gave me the perfect excuse to say, 'No thank you, I don't smoke.' I have never smoked since, first because of Ashton, and second because during the war my friends became so desperate for cigarettes, and suffered their lack so greatly, that I decided never to put myself in the same position.

Pamela May, June Brae and I were eventually nicknamed 'the triptych', and we shared rooms in the King's Parade in the centre of Cambridge. On a particular night in 1937 there was a party in our rooms. Two dark-haired brothers were dancing the new rumba rhythm to a recording made by the Lecuona Cuban Band. The music invaded my mind, overwhelming any conscious thought as I stared at their dance – which resembled nothing I had seen before. I wonder now if the younger boy looked at me or spoke to me that night. I just don't remember; but the next morning something very strange occurred – and this is absolutely true. After I woke up I stepped out of bed to find the floor was not as usual. My feet did not touch it as I moved across the room, so I returned and sat on the edge of the bed to think the matter out. I could not understand what was happening to me. The phrase 'walking on air' came to my mind, and suddenly I remembered the dark-haired boy dancing the rumba the night before. That was it! I must be in love! I did not even know his name, except that they called him Tito.

By a miracle he wandered into our rooms during the day, seemingly to see me, although he scarcely spoke a word to any of us. His presence set the world quivering; the room floated like a bubble in space. He touched my hand lightly, mumbled something inaudible, moved about restlessly for a few minutes and then went out of the door without excuse or explanation. The room reverted to normal. After that day he appeared frequently, in much the same manner, sometimes in my dressing room, sometimes as I walked by the river, never saying where or when he would see me next, never saying where he had been. I looked anxiously for him at parties, but was usually disappointed. Then, without warning, he would be standing beside me, holding my hand with an absentminded air as he talked to someone else. He never stayed long, but vanished again as mysteriously as he had come, leaving me with the feeling that a small whirlwind, after raising me up, had deposited me again on the hard ground.

Tito was slim, with a coffee complexion and beautiful hands, the fingers of which were very long and straight. His entire bone structure was so finely proportioned that, walking or sitting, he seemed always somehow relaxed and unhurried. Though incapable of a sharp word or an awkward movement, he was in no way weak or soft. He might have seemed thin, except that the handsome head was supported by a good neck. The thoughtful look on his rounded face gave an impression of a person who was light in weight but powerful of mind. His words, which were never very clearly pronounced, seemed to come from thoughts that were so far away that it was difficult to connect with them at such a distance. Having so little to say myself, it was perfect happiness to be with someone equally uncommunicative and yet totally compatible. Sometimes he held me so closely that I almost dared not breathe. I just wished he would take me away with him and look after me for ever. In the theatre, while I was making up, he would wander in casually and sit cross-legged on the floor, talking more than at other times, telling me about his life in Panama.

There was no way I could know what he felt for me. Certainly, since he sought me out each day to spend some time together, I thought he liked me. On the other hand, it was obvious that his feelings were nothing like mine were for him. But I lived on a cloud until he sailed for Panama to spend the long vacation at home. He had given me a Panamanian coin bearing the date 1936, the last year of his father's second presidency. I gave him a photograph, dedicated in my tiny, shy handwriting and, after much consideration, with the words *For my dear Tito from Margot*. I was deeply concerned that the message should not overstate the feeling for him that it would be correct for me to hold, in view of the fact that he had not expressed the degree of his regard for me. On the other hand, I did not want to understate my love in case he should think I did not care at all.

After he left England I was on a cloud, waiting for a letter, yet half trying not to expect it in order to forestall the dreaded disappointment. I hoped I kept my feelings secret from everyone except Pamela and June, and even with them I was as casual as I could manage when talking of Tito. It was inadmissible to be in love with a boy who did not love one even more!

As the days and weeks passed I convinced myself that it had indeed been a mistaken love, and that he was just a playboy who had forgotten me already. Otherwise he would at least have written some message, however wispy, to maintain the thread of understanding between us. How the young heart can suffer! Perhaps in later years pain is deeper because it has more knowledge to relate to, but innocence is utterly vulnerable. That year may perhaps have confirmed my escape into the reality of my ephemeral world of ballet.

By the time I saw Tito next May in Cambridge, my heart had hardened by a small but perceptible amount. Never again would I float on air. My feelings were unchanged, but were now fenced in for self-protection. To my surprise he again held me closely, and asked, 'Are you still mine?' Turmoil and confusion in my mind! I had prepared myself so completely for his lack of interest. In a tiny voice, I said a reluctant 'No.' At any rate I would not lie to him. It seemed, however, that Tito was saddened by my reply.

Despite my breaking heart, I must admit that during the winter I had been extremely preoccupied with dancing, especially as I was preparing for the three acts of *Swan Lake*, which I danced for the first time on 21 December 1937. Odette/Odile is a formidable role, climaxed by the virtuoso feat of thirty-two consecutive fouetté turns on one leg without touching the floor with the other. Some dancers can do dozens of these turns with ease; others

find them an impossibility. I have always found them difficult, and frightening, too. How I worked and worked on
this demanding ballet, and what a drama it was for the
entire company, wondering how I would get through it.
Robert Helpmann was all kindness and patience, making
light of my fears: 'Don't be stupid,' he said, 'of course you
can do it. Come on now, try once more.'

Had I not been so frightened of de Valois I might have
backed out of the whole nerve-wracking experience. Her
word, however, was law, so there was no alternative but
to get on with it as best I could.

My poor mother was more of a wreck than anyone by
the first night. She could only survive the strain with the
help of a stiff brandy in the bar between Acts II and III.
Well, somehow or other I did it, never guessing that almost thirty-five years were to pass before my obstinate
nature would finally give up the battle with fouetté turns.
In my last few performances of *Swan Lake* I substituted
another step.

All those years I would feel after the ballet like a run-
ner who has put his last ounce of effort into the race – the
glorious satisfaction of having given everything to the
moment. Exhaustion was cloaked in relief as I removed
stage makeup and dressed for a victory supper – followed
often by tribal celebration dancing on the ballroom floor.
The following day happiness and fatigue in equal measure
mingled with the beginning of apprehension for the next
challenge.

Apprehension grew into fear and fear into terror as the
new ordeal approached. Ballets rated fear in direct ratio
to the degree of absolute physical control and stamina
they exacted. Thus: *Swan Lake* and *Sleeping Beauty* –
terror; *Giselle* – dread; *Firebird* – fear and so on down to
Ondine, which was a joy from beginning to end – my
happiest ballet. The acting aspect of these ballets never
bothered me.

In those pre-war days we received no pay for our six
weeks' holiday. Nevertheless, we somehow managed to go
off to Paris to study with the famous Russian ballerinas of

the last Czarist days in St Petersburg. There were three of them living in exile, each with her own ballet school, and each offering different qualities as teachers of the pre-revolutionary period before Vaganova collated and standardized a system for training under the Soviet régime. Senior of the three, and the one to become my favourite, was Olga Preobrajenska. She was small, about four foot ten in height, with a slightly hunched back, a face full of character and an impish sense of humour. This was the woman whom Gontcharov, in Shanghai, told me had terrified all her students because of her severity and terrible temper. Naturally I was most apprehensive of attending her class until I found that, at the age of sixty, she was considerably mellowed, though still able to get extremely angry. Her daily class followed a very set pattern, to which one quickly became accustomed, though the pianist, another little *émigré* old lady, never could get it quite right. 'Pourquoi *poum – poum – poum*?' complained Preobrajenska towards the piano. 'Je veux *Poum – Poum – poum – po-poum*! No *Poum – Poum – Poum*!' And she would turn back to glower at the class until someone danced especially well, when she would rediscover her smile. As a matter of fact, none of the Russian teachers adhered to strict musical patterns. The accompanist was expected to lengthen some measures and add a few flourishes at the end of a phrase as required. Conductors were expected to do the same thing, pandering to the dancer's whim, and this created some rather unmusical traditions. In the English ballet, however, we were brought up very strictly and subjected as likely as not to a curt reprimand if we dared to ask for a change of tempo. Constant Lambert was not a man to be ordered about by a handful of ballet dancers. He understood ballet as a genuine marriage between music and dance, with music the senior partner.

Preobrajenska had always been the poorest of the three teachers. She told me that she had only succeeded because she watched every role in every ballet so that if a ballerina was suddenly taken ill she would be able to replace her instantly. Now, in exile, she was the only one who did not have her own studio. She rented one at the extraordinary Salle Wacker rehearsal rooms at Place Clichy. This building in the Montmartre night-club area consisted of steep iron staircases and small studios, two or three to a floor, each with its piano pounding out a conflicting tune for a different group of dancers. It was a long climb to Preo's studio on the fourth floor, but once there one found a light room with windows on two sides and a big mirror covering the whole third wall. Parents or visitors could sit near the piano. It was said that M d'Artemovsky, brisk, white-haired, with a little moustache, a little paunch and a monocle, who acted as her secretary, welcoming one effusively and collecting the money, had been cheating her for years, stealing most of the profits and giving her just enough to live on. She was a darling. I worked very hard with her, learning much about presenting oneself to the audience. '*Regardez publique,*' she would shout, indicating the mirror. 'Don't look at the floor, look at public.'

She taught all day, with a short lunch break, during which she had a morsel to eat before climbing on to a chair to put the crumbs out on a high windowsill for the birds, whom she loved much more than humans. There was a peculiarity about her main class of the day for professional dancers. At the end of one hour and a half the door was opened to allow the children in to start their junior class at the barre. Meanwhile our class spent fifteen or twenty minutes in the centre of the room, practising the difficult fouetté turns (featured in *Swan Lake*, Act III) for which the pianist accompanied us. This meant that the children got on as best they could against our music and with scant attention from Preo. My mother used to puzzle over it. 'I see the children with terrible faults getting no correction. I can't understand at what point they turn into the accomplished dancers of the senior class. I just cannot make it out,' she said.

*

The ballerina Mathilde Kschessinskaya, by marriage La Princesse Romanovsky-Krassinsky, was a completely different personage. She lived with her husband, the Grand Duke André of Russia, in fashionable Passy, where they had a charming little villa on a private road, and she had her own private studio near by. The studio was modern, clean, elegant, light and airy. Photographs of her best pupils adorned the walls above the positions they normally occupied at the barre. Pride of place beneath the picture of Tatiana Riabouchinska was offered to favoured visitors to her class.

Kschessinskaya, about the same age as Preobrajenska and also as diminutive, was very upright, with a rather aristocratic face, long straight nose and the most coquettish, sparkling eyes. By contrast to Preo, who invariably wore the same brown dress, school-tunic style, over a white short-sleeved knitted blouse, she had a variety of different-coloured floral chiffon dresses made to the same becoming pattern and worn with a matching single-coloured chiffon bandana tied round her coiffured grey hair. Everything about her class was happy, smiling, enchanting, light and free. She had, after all, charmed the last Czar when he was a young cadet, and had become his mistress. Later she was protected by the Grand Duke Sergei Mikhailovitch, who covered her in jewels and built for her the small palace that Lenin was later to find so appropriate for his famous balcony speech to the revolutionary crowds. It was on an Italian holiday with my beloved Princess Astafieva that Kschessinskaya had fallen in love with the Grand Duke André and conceived the child she was somewhat embarrassed to bear while still protected by Grand Duke Sergei. Not daring to reveal the true situation she continued dancing on her return to St Petersburg – but had her costumes cunningly altered, and changed the direction of certain steps so that she should never be seen in profile from the Imperial Box. She loved parties, jewels and gambling, even though this high life was incompatible with the daily routine necessary for a Prima Ballerina Assoluta. Therefore she cleanly – and cleverly – divided her life in two. Four weeks before a performance at the Imperial Maryinsky Theatre – now the Kirov – she closed her house to guests, followed a strict régime, practised for hours each day and retired early at night to prepare herself for the triumph of her appearance and for the several encores which the Grand Duke requested by a nod of his head from the box.

When the curtain fell on her last *révérence* she resumed the lavish entertaining in her palace and the bewitching of handsome men. At times she retired with the Grand Duke to the country estate he had given her, for a restful summer idyll.

As an exile in Paris, after gambling away in Monte Carlo the fortune and jewels with which she escaped from Russia, she was still vivacious, captivating, full of life and allure. Her lessons were unusually musical and were bent on charming an imagined audience behind the wall of plate-glass mirror. She was really a delight. June Brae, who loved Kschessinskaya's style, was always one of her favourite pupils. I loved her, too, but found it difficult to chose between her, Preo and Lubov Egorova, third of the famous Paris teachers.

Egorova, perhaps ten years younger than the other two, was married to one of the Troubetskoi princes, and she, too, had her own studio, near the Place de la Trinité – not as fashionable as Passy and not far from the Montmartre area. Egorova was taller, more like Astafieva in build, dark-haired and full of the dignity and soul of old Russia. I felt her to be very warm-hearted, but remote. It was as though the other two had remained children at heart, while Egorova had grown up and experienced the sufferings of the world. As a teacher there was a depth of emotion in her class arrangements, particularly in the long adagio sections, that no one else I know has offered. I felt a deeply respectful adoration for her.

On two separate occasions in 1938, Tito, who was holidaying in Paris that year, took me out – once to lunch and once to supper. Again there was that feeling of profound, unvoiced sympathy between us, which I then supposed to be only a product of my own imagination. I had other companionable friends and admirers by now, so I doubt whether anyone knew of my secret love for Tito. Even my mother quite believed me to be romantically involved with a quiet young Englishman who talked to me about art and painting. The truth was that he was fair with grey eyes; but Tito's eyes were black.

On the threshold of maturity, after three years of dancing major roles, I suddenly realized that it was no longer a question of being a promising newcomer. Difficult as it had been to dance my first *Giselle* and *Swan Lake*, there had at least been the excuse that I was young and inexperienced. Now I could see that with each new success the burden of expectation grew upon me. In particular, the standard by which I would be judged in classical ballets would be raised each season, and the same went for new works – though to a lesser degree, as no one could make comparison with the performance of past ballerinas. I thanked heaven for those glorious Ashton creations into which I put such heart and soul that I suffered searing jealousy when another dancer had to replace me because of some minor ailment, like an attack of influenza.

At this point in my young career I came upon the most difficult challenge, one that it would take me years to meet on equal terms, and curiously enough the one that eventually became my greatest triumph. It was, too, the one single ballet above all others that would carry the fledgling Sadler's Wells company to international fame, for *The Sleeping Beauty* became the cornerstone of our American tours, traditionally opening the New York seasons for almost two decades.

There was a day in 1938 when de Valois, Ashton, Helpmann and Billie Chappell were discussing over lunch the decision to mount this great Russian masterpiece on our little company the following season. All of them had seen the performances presented so lavishly by Diaghilev in London at the Alhambra Theatre in 1921. Indeed, Ninette de Valois had then danced one of the important fairy solos – the quickest one, of course, since her speed and precision exceeded even that of the Russian dancers. Diaghilev's production, with costumes and scenery by Léon Bakst, an enormous cast and five famous ballerinas to alternate the part of Princess Aurora, was nevertheless a financial failure. It was then that he uttered the words, 'I am fifteen years too early with this ballet,' and it was Ninette de Valois who now, just seventeen years later, was testing the truth of his prophecy. Not only was the Diaghilev version of *Sleeping Beauty* still clear in the memories of many balletomanes, it had actually been a unique landmark in the history of ballet.

I listened to the discussion of Karsavina's perfection, Trefilova's pure line, Spessivtzeva's fragile-seeming strength, Lopokova's bubbling vivacity. In awe I ventured to ask whoever would dance Princess Aurora this time. 'Why, *you* will do it!' said de Valois unhesitatingly, and continued with her theory that the Diaghilev version had failed because the costumes so overpowered everything else on stage that the dancing could hardly be seen for plumes and riches. This time the staging would be simple and clean, without feathers or sequins. She added that, as we were very short-numbered, cuts would have to be made in the music as well as a severe reduction in dancers for the big waltz and other corps de ballet scenes. However, the resident opera company at Sadler's Wells could provide some of the character roles, notably Carabosse, which would ideally suit Jack Greenwood – a darling jovial man, who loved appearing with us in *Coppelia*, *Swan Lake* and various other ballets – and Catalabutte, which Carol Bertram would do very well.

My imagination went back to Mr Olson on the beach at Hong Kong, telling me about his memories of Karsavina dancing *The Sleeping Beauty*. I thought of the wistful, nostalgic look in George Gontcharov's eyes as he talked of the Rose Adagio and the Grand Pas de Sept at the

Bolshoi Theatre, Moscow, while he gave us class in Mrs Brae's front room in Shanghai. In those days it had been quite impossible for me to re-create in my imagination the scenes they described. Even now it was as though I had just been told I would climb to the moon on a ladder woven from sand. To dance *Giselle* and *Swan Lake* I had the example of Markova in my mind's eye, even though she presented an ideal totally unattainable. Now I was forced back on the memories of other people as my guide to the style I should pursue as I embarked on rehearsing the part of Princess Aurora.

In England the story would normally be called *The Sleeping Beauty*, but this title was so associated in stage versions with the traditional Christmas pantomime that it was decided to follow Diaghilev in calling it *The Sleeping Princess*. I found this rather a relief, as 'Beauty' was a word I did not feel able to live up to – I had enough to contend with in the dancing without having to worry about my face as well, for at that time I was going through a fat period and was quite podgy all over. Another change: the prince's name was originally 'Desiré'; this was a bit much, so they changed it to 'Florimund'.

Nicolai Sergeyev, together with his pianist Ippolit Motcholov, came every afternoon to teach the ballet. Sergeyev pored over his manuscripts, consulted with Motcholov, then demonstrated the steps to the best of his limited dancing ability, trying to clarify them with some mixed Russian–French–English vocabulary. Often there would be confusion about fitting the steps to the music, accent up or accent down. De Valois had so little confidence in his ability to get everyone together in the same rhythm that she called 'secret' rehearsals to 'tidy it up', telling Sergeyev that other ballets were being rehearsed that day and that he was not required. As soon as he started work the next afternoon, his beady little eyes saw what had been done, and he got pretty ratty with us, banging the malacca cane on the floor and shouting, 'No, no, no. Not change! Not change!' At the piano, Mr Motcholov would seem to shrink a tiny bit into his stiff collar,

86

while his lower face tensed a little like someone who has just taken his first sip of an extra-dry martini.

When I saw my name on the notice board for costume fittings, I ran up to the wardrobe full of excitement at the prospect of seeing myself incarnated as a glowing princess. The wardrobe mistress showed me the sketches and the chosen fabrics. What a terrible shock! The bare tutu designs, one peach-coloured, one pale blue and one white and gold, were almost totally unadorned except for some sun-ray points on the skirts. The headdresses were merely cardboard crown shapes covered in plain satin fabrics. Not one sequin or jewel was to be allowed to mar the austerity. I could not believe that the scintillating princess described by all who had ever seen the ballet was going to burst on to the stage in such stark, ugly dresses. I nearly cried when I got home to tell my mother that the costumes would be like 'little cotton house frocks' instead of the rich costumes suitable for a ballerina.

As well as being at war with my attire, I found the characterization of the role elusive. There was nothing to act except a young girl celebrating her birthday. In other words, I had to be more or less myself, which was the hardest thing to be. The other ballets I danced offered meaty opportunities to be mad, forlorn, tragic and so on; I could fling myself about the stage, happily tearing a passion to tatters. But in *Sleeping Princess* there was very little emotion to use as a cover for my technical deficiencies.

Ironically enough, the production was more successful than the magnificent Diaghilev disaster. The first performance took place in February 1939 in one of the 'pea-soup' London fogs which seemed to gather themselves up for so many of the pre-war Sadler's Wells premières. Emerging from the stage door after the congratulations and kisses, with armfuls of bouquets and having made a mental note of the next morning's rehearsal hour, we encountered a murky world, with visibility at about ten feet and an eerie silence prevailing on the streets. Those cars and buses that still ventured forth had to inch along the curb at a snail's pace, unless they could follow in the wake of another driver, profiting by his tail lights as well as their own lamps. It added to the excitement of the evening as we wondered whether we would ever get home.

Like Princess Aurora herself, I was undoubtedly blessed in my youth by fairy godmothers. Few ballerinas can have had so many opportunities, or so much attention and advice showered upon them. The only thing I can say for myself is that I grabbed it all with both hands and held on with all the tenacity of a true Taurean. One of the remarks which influenced me more than anything else came from Ashton, soon after he had returned from producing a new ballet in New York. He told how Alicia Markova and Alexandra Danilova were vying with each other in the same part at rehearsal. Markova was dancing with her effortless grace and creating a great impression on the surrounding corps de ballet; Danilova, when it came to her turn to repeat the same dance, announced, 'I am Russian. I dance strong!' Whereupon she went into a spitfire attack on the difficult solo. From that day on I danced strong, with every bit of energy I could muster.

SEVEN

I saw little of Tito in that last summer before the war. The die was now cast for my career, and even if he had suddenly, miraculously, declared his love and asked me to marry him, I believe I would have refused. I would have found it hard to relinquish my considerable foot-hold on the climb to success in my make-believe world in exchange for the realities of marriage and motherhood, the latter role presenting no attractions for me whatever.

A chance remark by one of our Cambridge friends, intimating that Tito had been living with an American lady in Paris during the vacation, cut me deeply and confirmed the playboy tag with which I labelled him for the next fourteen years. I reckoned I had been mistaken in loving him. And that was that.

A short provincial tour before the new season had us all hard at work dancing in every performance. I still took little notice of the war talk, even when a trial 'blackout' of city lights was ordered for Saturday night as we closed our week in Liverpool. On Sunday morning the Sadler's Wells Ballet boarded a train to Leeds for our next engagement. As the train moved out of the station I thought I heard a porter shouting, 'War declared!' as he ran along the platform closing the last doors. Tentatively, I mentioned this to the others in the carriage. 'What, dear?' someone asked, so I repeated it. 'Oh, rubbish. He was saying "all clear", of course,' said one of the adults. And so the matter was dismissed. It was 3 September 1939. Two and a half hours later we disembarked at Leeds, to learn that war had indeed been declared that morning. No one could believe it and most of us were too young to have much idea of what it meant anyway. Fred Ashton was silent and gloomy. Constant Lambert, untypically, was at a loss for an amusingly highbrow comment to fit the occasion, and even Helpmann could think of no way to turn this situation into absurdity.

War meant instant disaster and death: at least, that was how I imagined it as we stood about on the station platform wondering if the government would order all theatres to close immediately. Since the government had more urgent things to attend to first, we stayed overnight in a local hotel awaiting the decision. Pamela and I, sharing a room, were awakened in the night by the eerie sirens giving an air-raid warning. Of course I panicked, thinking that a bomb was on its way through the sky to me, personally, at that very minute. Unable to put the lights on for security reasons, we bumped about the bedroom, like bats in daylight, feeling for our clothes. In the dark I said to Pamela, 'I can't find my things, let's wrap ourselves in the bedclothes and hurry down to the shelter.' De Valois emerged from her room just as we were passing her door, swathed in blankets. 'Don't be ridiculous, you two,' she said. 'Go back and get your dressing gowns at once.' In the dusty cellar, which smelt of stale beer, a couple of hours passed while nothing at all happened to the city. Afterwards I felt extremely foolish about my hysterical behaviour.

We returned to London next day and the company was disbanded, since the government had after all decided to close places of entertainment. No one knew if and when theatres would be allowed to reopen. My mother was so calm I could not understand her. Why wasn't she making plans to leave London as quickly as possible? Why was she just sitting there waiting to see what would happen? In short, why wasn't she as frightened out of her wits as I was? She thought I should go off to the country to friends if I wanted to; she would stay in London as she had lived through World War I and didn't think there was such a desperate necessity to escape. Two weeks later the ballet was recalled to start immediately on a tour of undetermined length. Oh, what sore muscles and bruised toes we had as we went straight into performances without practising a step for fourteen days! The first week was physically painful, but soon our limbs accustomed themselves to dancing seven shows a week, which we continued to do for the next five years with only occasional short breaks. Engagements at military camps were not always well received by soldiers who did not think that war meant having to watch fancy ballet dancing. They banged their seats loudly to express their disgust as they left the theatre during the quietest moments of *Les Sylphides*, which was normally first in the programme. Some were heard to complain on the way out that it was more fun to spend the money on a postage stamp and write home. Others did not trouble to turn so delicate a phrase in expressing themselves. Most of this could be clearly heard on stage because the musical accompaniment came only from two pianos, one played by our conductor, Constant Lambert, and the other by our rehearsal pianist, Hilda Gaunt.

One night, in our theatrical lodgings, over cold meat, apple pie and hot tea, Fred Ashton announced that he was going to read the Bible from beginning to end, and that by the time he finished it the war would be over. Finding some passages monotonous and heavy going, he made a further announcement: he would read it aloud to us. Billie Chappell protested, saying: 'Freddie, you can't do that to your friends.' Nevertheless, Freddie did, but he miscalculated by about four years, and was to read a great many other books before the holocaust ceased.

During the 'phoney war', so called because there were no attacks on England, it was arranged that in May 1940 the company should dance in Holland. There were some misgivings when we were about to depart, but an official came to tell us that we would be perfectly safe. Moreover, we should realize that our visit might be important in helping the morale of the Dutch people, who were so courageously facing our common enemy across their land frontier. So we set off cheerfully across the blessed English Channel, soon to save Britain from the fate of our allies on the mainland.

In The Hague an extraordinary calm masked the tensions of a country that sensed its imminent fate and wondered only when and where the first blow would fall. Perhaps the arrival of an English ballet company, laughing and sightseeing for all the world as though nothing unusual was going on, did indeed ease the spirits of some people, for our opening performance was received with almost heartbreaking enthusiasm, and tulips were rained upon us from above as we took the last curtain calls. There was an exceptional bond of intimacy between performers and public that night, as both sides joined in an elaborate pretence, never admitted, that time could be made to stand still and impending doom held for ever at bay.

The gravity of the situation became more obvious every day. The generation above mine reacted according to their different temperaments. De Valois showed her anxiety only when caught off guard. Constant Lambert tried to look cheerfully fatalistic. Ashton's hypersensitive imagination worked like an antenna to pick up new signs of the impending German invasion. Helpmann, the court jester, wrapped truth in humour in order to break the tension he perhaps felt more than anyone else. He made a joke out of everything so that even de Valois, who felt personally responsible for the whole troupe, relaxed and laughed, particularly when he said that the covered barges we saw on the canals were packed with German soldiers dressed as nuns with machine-guns concealed under their habits – which, for all I know, may have turned out true, though we all thought it just a hilarious fantasy.

On the fourth day we danced at Arnhem, getting there early enough to see something of the town before going into the theatre. In the afternoon sun we stood on the bridge looking towards Germany. 'The frontier is only half an hour in that direction,' said our guide. 'Half an hour by car or ten minutes by tank!' said Helpmann. 'Now I understand why they decided to send us straight back to The Hague tonight instead of tomorrow morning.' The journey back was very slow, due to the sudden flood of armoured vehicles coming towards us in the small hours of the morning. 'It must be a general mobilization. They are all going to the border.' In our darkened bus we all fell silent. Even Helpmann was serious.

At dawn there was a sudden commotion in the hotel corridors. 'Invasion. The Germans are invading; they are landing by parachute all around us.' Someone found that the roof offered a perfect lookout, and indeed it was a fascinating and rather beautiful sight as the earliest rays of sun caught the distant parachutes like little puffs of silver smoke, slowly sinking down and vanishing beyond the city skyline. A brisk burst of gunfire sent us scampering down the stairs, and we were soon ordered to the cellars. But, as the day wore on, groups ventured out to the square to sit in the sun. Again, exposure was short-lived. A single bullet, narrowly missing Fred and Bobby in a sidewalk café, provoked an order that everyone must stay inside the hotel until instructions were received from the British Embassy. Only de Valois and Lambert went out to discuss with the Ambassador and the Dutch authorities what could be done. A suggestion that the girls could return to England, leaving the men behind, was brusquely dismissed by de Valois. Hours passed. All was tranquil on the surface. Rumours, alerts, counter-rumours, cancellations: 'Arnhem fell early this morning'; 'Be ready to leave in half an hour'; 'We can't leave, the transport has been commandeered'; 'More divisions have landed.'

The following night two buses drew up in front of the hotel. We clambered aboard, taking with us only what we could wear and with no clue to the destination of our journey. At the front and rear of each bus was a young soldier, well armed. One of them tried to converse in short phrases, using German words among the Dutch. We had difficulty in getting the gist of what he said: 'Juda; nicht aryan.' Then we realized he was telling us that he was Jewish. He must have felt such a need to communicate with friendly people in that unlit bus, which halted every few yards on its way through the ink-black night. 'Poor boy!' we thought. 'He is certain of death at German hands.' We were suddenly aware how cold it was in the bus.

Perhaps the ride lasted six hours; anyway, it was still dark when we halted for the last time. Everyone was happy to unfold stiff limbs and enter a large château, but since it was overcrowded with other refugees we went out to walk a little before trying to find a corner in which to lie down. The faintest grey light was breaking through the dense night sky. We were in a big garden. The chilly air was sweet and fresh, and trees took shape as the light grew. Slowly there came the miraculous unfolding of a picture so serene and exquisite, touched with morning dew and the promise of a fine warm day. It was like a Japanese landscape. A mist-laden lake, rushes, flowering shrubs, pathways and broad lawns came into view as the first vigilant birds alerted others to the hour of awakening. These stirrings of dawn quickly provoked more movement by the water's edge, as a variety of ducks shook their feathers, while herons, treading with extreme care, delicately lowered their long legs and stirred life into some deer who softly stretched and wandered away into the park to start a day that, for them, would not be different from any other.

The day we spent in this blissfully rural paradise was disturbed by occasional bursts of gunfire and rumours that, by a new landing of the enemy, the area was encircled. There was nothing anyone could do, so some of the company organized a game of football with the Dutch soldiers, for all the world as though it were midsummer's day on the village green.

With nightfall our buses moved on again, haltingly as before, until we reached a quayside where we joined a long queue of people waiting to board the ship that was tied up alongside. We were at the port of Ijmuiden, though there was no way of finding that out at the time. Docks and harbours were obvious targets for enemy bombers, and it was an unpleasant feeling edging along in a queue, wondering why those in front couldn't hurry themselves so that we at the back could get under cover, too. Once on board we sailed immediately: I didn't know that a ship could get away so speedily.

The English Channel was mined, and one's instinct was to stay up on deck with the chance of landing on the surface and floating if trouble came. Of course, there was no space, and everyone was ordered below decks. It transpired that we were not in a passenger ship at all. The huge gloomy area of the aft hold was already crowded with women and children, settled on the floor; one could hardly look around for a small space and get down likewise on the hard boards among the straw, imagining the horror that would follow if we were blown up. Such thoughts, together with the cold and the discomfort, didn't encourage sleep. But at last the night gave way to

94

another fair day, and we sailed into the safety of Harwich and home.

Back home at long last I recounted it all to my mother, then fell fast asleep for twenty-four hours.

The 'phoney war' was over. Holland was overrun and defeated in five days; we had been among the last to get out. The horror in Europe spread from East to West; the disaster of Dunkirk seemed almost a victory, and Britain took up her solitary stand behind the English Channel.

Often during those days I tried to remind myself how lucky I was. I was distressed to find how much I cared about material things such as my books and little ballet treasures, including my photographs of the old ballerinas. I really did not want to lose these things, and yet I was ashamed to hold such petty thoughts when there was agonizing human suffering all about me.

For what was I doing all this time? Dancing! I remained in my chosen profession, with little privation or real discomfort, and without losing any close relation. Even my friends were spared, with the exception of Painton Cowan, who had fallen in love with Pamela May in those happy Cambridge days. When the war came they married, like thousands of other couples, to try to snatch at least a few moments of happiness. Painton was killed three weeks after their son was born.

In the ballet we became an even more closely knit family. Most of the men were called up to do national service, Michael Somes among them. His case was typical: he was away for four years, from the age of 23 to 27, perhaps the most vital period for a dancer. But after it was all over he struggled back into training, shrugging off philosophically the disruption of his career like all of them. Ninette de Valois was adamant in her refusal to invite as guest artists any of the new young dancers from abroad who, not having lost a slice of their careers, were then more inspiring to watch. Said de Valois emphatically, 'I will not do it. If I take any of these foreign boys it will discourage our own dancers and we will never develop a tradition for male dancers in England. It is not fair to our boys.'

Frederick Ashton, being a true creative artist, had quickly absorbed the impact of war. Even before our visit to Holland, he produced *Dante Sonata*, which he saw as a struggle to the death between The Children of Light and The Children of Darkness. It was created in the modern dance idiom in bare feet, and we were for ever coaxing splinters out of our bodies, since there was a lot of dragging each other across the stage and no one ever thought to lay a covering over the ancient wooden floorboards of English provincial theatres. But we felt so deeply the passion for Ashton's heart-cry for humanity that we cared nothing for the splinters. It was a ballet impossible to reproduce after the war, danced by a generation too young to understand the time of its creation.

Dante Sonata was conceived during the 'phoney war'. The next phase, that of bombing the cities, brought a different Muse to Ashton's side, and he choreographed an exquisite ballet called *The Wise Virgins*, based on the biblical parable. It was an escape to spiritual thoughts in a time of human agony. This ballet, too, we performed with intense fervour – though there was a lot of mirth when we saw it advertised on a billboard as '*The Wise Virgins* (subject to alteration)'.

As more and more male dancers were called up, so boys were taken early from the school to give them, and us, two years of their dancing before they reached eighteen and went to fight. Naturally, they were not the strongest partners, and the girls learned to fend for themselves in those pirouettes called 'supported' in which their partners should help them. Lifts were another matter, and I was not alone in being nervous when thrown into the air by these youngsters!

The person who more than any other kept the company going during the war was Robert Helpmann. Not only did he support our morale with his humour, he was the one star who could help the company reach dancing maturity. While Fred Ashton was serving as an officer in the Air Force, Helpmann began to create ballets, of which *Hamlet* is definitely a masterpiece, while the others were all original and exciting theatrical experiences. It was a godsend to us that, as an Australian, he was not called up.

De Valois, meanwhile, remained a supreme leader. We would one and all unhesitatingly defend her and obey her commands. We would, metaphorically speaking, have died for her. Part of her secret, like that of all great generals, was that she cared deeply about our lives and our personal problems as well as our careers, although it took me a long time to find that out. It was Gordon Hamilton who decreed that she should and must be addressed as Madame, not Miss de Valois. So she has been Madame to her dancers ever since and in that form still signs her letters to me, but in quotes, thus, 'Madame'.

Like most people in wartime, we had little in the way of personal lives. We spent long hours in the theatre, and we alternated provincial tours of eight to ten weeks with shorter seasons in London. I still did not feel very grown-up, though I had passed my twenty-first birthday, but at least I was no longer afraid of the others. Helpmann, Ashton and Chappell were Bobby, Freddie and Billie; their dressing rooms were always ringing with laughter. One evening Bobby ran into my room to tell me the latest, somewhat indecent, cause of amusement, and then stopped suddenly: 'I wonder,' he said, as he looked at me in the mirror putting on my makeup, 'if Karsavina and Nijinsky used to tell funny stories in the dressing room, too?' Somehow the idea seemed sacrilegious.

Outside the theatre, life became more and more drab, food less and less adequate. This was a problem because of the energy that dancers burn up. Ballet fans were marvellous about sending little parcels of sugar, choco-late, butter and other rationed food, depriving themselves of their own very meagre allowance to help us. I missed the butter more than anything, for the two ounces allowed per week was the amount I had previously eaten at one breakfast. We started looking for other sources of energy and drank lashings of a strange green tonic which was described as 'giving you tomorrow's strength today'. All that happened was that tomorrow we felt even more tired, and drank more green drink. Dancing every night with three matinées made a very heavy week, so as an experiment the Thursday afternoon show was moved over to Saturday, giving us three performances that day. But at least we had all Sunday to recover. The three Saturday performances had to run nonstop, with only a half-hour between them, in order to finish early enough for the public to reach home before the bombs fell. After one or two girls had fainted on stage, this Saturday schedule was abandoned. I was quite sorry. It had been rather fun, in a way, while it lasted.

Pamela May was away from the ballet for quite a while having her baby. June Brae, the other member of our 'triptych', had met David Breeden at Cambridge at the same time that I met Tito and Pamela met Painton. June and David married early in the war, and their daughter was born soon after Pamela's son. I seemed to be the odd girl out.

Alone in No. 1 dressing room, without my closest friends, I developed a star complex, and for a time I was really impossible, imagining that I was different from, and superior to, those around me. Then Pamela came to see us. It was soon after she had been widowed. Completely broken up by her loss, and living as she did facing up to stark reality, she was in no mood to put up with my fanciful airs. She told me outright that I had become a bore. Thinking it over, I decided that I far preferred the company of my friends to the isolated pinnacle implied by the title Prima Ballerina Assoluta, which I had been trying to reach, so I climbed down. As a matter of fact, it had been partly the fault of what I call false friends — those who, with the best will, and believing themselves your warmest admirers, unwittingly destroy you with such talk as: 'People don't realize how great you are'; 'You are the greatest ballerina alive; people should fall back in awe when you leave the stage door'; 'You should be treated like a queen.' All of which is, of course, rubbish. Great artists are people who find the way to be themselves in their art. Any sort of pretension induces mediocrity in art and life alike.

I received some sad stage-door calls. A few months after the Dunkirk debacle I was told by the stage doorman that two ladies were asking to see me. 'They say they are good friends of your husband; he stayed with them after Dunkirk.' 'But I haven't got a husband,' I said. He looked concerned. 'I think you should see them; they are sure you will know them.' So they came in and I learned how a soldier had been billeted with them for several months and how he had said I was his wife. They were very fond of him and showed me his picture taken in the garden with the family and the dog. It was hard for them to believe the truth. Indeed, I hated to upset them, and I have often thought sadly of the boy, so obviously lonely and lost. This sort of episode was not uncommon.

A little old lady came to my dressing room in London. At first I thought she wanted a job as wardrobe mistress, but her conversation ruled that out. 'This is something that will help you very much; many people have been helped.' She didn't say what it was, but I guessed it must be religion. 'Well, thank you very much, but I think I am all right,' I said. She persisted, however, and suddenly asked, 'You know Miss So-and-so, the Chinese dancer, don't you?' 'No, I'm afraid I don't,' I replied, thinking, *Well, it can't be religion so whatever is it?* 'Yes, I know you know her. She has been helped very much by this, too.' Eventually I got rid of the lady, still mystified by her visit until I realized the only possible explanation was that she peddled drugs and had mistaken me for someone else. It was an alarming occurrence.

'There's a G.I. asking to see you,' said the doorman one day. That was a surprise, too, for although London was full of G.I.s, I had not met one. 'Shall I show him in?' I was intrigued, so I said, 'Yes.' He introduced himself as Joseph Stuhl from Philadelphia. 'I saw you dancing to-night,' he said. 'It was marvellous. I've brought a box of chocolates for you. I know they are rationed here.' He was a charming young man, so well-mannered and correct. It happened that he came to the ballet on D-Day, and crossed to Europe the next morning, so I did not realize at the time that I had made a lifelong friend. He was the first of many American friends, whom I have found the kindest in the world.

The only other encounter I had with an American sol-dier was once as I was going home in the blackout after the ballet. I did not like the drunken crowd around Picca-dilly tube station, so I decided, even though I was fairly frightened of the unlit street, to walk to Green Park station. I always walked close to the curb, not liking the idea that someone might jump out from a dark doorway and grab me. I heard footsteps close behind, so I moved a little faster. The footsteps came nearer and I hurried even more. Just as I turned to enter the station, a gentle American voice said, 'Pardon me for speaking to you. I just wanted to say that I noticed you are the only girl in Piccadilly tonight who isn't trying to get picked up.' 'Oh, thank you,' I said. 'Good night.' And he replied 'Good night,' very politely. I thought he was an officer, but I never saw his face because there was no moon that night.

In the days – or rather, nights – of the blitz we welcomed moonless nights. But then came a new horror, which cared for neither moon nor sun. The buzz bombs. They came through the sunny skies, their engines making plenty of noise so that everyone would know death was approach-ing. As in a game of musical chairs, one listened for the moment when the music stopped and, if it seemed over-head at the time, one dived behind the settee and hoped for the best. One might not be able to do much about a direct hit, but it would be silly to be caught by the flying glass if it only landed near by. After the buzz bombs came the V2s, which landed indiscriminately without any warning. But throughout the war, no matter what happened I never heard of anyone getting up from his or her seat to leave the theatre because of an air-raid alert.

I was reminded of this period, and of our spirit, when I came across a letter I had written on 28 June 1944.

Dearest Grandma and Auntie,

I expect you will be worrying about us in the raids which are none too pleasant I must say. However, we are absolutely safe and well so far despite the fact that the house has been blasted to bits, more or less, on Monday night at 12 o'clock. I was out and missed all the fun but Mother was by the front door which gave her a slight bang on the backside before landing up against the wall. The bomb hit the top of a big block just opposite us in the main road, about 200 yards away, and the blast has broken every window but one in the house and removed most of the doors, part of the roof and brought down part of the ceilings and walls, so it is in a pretty state. Rather draughty in this weather! And the dirt and mess are unbelievable. But practically nothing is broken, no furniture, glass or china. I just can't understand it. Poor Mother is in the throes of trying to clean up the mess. She is really wonderful about it, having had no sleep Monday night and worked ever since. She is rather tired and getting a slight reaction today but is cheerful. It all might have been much worse and where we are at the moment is as safe as anywhere else. Certainly downstairs is the place to be as the blast goes upwards and the bombs almost always explode on impact with the top of a building so don't worry about us.

The theatre is still full every night.

Must go to bed now.

All my love,
Margot.

*

At the outbreak of war my mother had initially leased an Elizabethan house in the country to avoid the expected air raids. When they became routine she moved back to London, knowing that she could not miss all those performances and that I needed home cooking and comforts. Every bit of my energy went into dancing, and she did the rest.

Felix was in the Army, where in the course of time his mechanical skill and patience, inherited from our father and grandfather, were put to work on testing new tank weapons. For his peacetime photographic career he had adopted the name of Fonteyn, at my suggestion.

My father had been able to see some of my early Sadler's Wells performances when he came home on leave in 1936. His next leave, due in 1940, was postponed indefinitely because of the war, so that we did not see him at all for ten years. When the Japanese overran Shanghai he was among the enemy aliens taken into internment camp, where on his arrival he wisely volunteered for kitchen duties and spent the next two and a half years boiling rice but remaining cheerful and adequately fed.

Among the marvellous 'fans' who sent bunches of flowers, and still do to this day, were two sisters, Charlotte and Irene Armspach. I had not met them but knew their names well from their many little messages of goodwill. So, when a young sailor wrote asking if I could occasionally send him some news of the ballet, which he greatly missed now that he was in the Mediterranean, I fowarded his letter to them suggesting that they might write. My scheme had the happiest result. Sidney Dawlson, the sailor, and Charlotte later married, and I still hear from them whenever I dance in London. I was also flattered to hear that my photograph hung in the Officers' Ward Room of H.M.S. *Aurora*, because of my role in *The Sleeping Beauty*.

In ordinary life, elegance had all but disappeared with the shortages and rationing of fabrics. Our silk stockings were sent for repair again and again to the countless little shops where girls sat in the windows invisibly mending the runs. In the ballet we were quite adept at picking up the ladders in our irreplaceable silk tights, using little hooks. It was a slow job, but it restored them perfectly. Before the Dunkirk retreat some friends in the Navy had been able to buy a supply of tights from the maker in Paris and had smuggled them into England, and these were made to last out the duration of the war. Most fortuitous of all, the ballet-shoe makers were permitted the necessary materials to continue their trade.

There were rumours of a remarkable new fibre called nylon, which could be made into stockings that would never wear out. This was not true, of course, but the real difference was that nylon is very much finer than the sheerest silk imaginable. Until that time, all ballet shoes were made in pure silk slipper satin, which has a sheen finish unmatched by any artificial material. I have always steadfastly insisted on pure silk for my shoes, with double satin ribbons to tie round the ankle. I also insist on silk ballet tights. The ribbon is virtually unobtainable these days, and now the manufacture of silk tights has been discontinued. Since, after so many years, I cannot accustom myself to dance in any others, this might just turn out to be the factor that will finally decide my retirement.

At last the tide in Europe turned in favour of the Allies. The enemy was beaten back through Italy and from the Russian front and from France. Paris was liberated on 24 August 1944. What a time of celebration! Cheers and songs ran through the blacked-out streets of London and far into the night. In our favourite French restaurant after the ballet we drank more bottles of Algerian burgundy than ever before, and cried tears of happiness with the proprietor's family. Early in 1945 the Vic-Wells Ballet was assigned to entertain British forces stationed in Brussels and Paris. Our hearts rose at the idea, but the news that we would be kitted out in service uniforms brought cries of protest, which no one heeded. We were issued with the straight khaki skirts, military jackets, sturdy over-coats, ghastly khaki stockings and flat-heeled shoes. Each of us got two shirts, a tie, a wool scarf and a very unbe-coming soft military cap. Even Madame de Valois decided to go against regulations and wear her scarf as a turban. Pamela and I went to Aage Thaarup, the Queen's mill-iner, and had our caps blocked in rather smart styles. We despaired altogether over the shoes and wondered if we could not wear our platform-soled ankle-strap shoes, which, now that I see them back in fashion, I am amazed to think I once loved so much. Reluctantly, we decided they must be left at home.

Despite the years of occupation, Brussels seemed a para-dise to our eyes. The shop windows held unfamiliar treasures, food was plentiful in our Army-requisitioned hotel and champagne cocktails were as nectar to the Algerian burgundy!

In addition to our entertaining the forces, and their entertaining us, we danced for the civilian public at the Théâtre de la Monnaie. It was a beautiful little opera house with a vile stage – not that it worried us much, even when loose floor boards stuck up at one end as one trod down the other. The old, almost soft, ballet shoes I was in the habit of wearing absorbed the uneven surfaces. Fred disapprovingly called these shoes my carpet slippers, but I could never bear hard toes that make a noise on the stage. We danced with tremendous abandon in response to the inspiration of a fresh and enthusiastic audience who had known the horrors of enemy occupation.

We went on to Paris in the first days of spring. Those of us who were old enough to have been there before the war were overwhelmed with feelings of nostalgia. One had forgotten the space and beauty of the city. There were none of the random-bombed buildings, like gaps in a row of teeth, that we saw at home, but there was some-thing more chilling – the bullet marks on the walls and the little crosses commemorating a patriot who had fallen dead in the street. 'The enemy' had meant to me a name-less, faceless mass in helmet and jackboots, hundreds of miles away in another country. Here, people had faced the reality. It presented a whole new aspect of the war that I had not thought of as we danced through the air raids.

The lack of transport led us to being extremely thank-ful for our sturdy military shoes. Our strategy for eating in a city near to starvation involved a lot of walking. The Parisians had practically no food, no fuel, no cigarettes, or soap, and these items were only available to us in mili-tary establishments or service clubs.

The bulk of the ballet company were well catered for in a requisitioned hotel, but three or four of us were allo-cated rooms in an otherwise civilian hotel. There was no hot water, and breakfast consisted of some gruesome bread with a scrape of uneatable preserve and coffee that tasted like ground acorns. Inquiring about supper after the show it sounded too good to be true to hear that the only thing they could offer was pâté de foie gras and champagne. Our dull English rations included no such rich delicacies. Gluttony prevailed for three nights, followed, in my case, by a shattering liver attack and a subsequent aversion to foie gras. That was when I had to start weighing the choices of going without supper or walking home from the Canadian Officers' Club near the Opéra, which was the only place we could get a meal so late at night. It was a long walk to our hotel on the Champs Elysées, though one might get a lift if one was lucky. On the other hand, it was a long time to go without food from lunch one day to acorn coffee the next morning.

Our French colleagues suffered extraordinary hard-ships. At the Paris Opéra it was so cold on stage that the dancers had permission to wear sweaters during per-formance. They all chose discreet little white cardigans, ex-cept for one coryphée who, determined to be noticed, wore a fluffy angora that made her stand out like a polar bear among the Sylphides.

Our beloved Preobrajenska was still teaching at the

Salle Wacker, which we could not reach. But we managed to get her brought officially to the Théâtre des Champs Elysées to give us special lessons. She was quite unchanged and so happy to see us. She walked to her studio every day with amazing fortitude, taking two hours there and two hours back and resting in the Parc Monceau en route. She wouldn't give up teaching, though she was over seventy, and undoubtedly she shared generously what little food she had with her pet birds. She also kept a tortoise called Hortense, whose back legs became paralysed; so she attached two little wheels to Hortense's shell to restore the creature's mobility.

Preobrajenska was the unwitting cause of de Valois's being more angry with me than she has ever been before or since. Preo's last class before we left Paris coincided with an important social reception, for which Pamela and I arrived late, riding three on a bicycle with a French sailor. As de Valois was leaving the party she caught sight of us and flew into a rage. She felt personally responsible for the good manners of her dancers, and considered our behaviour downright insolent. We felt justified in giving the demands of our art priority over a cocktail party and indeed, considering how much we liked champagne, one could more easily have expected to give de Valois the opportunity of berating us for party-going when we should have been practising. She gave us a terrible dressing down, then stormed off down the gravel sidewalk of the Champs Elysées, literally vanishing in a cloud of dust.

The French thought it quite extraordinary to dress a ballet company in military khaki: they couldn't get over it, particularly the younger generation of dancers, who managed to look very chic themselves. We eyed each other curiously but did not know each other's language. Only de Valois could speak adequate French. She immediately took the young dancers to her heart, singling out a nineteen-year-old boy who had just choreographed his first ballet. 'He looks exactly like Massine at that age,' she said. 'The same black eyes. He has a remarkable talent.' That was how we first met Roland Petit, together with

Jean Babilée, Nathalie Philippart and many of the group that was soon to bring fresh air to our art as the Ballets des Champs Elysées.

A few weeks after the Brussels–Paris tour, the war in Europe was over. We had 'V-E Day' for Victory in Europe', and that was it. The war years closed up like a book. Five and three-quarters years and what had I done? Totally immersed in my tinsel world, I had hardly changed at all. I saw my friends marry, have children, give up dancing and wondered why I could not possibly imagine myself in their place. At Felix's wartime wedding I was very overdressed and cried at the marriage vows. He looked very handsome in his officer's uniform. Pamela had said, 'It's so easy to be married.' Fred said, 'Margot loses her head but not her heart.' In truth I lost neither. Marriage appeared unbelievably difficult.

With the ending of the war, exhaustion and the restricted diet together left me quite ill for a while. An infection on my face threatened to leave a nasty scar, and the specialist treating me, Dr Isaac Muende, was so deeply worried about this that he decided to try a completely new technique. He injected the recently discovered penicillin directly into the point of infection, which, to his delight, healed up without a trace. Seeing him so anxious about the scar, I said lightly, 'Oh, my feet are much more important than my face.' I think he could not believe I was so silly as to mean it. He treated me as delicately as a film star, never realizing that, the stage being the only thing that mattered to me, I attached no importance to any blemish that would be invisible at a distance. But, now that I have come to my senses, how grateful I am for his concern.

EIGHT

During the war Vera Volkova, whose black straw hat had impressed me so much when I was twelve, was living in London and had started to teach in a shabby studio near Cambridge Circus. She had an absolutely unwavering vision of the ideal, from which nothing distracted her. I worked hard every day to be prepared for the time when Ashton would return to the company and make new ballets for me – I had long dreamed of Ravel's *Daphnis and Chloë* and of a three-act ballet to follow the great classics of the nineteenth century. Often in class I would think I had made a little progress on a step, only to hear Volkova say regretfully, with her head slightly on one side, 'Yes. Well, somehow it didn't quite come out, isn't it?' She had a beautiful way of getting her colloquialisms mixed – 'Here and then' instead of 'Here and there' – and imaginative descriptive phrases such as, 'Head is like you are smelling violets over right shoulder'; or, 'Arms are holding delicate flowers you must not crush.' I was greatly charmed by 'Leg does not know is going to arabesque.' It gave me a new perspective on my limbs as though they were independent of me. I was reminded of another teacher who really unnerved me by saying, 'Don't trust your right foot.'

I worked so hard in Volkova's class that I used to wish I could faint, as the great Taglioni is reported to have done every day at the end of two hours' training with her father. Anyway, though I felt sick and ready to die, I remained, to my annoyance, conscious and quite healthy-looking.

After the war Volkova's studio attracted all the top foreign dancers who passed through London. It was almost like attending a morning levée, with eminent critics and guests coming to watch. It is not very enjoyable being observed in class, though doubtless good for the soul. Matters of technical accomplishment such as turns and balances are never completely under control; they desert one at the very moment when one wishes to show them off to the spectator.

An attractive dark-eyed girl was standing by the barre one morning waiting for the lesson to start; she wore a chiffon tunic reminiscent of old photographs of Anna Pavlova. She came up to me and asked shyly, 'Are you Margot Fonteyn? I am Violetta Prokhorova Elvin; I come from Moscow.' Her voice was unusually deep and melodious. She was our very first breath of Soviet Russian ballet. Before and during the war no dancers had come to us from that reborn land to whose ancient traditions we aspired. Of the *émigré* teachers Volkova was much the youngest, and had left Leningrad some time after the Revolution, but still I could not grasp some of the things she described without seeing them actually performed, for I had been too long walled-up in my own way of dancing without the opportunity of watching other styles. When Violetta joined the company she brought with her many innovations. Little touches of her own made ripples that influenced our dancing long beyond the ten years that she stayed with us. In particular, she broke what was tantamount to a sound barrier with regard to the choreography of our classical ballets. No one had ever been allowed to alter a single step of Nicolai Sergeyev's productions until Violetta insouciantly remarked, 'In Russia ballerinas often make other step if original not suit. We think more important make beautiful effect.'

Watching her dancing, I was afraid that my own style would disappoint Russian audiences. She reassured me, saying, 'No, Margotchik, you are wrong. In Russia, we have phrase for dancers with no high jump. We call mezzo-tint dancer. Can be very beautiful, too.' It was typical of the tactful way she presented any situation.

Another dancer who brightened the company like a jewel was Moira Shearer, fair and fragile-looking, her dancing as light and airy as an autumn leaf. She always had star quality, and when she appeared in the film *The Red Shoes* she brought ballet to an enormous new public. I think it was a major factor in creating the world-wide enthusiasm for ballet that exists today.

One might say that Sadler's Wells Ballet graduated from college in 1946, when it moved to the Royal Opera House, Covent Garden. (It came of age in 1949, when it first appeared at the Metropolitan Opera, New York.) Before the war there had been no resident opera or ballet at Covent Garden, only limited seasons and guest companies, so we established a new era. I loved the Opera House so much I would have lived right in it if possible. Since that was hardly feasible I took a small flat near by in Long Acre. The old Covent Garden fruit and vegetable market filled the street below my windows with bustling activity all night long, so I was never frightened of living there alone.

The Sleeping Beauty was the ballet chosen to open our first season at Covent Garden, and to reopen the Opera House itself. It was a new production, designed with extraordinary distinction by Oliver Messel. The muted settings were calculated to give prominence to the dancers, and the costumes had all the splendour one could wish for, without exaggerations of colour or proportion. Never were dancers shown to better advantage.

For the new production the correct title of *Sleeping Beauty* – not *Princess* – was restored, and some of Diaghilev's alterations were incorporated into the new version. It is curious that the classical ballets become stale from time to time, and attempts are rightly made to revitalize them. But the more sweeping the improvements the less likely they are to succeed. Luckily, in England we are traditionalists ready to discard innovations that prove unsatisfactory, thus making the distinction between updating and modernizing. Luckily, too, these sturdy old ballets, like Shakespeare's plays, can withstand countless different interpretations.

Oliver Messel was exigent about every detail of the 1946 costumes, for which fabrics and trimmings had to be found when there was still strict rationing. Time was short, and, as his sketches started coming to the wardrobe department, there was tremendous pressure to locate the desired materials. My mother was delighted to be enlisted as a searcher, and she spent day after day unearthing brocades, feathers, braids, gimps and all kinds of un-rationed bits and pieces that could be utilized.

The Opera House had been dormant as a theatre for so long that it might have been Sleeping Beauty's palace in need of cleaning up and refurbishing after a hundred years. In long narrow store rooms high above the stage, forgotten opera productions were unearthed dating back thirty years or more. Dressing rooms were cold and bare. The stalls seating area had been covered over at stage level to make an immense ballroom floor for the Palais de Danse which had operated throughout the war. I had gone with Michael Somes to take a possible last look, in case the building was bombed and we should never see it again. I vividly remembered the jiving dancers, the popular tunes and the smell of stale beer. Some resident rats from that era were still in occupation during our first ballet season.

It was difficult to adapt to operatic stage dimensions after the intimacy of theatres where faces in the front rows were visible at close range. Only Violetta Elvin, who came from the Bolshoi – meaning 'Big' – Theatre in Moscow found Covent Garden quite cosy. But at the opening performance she, too, was full of excitement as she whispered, 'You know, is very funny *real* King and Queen will be in audience. In Russia they existed only in fairy tales and ballet.'

There were so many 'Royals' present at the opening that, when I came to the last presentation curtsy, I was dizzy from bobbing up and down. I almost overbalanced, when to my astonishment the young Princess Margaret, then fifteen, expertly and unobtrusively steadied me with her handshake. I thought, 'They must be trained for this from childhood. I suppose it happens all the time.' Professional training must start early, for royalty as for ballet dancers.

Mr Jackson, the stage-door keeper, well know to famous foreign opera and ballet stars of pre-war days, was overjoyed at the reconversion from dance hall back to theatre. He ruled his stage door like a feudal lord guarding his castle, which wasn't easy for those he did not favour. To my eternal shame, I was one day to ask him not to call me 'Margot' but 'Miss Fonteyn'. I was having a touch of star-mania that day. I should have been honoured that he bothered to address me by my Christian name – and so I realized once I'd come to my senses. It was just that, with the war over at last, I longed to enjoy the luxury of being a great star, spoilt and adored, swathed in rich furs as I left the Opera House to sup on caviar and champagne. As Volkova would say, 'Somehow it didn't work out, isn't it?' I was just an English ballerina with a dash of Brazilian blood. If a few did succumb to that expression of the inner soul transmitted through my dancing, I was scarcely aware of it. My heart and life were in the theatre, while relationships with people outside the ballet circle were unreal or at best uneasy.

When Frederick Ashton was restored at last to civilian life, the idea came to him to choreograph César Franck's *Symphonic Variations*. It was the first 'abstract', or plot-less, ballet that Fred had undertaken for our company, and, as always, he drew some part of his inspiration from the dancers he had chosen. These were Pamela May, Moira Shearer, Michael Somes, Brian Shaw, Henry Danton and myself, of whom Michael had been exiled from our world for four years of war. Moreover, he had suffered a serious accident before his release from the Army. He needed time and encouragement to regain his prowess in the ballet. As it happened, the ballet had an unexpectedly long period of gestation.

Sophie Fedorovitch, who designed the scenery and costumes, was as much involved in the choreography as the dancers. She understood Fred better than anyone in the world. She was beside him at rehearsals and sat up with him at night, giving comfort and wisdom in her strange, mumbling way and making him laugh when need be. The Covent Garden stage, so much bigger than those we had worked on all our lives, still made us uneasy. Fred had never encountered the problem of filling a large area with only six dancers.

The ballet was just about finished when the first night had to be postponed because Michael tore a cartilage in his knee and no one could replace him. During Michael's recuperation, Fred reassessed the work he had done and eliminated every insignificant or superfluous movement. Vera Volkova often came to rehearsals, and tiny details were discussed and reworked as though they were part of an architectural plan for a building that would last for ever. The final pose in particular was unresolved for several days while different versions were tried.

The unexpected extension of time before the birth of *Symphonic Variations* accounts, I believe, for its perfection. I have noticed that, although improving and polishing the choreography can continue right up to the final rehearsal of a new work, alterations made after it has been seen by the public are rarely for the better, except for cuts and matters of production rather than dance invention. Even more strange is the fact that, left untouched, new ballets improve by themselves with repetition in performance. In other words, the first night is the worst possible time to make a hard and fast criticism; the baby never looks its best on the day it is born. Critics have caught on to this and, realizing the dangers, try to circumvent them by watching the dress rehearsal – which only compounds their problem, because what they see there is not by any means the thing they are trying to assess. An old theatre adage runs, 'Bad dress rehearsal – good performance', and it generally runs true. The French invented the Répétition Générale, which must have been a device for trying to reach the second performance without living through opening night. Unfortunately, the Smart Set, and the critics, attend the Générale, and so defeat the object of the exercise. There is clearly no easy solution to this dilemma.

Although I was dancing regularly, my health was still not fully recovered, and I felt stale and uninspired. So, gathering my courage, I asked de Valois for a weeks' leave of absence to study in Paris. She agreed, and off we went, my mother and I, with our austerity wardrobes. Gordon Hamilton, who had defected to the French ballet, had arranged hotel rooms for us. To my surprise, his colleagues thought rather highly of me. However, they spoke no English so I made an attempt to converse in French. But mostly I listened to their animated talk until I came to understand it quite easily.

Paris certainly gave me a much needed change of atmosphere in work and play. The dancers wanted to show me everything from the Bois de Boulogne in spring to the night clubs of the rue de Lappe, where my mother was not at all dismayed to see men dancing together, and the famous Mme Arthur's all-male cabaret. Wandering about the city in the warm night air we once dived into the Seine for a midnight swim, and we always got home in the small hours, only to get up a few short hours later to be at the class of Boris Kniasev, a teacher of oversized personality and enthusiasm, who gave me renewed confidence in my dancing. A big man, with powerful voice and generous laugh, talking, correcting, explaining throughout the class until everyone excelled themselves in effort and accomplishment, he was exactly the teacher I needed at that time.

It was de Valois's favourite, Roland Petit, with the black eyes like Massine, who thought up our various exploits. He was a veritable dynamo of energy and ideas – dancing, choreographing, seeing new designers, composers, writers, his mind everywhere at once. We developed a deep but harmless crush on each other, born of the mutual stimulation of his inventive imagination and my restrained classicism. We were perfect opposites in temperament. He told me I should leave the Sadler's Wells Ballet, where I was too restricted, and get out and dance new, exciting ballets. I told him he needed the stability of the Paris Opéra, from which he had broken away. Neither of us took the other's advice. I was not too swept off my feet to forget that my success was based on the position I held in the Sadler's Wells, while Roland knew he wanted complete freedom to create ballets in his own way.

Roland was going to take me to an opera première at the Théâtre des Champs Elysées. No doubt he was justifiably nervous about what I might wear. He said, 'There's a marvellous new couturier who has just shown his first collection. It's a sensational success. He's called Christian Dior.' He took me to Dior, where they lent me a striking dress to wear that evening. Everyone complimented me on the gown, and I had never felt so elegant in my life. The Maison Dior decided to take me under its wing, and I bought one of the first season's outfits. It was called 'Daisy'. It was the New Look line, with small waist, narrow shoulders and bell-shaped skirt to the calf, in complete contrast to the unfeminine war and post-war styles of short, straight skirts and padded military shoulders. 'Daisy' was quite stunning. When I finally wore my elbows through the sleeves, I gave it to my friend Doris Langley-Moore for her collection, now housed in the Museum of Costume in the city of Bath. Subsequently I bought some ravishing dresses from Dior and, of course, ordered my wedding dress there. When Christian Dior died ten years later, I changed to Yves St Laurent.

Now Paris had given me new life. My batteries were recharged and my powers of total involvement in the role, and of utter concentration on stage, had been restored.

I returned to London full of enthusiasm, but I was afraid that Fred Ashton might be rather hurt that I had found inspiration in another setting. He had spent so much time away during the war that it must have seemed treasonous of me to be enamoured of the French, even though he himself greatly admired the fresh young company. But art and artists must feed on whatever is necessary at the time; the muse is not always located in the expected and convenient place; a temporary defection is sometimes required in order to catch up with her. Emotionally and physically, too, I had been exhausted. There was a time towards the end of the war when my main concern was to prevent myself from giving up in the middle of a dance and just running off stage. More than once I forgot which ballet I was dancing and almost panicked. I also experienced that strange illusion of hearing my name called out loudly when it was not so; it might be in a restaurant or the dressing room or just at home. Bobby said he had experienced the same thing.

It was only during the war, after Mary Honer and Elizabeth Miller had both left the ballet, that I started to dance *Coppelia*. It frightened me to try comedy and I thought I would be terrible. Bobby said, 'You can do your tragic roles, your romantic roles and of course you can do comedy too. Just do it and don't worry.' But he was such a great comedian himself that his characterization of Dr Coppelius monopolized the stage with its absurdity and pathos, laughable and endearing at the same time. Trying to draw any of the public's attention to myself while sharing the stage with him in *Coppelia* was one of the greatest lessons of my career.

NINE

Early in 1947, Léonide Massine came to produce and dance in two of his ballets, *Le Tricorne* and *La Boutique Fantasque*, both of which he had created for Diaghilev. I knew the ballets, having seen them danced by Colonel de Basil's Ballets Russes before the war. As usual, I was intimidated at the thought of stepping into the shoes of a long list of famous predecessors. 'What a beautiful step, I shall never be able to dance it!'

The great Massine was already a legend; a strange, quiet man, with those marvellous eyes that fascinated yet also had the effect of a closed door. Occasionally a quick smile lit up the impassive face, and the door opened briefly. But even then I felt at a great distance from him. It was the first time that I had danced with a famous guest artist. A chance meeting quite recently found a smiling, friendly, well-preserved Massine in a neat suit and a black homburg hat. His eyes seemed larger and deeper than ever. He agreed that he had been very serious, as I remembered him, and explained, 'I am a primitive man. If I am engrossed in work I cannot laugh at the same time.'

I had always loved Spanish dancing. When I joined Sadler's Wells my ambition was to do the national dances in Act III of *Swan Lake*: the Czardas, the Spanish and the Mazurka. (Actually, I danced them only a very few times.) The de Falla music for *Le Tricorne* fired my spirits and enthusiasm, and I danced almost to kill myself, nearly fainting in the wings from exhaustion. I loved every minute.

I don't think I was particularly good in the role, but the exaltation of swirling about in the Fandango opposite the intense face of Massine, and then watching him stand absolutely motionless at the end of the Miller's dance while the audience cheered wildly for five minutes, was so overwhelming that I am not surprised my life at that time had more substance in the theatre than out of it. Only a fatal passion could have been more engrossing.

'Theatre', obviously, is what I care about and, since my particular form of expression is the dance, I try to follow the laws of 'theatre' in the field of ballet. These laws are very clear in my mind, and always have been. I don't remember ever being told about them.

First, the audience is always right. They buy their tickets in expectation of entertainment, laughter, beauty, tears, intellectual exercise or whatever. If they are disappointed it is our fault, not theirs. Every performance carries a burden of responsibility, and the performer must strive to match the expectations of his public.

Second, it is no concern of the public how we achieve our purpose or at what cost. They should not be aware of how difficult it is to dance to the conductor's wrong tempo, in a bad pair of shoes, with an uncongenial partner or with a cold in the head. We should try to conceal all these things from the public. They don't want to know that we are subject to the same inconveniences as they themselves.

In this second respect there is one distraction to which I have never been able to adapt. It is the sound of a camera clicking during performance. All other disturbances are a part of the essentially ephemeral aspect of theatre. The performance goes on, with all its imperfections, from beginning to end. Then it ceases to exist, except in the mind of the beholder. Some embellish the memory, some dismiss it; but it cannot be grasped and preserved. That is the magic of theatre: it is born and dies each evening. It is never the same twice. It can no more be put on record than can the beauty of a sunset, which reproduced on a piece of paper gives no idea of the subtle interplay of light and colour, of the glory and power of the sun, and of the sense of space and distance reaching into the universe.

The result of catching a dancer in mid-movement can be disastrous, exposing transitory positions never caught by the spectator's eye. These pictures showing a grimacing dancer with turned up toe and bent knee are apt to appear in print without one's knowledge or consent, and give one a strong camera phobia. The sound of a shutter click during performance interrupts my concentration while I put myself mentally in the position of the camera and consider my pose at that instant. A performer should never picture to himself how he looks from the stalls. That can only be done in rehearsal. The performance should come, as it were, from within, the result of complete concentration. For this reason I find it intolerable to be distracted by an active camera and, to my shame, I have created several scandals by walking off stage and stopping the performance. My belief in the sanctity of theatre law is gravely wounded by such behaviour. How happy to have lived before the age of the action photograph!

The worst offenders are what I call 'tourist' photographers, who must surely forgo their personal enjoyment of a live performance as they block their own view with a little contraption that will give merely a static, cardboard reminder of something that can be preserved only in the mind's eye. Journalists are at least trying to carry out their job, but the 'tourists' mar their own pleasure as well as that of more sensitive neighbours. A strange hobby!

In 1947 we went to dance in Prague. We saw a city re-awakening, like Princess Aurora, after the long dark night. The people who had suffered so much in the war were incredible in their expressions of warmth and friendship, and in their enjoyment of our ballets. Next we went to Warsaw, almost unbelievable in the extent of devastation wrought by the Germans in their determination to obliterate the city for ever. As they retreated they left barely twenty buildings standing. Each inhabitant, each week, spent so many hours carrying bricks from one place to another to bring back some semblance of order, although it appeared a hopeless task. I think we never in our lives were more deeply moved than by the Polish people at that time, as they cheerfully reconstructed their city of rubble, inch by inch.

In the middle of this shambles of broken buildings was one area completely and totally flat, razed to the ground. It was the Ghetto. As we stood at its edge we were told how it had been sealed off, and systematically destroyed, with no possibility of escape for those inside. The gruesome place was to be kept untouched as a memorial.

We danced in the Teatr Polski, one of the first buildings to be restored. We asked, 'Why do you think of rebuilding a theatre when thousands of people are homeless?' 'Ah,' they replied, 'the Polish soul needs music and beauty when faced with so much tragedy. These things are symbols of our city; we must rebuild them first for everyone to share.'

It was in Warsaw that we first heard the phrase 'Iron Curtain'. People spoke guardedly about the future, their optimism tinged with doubt and anxiety, thus creating an atmosphere quite different from that in any other countries we had visited. It drew us closer to the people we met and worked with, and our admiration grew into deep affection. It is hard to describe our feelings as we came, a happy, well-fed, well-blessed ballet company among people who had lost everything and were menaced by the future. As usual, Ninette de Valois was the one to sum it up for us in a speech that she made at a reception to meet some Polish dancers, and she brought everyone to tears. At the end they sang a Polish song for us, and de Valois made us sing 'For He's a Jolly Good Fellow'. I can't abide the song, but it was perfect for the occasion. We knew then why, despite her often incomprehensible thinking and paradoxical behaviour, any one of us would defend de Valois to the death. She has the rare quality of leadership which unites people in pride and loyalty.

There were floods of tears next morning as we boarded our train for the Baltic port of Gdansk and so on to Sweden. A few weeks later the Iron Curtain came firmly down between Poland and the West, and in February the following year Czechoslovakia, too, was suddenly on the other side. Our Czech friend, the ballet master Sasha Machov, who had spent many evenings in our house in London just after the war, stepped out of a window in Prague and died. He chose the same end as the great Czech patriot Jan Masaryk.

We were on our way home to London, but we found time for an overnight stop at Copenhagen to see the Royal Danish Ballet. Soon afterwards the American Ballet Theater came to London, bringing marvellous dancers and exciting new ballets. What a stimulus we found in these foreign companies, each so different from the other! The French so original, the Americans so exuberant and the Danes a revelation of ballet as it had looked a century before. At the time of our visit to Denmark the training and much of the repertoire had continued unchanged, handed down from generation to generation, for almost one hundred years. The lithographs of that period before ballet was photographed had always been something of an enigma to me until I saw the movement, style, elevation and charming stage manner of the young Danes. I gained another new perspective.

Of course Frederick Ashton, with his sensitive eye for every detail, absorbed a myriad fleeting impressions from these tours, and in due time his replenished creative spirit poured forth a richness of new ballets. But before I danced a new Ashton ballet, I was to dance for Roland Petit.

Roland Petit had by now formed his own ballet company. I was upset that the group of dancers of the original Ballets des Champs Elysées had broken up, no longer able to work with each other. Loyalty and team spirit were so much a part of Sadler's Wells that, to me, it was shocking to see a marvellous young company fragment after only two years, instead of realizing that strength lay in holding together. Jean Babilée and Nathalie Philippart, magnificent protagonists of *Le Jeune Homme et La Mort*, one of the most gripping and unusual ballets ever created, went one way; Margrethe Schanne and Kjeld Noack went home to Copenhagen, she as the leading ballerina; and Roland, too, went off, taking several of the others with him. Still impatient with everyone, and full of ideas, he produced new ballets like rabbits out of a hat and never lacked for dancers to work with him. There was a dark young boy, with unusual blue eyes, in the corps de ballet. His name was Maurice Béjart.

Roland brought me *Demoiselles de la Nuit*, from a story by Jean Anouilh. He was to choreograph it and wanted me to dance the part of a white cat called Agathe. I agreed. The early rehearsals took place in London. I was, as always, very nervous that I would be unable to do the steps he wanted. I felt my technique inadequate, and I was more at ease with Ashton's way of working. He allowed his dancers to contribute ideas if they felt inclined, accepting or discarding them as he saw fit. When I volunteered a suggestion to Roland, his look suggested that he thought I was trying to teach him his own business. I didn't make the mistake again.

In Paris I became even more nervous, rehearsing with a company of strangers after the protected family life of Sadler's Wells. I was sure they would find my dancing terrible. In fact they made a great fuss of me. Several new ballets were being rehearsed at once, and Roland's assistant, Jacqueline Lemoine, kept me posted, in English, of the dramas, crises and comedies which arose each day. She had a wonderfully mischievous sense of humour. Janine Charrat was choreographing a ballet written by Jean Genet, who could rarely be located except when he was in jail. Then, of course, he was unavailable. Jacqueline was very pleased one day. Genet was at last going to appear. 'The police are looking for him,' she said, 'but he has promised to be here today.' Sure enough, he came to rehearsal looking rather like a mole, furtive and shy of daylight. I thought he had enormous charm, the charm of a sensitive poet, and I was sorry when he slipped back into his preferred world of vice. The only blue movie I have ever seen was by Jean Genet, and I found it quite inoffensive because it was touched by poetry. His ballet was about sailors, as I suppose one might have expected.

We were all at fever pitch as *Demoiselles* came to the orchestra and costume rehearsals. Leonor Fini, the designer, had an obsession about cats and had made perfect cat masks complete with pink noses, whiskers and all. The trouble was that I could not conceive of expressing anything with my head shut in a kind of cat-box. A love duet was out of the question. I felt grotesque. Leonor Fini was unwilling to change the design, and I suddenly found myself shouting hysterically in French that I refused absolutely to wear it.

I was horrified at myself! Never could I imagine myself doing such a thing at Covent Garden! But it worked, and the mask was cut down to an attractive size covering the eyes and a bit of nose with the whiskers remaining. Altogether my two costumes for that ballet were ravishing. They were made by Irene Karinska, whose mother had made the beautiful *Apparitions* costumes that were delivered at the theatre almost too late for the opening night in 1936.

The Répétition Générale was a riot. To the last minute I didn't understand whether it was going to be a rehearsal (répétition) or a performance. Jacqueline explained that it was a rehearsal that ran straight through, like a show, and was watched by a full audience of selected people. 'Then it is a performance,' I said. 'No, it is a rehearsal, but a Générale. You can't stop in the middle or repeat anything.' Whatever it was went surprisingly well until the last scene, when the poet (Roland) follows Agathe and her cat friends across the rooftops. Leonor had designed a sensationally realistic roof setting and, as we all pounded about chasing each other over the tiles, the structure collapsed. Holding a pose centre stage, I expected the curtain to be lowered. Instead the orchestra stopped playing and, since the curtain remained open, I gesticulated to the conductor, saying loudly, 'Play! Play!' which, after a moment or two of bewilderment, he did. We brought the ballet to a close amid a mass of splinters on stage, and to cheers from the public.

Remembering my beloved Preobrajenska's affection for animals, I was careful to see that she had seats for the official première the following night. Afterwards the darling little old ballerina came backstage and kissed me warmly. Then she sat down and I asked her how she had liked it. 'Oh dear! Oh dear!' she said, shaking her head and with a sly sort of twinkle in her eye, 'whatever would Petipa have said?'

The dressing room was massed with flowers and telegrams, the ballet was a great success and Paris gave me the 'lionizing' treatment. The oddest compliments came my way. *'Elle a les jambes spirituelles'* – which I took to mean that I had 'spiritual' legs; but it turned out that they were 'witty'. I thought only Danilova had really witty legs, and I was pleased. Someone else sighed *'Ah! la derrière de Margot!'* and several others took up a similar theme. It was true that my skirt was very short at the back. I found myself surprised but flattered at this very un-English compliment.

Among the little bistros we frequented was one called Chez Manouche, owned and presided over by the lady of that name. She had been the mistress of France's most notorious gangster, though he was but one of a list of well-known names. She was middle-aged, fat, wise and above all a woman. To Jacqueline she lamented the loss of her gangster lover. 'Ah, if you could only see the beauty of the man as he lay naked on my bed,' and she dried a tiny tear in the corner of her eye. His enemies had come right into her restaurant at the dinner hour and shot someone dead at the bar, but I was never quite sure whether that had been the gangster lover or another. She confided to Jacqueline that a very gentlemanly foreign general was taking her to the Plaza-Athénée. 'The upper part of my body is still very good,' she said, 'but to hide the other signs of age I cover myself with a delicately embroidered cloth until the last minute.'

In Paris I began to show a touch more vanity about my hair, which, before the invention of hair spray, invariably had loose wisps well beyond my control. When I kept my friends waiting while I redid my coiffure several times, they would say I was being coquettish. Everything I wore drew comment, favourable or otherwise, and I was very happy to let my friends Suzanne Luling and Yvonne Minassian from Christian Dior supervise my clothes. But the critic I respected most was Ashton. If he praised my new dress, I was really happy. I sought his opinion in everything I did, to the extent that I thought I would never be able to marry anyone who didn't have his approval.

That summer Nora Kaye, whom I had got to know well when she was in London with American Ballet Theater, came to Paris for a holiday. Fred came, too, and we laughed our way from morning to night through idiotic adventures. Nora had never been to Paris, but a quick taxi tour round the main attractions was enough for her. 'Good, I've seen that,' she said as the Étoile, the Louvre and the Invalides flashed past the cab window. Nora, with typical American generosity, insisted on giving me a silver fox stole.

At the Bal Nègre I was entranced as I watched the black dancers. One of them invited me on to the floor. I

thought it rude to refuse, and nervously stepped out, trying to follow his rhythm and movement. He steered me
once around the hall then returned me to my table saying,
'You're an attractive girl, it's too bad you can't dance!' I
did so agree with him. I thought yet again – 'What a
beautiful step . . .'

ELEVEN

I have written about many of my teachers, for they are
vital to a dancer's life and career. Their classes are the
foundation stone of the whole edifice. In 1947 a Latvian
ballet master came to Sadler's Wells Ballet. He was
Harijs Plučis, the most lovable of men. He knew Russians,
he knew Germans, he had taught in Paris, but he had
never encountered British dancers, for whose nonchalant
attitude towards work he was totally unprepared. He was
a forceful and dedicated teacher with a dramatic and endearing delivery of slightly incorrect English. Every remark was prefaced with 'My dear!' Our phlegmatic
reaction to his enthusiastic exhortations to jump higher
and dance harder made him actually bang his head
against the wall in despair. But he was a perceptive and a
worldly man. Quite soon he discovered that the only way
to make English dancers work was to make them laugh.
Thereafter he had us in his pocket. Instead of clasping his
head with both hands and saying, 'My dear! Vos is ziss?'
when someone was very late for morning class, he instead
remarked, 'Good afternoon,' in a comic tone of voice that
made us all laugh at the latecomer instead of at Plučis's
histrionics.

He had a theory about pirouettes which involved pulling one hip in as one started to turn and the other as one
finished. He called it 'Take sides', and he jabbed his finger

into one's waistline, to indicate which side, and constantly besought us to 'Straight the knees.' Through all the ten years he stayed with us he never learnt the words 'dressing room', but invariably said, 'I vill see you in your vardrobe,' which gave me a momentary vision of meeting him in a clothes cupboard. When I come to think of it, he wasn't far wrong. My dressing room at Covent Garden was not very much bigger than that.

For Plučis, the theatre was to be revered, almost as a holy place. 'My dear,' he would say, 'when you come into theatre is like church. Quiet must be. Very polite, very careful.' He clasped his hands together in front of his chest and spoke in a low voice to demonstrate the deferential manner to be adopted on entering the stage door. His dedication was complete. He sat through every performance and, after coming backstage to give encouragement or corrections, he went home to write up a sort of log book on the evening's performance, from which he could gauge our progress, or otherwise, in every technical detail.

He gave me many corrections, and it was hard for me to incorporate them immediately into my established way of dancing. I find that my brain takes in the message immediately, but it doesn't put it into operation until the body has learnt it also. This may take months. One day Plučis was very pleased with me. 'Margott, my dear!' he said. 'Now I understand you. I tell you corrections today and after two years you do perfectly.' No exaggeration! My dancing depends on my body knowing the choreography so well that it needs only slight prompting, leaving most of my concentration free for interpretation.

Plučis was a thickly built man, of average height. He had big hands, and one could see that he had been a strong and reliable partner who danced with heart and soul. Once he confessed that he had failed to catch the ballerina Fedorova as she dropped confidently into what she expected to be his arms. Covering his blushing face with both hands, he exclaimed, 'My dear! *Vot it vos!*' and I could picture the furious Fedorova, flat on her back on the stage, as he bent over her in horror. Even a good and reliable partner occasionally fails; or, as Tito puts it in a Panamanian proverb, 'Even the best monkey can drop a coconut,' which I find a comforting phrase to remember when one makes a real gaffe.

When Plučis arrived he was perhaps in his late forties, and I had the impression that he had never married. At the performance he was always alone and yet, when he suddenly said, 'Margott! I have secret to tell you,' I noticed an unusual light in his blue eyes, and I said immediately, 'You are going to get married!' He blushed pink and looked astonished. 'My dear! How do you know? But not vill be, *Is*! This morning *was*!' 'Who is she!' I asked, and he went pink again. 'Young girl! You don't know.' Indeed, Inez was probably twenty years younger, but she was the perfect wife for him, giving him three children and great happiness for the rest of his life.

Until 1948 I had remarkably few ballet injuries, considering the enormous number of performances I had given on dozens of different stages – some hard, some slanted, some slippery and some with a surface like a ploughed field.

During the first performance of Ashton's *Don Juan* I tore a small ligament in my ankle on the Covent Garden stage, which remained quite treacherous for twenty-five years despite our continued protests. To be fair, the Paris Opéra also has a very difficult stage, and many other famous theatres, too. The old 'Met' in New York became so rough that one had to select a suitable spot before daring to put a toe down on point.

My ankle injury came at a difficult moment in my career. I had risen to the top while very young, and now I had to concern myself with staying there. This is much the hardest aspect of success. Being completely occupied with the present, and looking only forwards, I did not notice the passage of time, nor take account of it. I simply had not thought about the dancers coming up from behind, and likely to overtake me. Beryl Grey was a lot younger than I and easily fitted her place as a ballerina, sharing the classical roles. Violetta Elvin brought new life from her Russian background and so gave more than she took. Then came Moira Shearer, with her incredible airy lightness and ease, to be a real threat to my position. Moira was young, fresh, beautiful and different.

Since my state of exhaustion towards the end of the war, I had insisted I must have a free evening before I danced a three-act ballet or else, I thought, I would not have adequate strength. I also took pains to work up a stage fright, even if I didn't feel it, knowing that sheer terror would produce the required adrenalin to 'dance strong'. What began as genuine fatigue had become a bad habit, and as I woke up in the morning I would think: 'My God! *Giselle* tonight,' and feel physically sick, convinced I couldn't do it.

At last Ashton was about to produce a three-act ballet. For years I had been waiting for this, and had tried to prepare myself for it. One morning I opened *The Times* and read that the principal role in *Cinderella* would be danced at alternate performances by myself and Moira Shearer. In the past, any part created for me by Fred belonged to me; or so I felt, with a possessiveness equal to jealous love. I had danced all performances until some-one else came in on an understudy or 'second cast' basis. The idea that Moira or anyone else would share *Cinderella* from the start, hit me like a slap in the face. I went to Fred almost in tears and asked indignantly why he had not even told me before it was announced in the press. He said calmly that the first performances had to run consecutively, and I had made it clear I could not dance a long ballet every night. He tactfully left it unsaid that younger dancers deserved some of the opportunities I had enjoyed at their age, and that I was too spoilt to have considered that aspect. Neither did I stop to think that Fred, too, might have been hurt when I so obviously enjoyed the success of *Demoiselles de la nuit* in Paris. I felt righteous in my indignation.

The prospect of losing my favoured position as undisputed head of the company made me ill at ease and defensive, and my normally shaky self-confidence was altogether undermined. Perhaps it was not wholly accidental, therefore, when I slipped and fell during that performance of *Don Juan*. Helpmann quickly lifted me up, and I continued dancing to the end of the ballet, by which time my whole foot was very swollen. Next morning I went to the hospital and came out an hour later with my leg in a plaster cast. There it remained for six weeks. The shock was unbelievable.

My life was so concentrated on the exigencies of dancing that I was utterly lost, aimless, without direction or purpose. When I was fully occupied with class, rehearsals and performances, I thought of a million things I would do if I had time, but as soon as the time was thrust upon me I had no idea how to organize myself to use it, and my spirit was too low to care. I could think only of escape.

So I escaped to Paris, in the hope of solving my psychological problems by imposing them on friends. I was miserable to realize the extent of my dependence on them. They were extraordinarily kind, but I remained despondent as I read the success of *Cinderella*. Moira danced the role with ease at every performance, the very thing I believed I could not do. *Cinderella* opened just before Christmas. I was too depressed to be there, so I stayed in Paris and learned how lonely it can be to spend an essentially family festival away from home.

The experience of being unable to dance and unable to find another direction in my life was a major personal crisis. It was a turning point, in that I was forced to take stock of myself for the first time. I was twenty-nine years old, I could dance probably until I was about thirty-five and beyond that I faced an abyss. Emotionally my need to love far outweighed my need to be loved. The person whom I loved most and depended on most was Fred, but in the way of a friend, mentor and master. The man I could marry did not apparently exist, and without such a love I would descend into the abyss when my career

130

ended, or so it seemed. When I spoke to de Valois about it, she said that I had so many interests in life that I would not find it hard to live without dancing. She thought her own life had been more single-minded, and the problem of retirement therefore more difficult. In this she was perhaps right. But her intellect is so brilliantly alive that she remains one of the most fascinating people one can talk to on any subject, and I cannot think of her as retired.

She was certainly right in that I now have no fear of retirement. Rather do I regret the books I will now never have time to read, and the projects I will never be able to complete. But my lack of fear is because an essential element, then missing, afterwards entered my life.

TWELVE

Early in 1949 negotiations were completed for our first visit to the United States. The company was to go under the auspices of the great Sol Hurok, an impresario in the grand old manner. In his own personality and style he was as much a star as many of the stars he presented in a long and courageous career. Nora Kaye had spoken of him so often, and so glowingly, that I felt I already knew him.

My first real meeting with him was in the house of Bianca Mosca, the couturier, at a party she gave for Hurok when he was in London to arrange the details of our tour. Bianca was one of the couturiers who had generously agreed to dress the entire ballet company for the New York visit, with the idea that we should be ambassadors for British fashion, then struggling to pull out of its wartime austerity image. Ashton, Helpmann and Nora

Kaye were among Bianca's guests. I was greatly in awe of Hurok and hovered near enough to hear what he was saying but far enough away to be in no danger of having to join the conversation.

He was not very tall, but strongly built and rather rotund. Perhaps egg-shaped would best, though not too politely, describe his compact figure. He was bald, with a worldly look about him. He had a sly Russian humour, which could be impish at times. He loved to make dead-pan jokes and to laugh at my gullibility.

Shaking hands with him was like shaking hands with a bear. He knew this, and liked to tell how he had taken the part of the Dancing Bear in one of De Basil's performances of *Petrouchka*. His manner was authoritative, and he had a deep voice with a fine Russian-Brooklyn accent. Fred asked him what a particular artist was then earning. 'About toity tousand dollars,' said Hurok. Until then I had thought that this accent was strictly for the movies.

Later we found that he pronounced 't' as 'th', and vice versa. My favourite example: 'Melba was a greath singer. She never had anyting but thea and thoast before singing Thosca.'

When I came to know him well, I found that Hurok reminded me of an old Russian peasant woman going off to market, basket on her arm, to pick out the best of the produce. Each year until his death at the age of eighty-five, Hurok went off to Russia to pick the best of cultural goods that were for sale.

He was always nervous about 'thicket' sales, and before curtain time could be found hovering in the back of the box office. His eyes seemed to click like cash register signs behind his glasses as he watched the crush of eager patrons.

In his latter days he implied that he had been in love with me twenty years earlier. If that was true, I was never aware of it. I think it was, rather, that he was in love with all his successes. And that was his secret. He was not just a man in show business. Show business was his entire life.

Preparations for the U.S. tour started months ahead, and built to a crescendo as gradually every single thing we did was judged in the light of its impact on New York. At first, *Symphonic Variations* was considered an essential for opening night. *The Sleeping Beauty* was regarded as a gamble, something that might be a disastrous failure and ruin the start of the season. In the end, however, it was decided that *Sleeping Beauty* should open after all. It was completely new to American audiences and presented the entire company on stage in one evening of dancing galore. When I heard the news I started an attack of stage fright that must be the longest in history. It lasted three months. Despite Nora Kaye's enthusiasm – or perhaps because she was so sure – I was utterly convinced I would fail. At rehearsals I worried over each step: 'I do this so badly, couldn't I alter it for New York?' 'How can I do this better? I look horrible!' Throughout the whole of that period it was like preparing for a journey into the unknown.

We arrived in New York something like eighteen hours behind schedule, to be greeted by a 'cheesecake' greedy press. The photographers ordered the girls to smile and show a little more leg. Skirts were at a modest mid-calf length that year, which did not make for newsworthy pictures. We looked as haughty as we could under the circumstances.

It was late at night by the time we were settled into our hotels. Nora took Fred, Bobby, Leslie, Pamela and me to eat at Reuben's. On the way I felt drawn to the scene of my forthcoming ordeal like a moth to a candle, so we ordered the taxi to drive past the Metropolitan Opera House. We found the ballet scenery being unloaded from a truck, and we were able to step straight on to the stage through the scene-dock entrance. It was moving to stand and gaze out at the beautiful old auditorium, dimly lit from the working light on stage. I was simultaneously in love with the theatre and filled with dread of what it held in store. As we drove to the restaurant Nora explained that Reuben's was where people went after an opening to wait for the reviews. I went cold as I imagined the critics' reactions in a few nights' time, and thought how much better not to know.

The Hurok public relations operation was in full swing, with a certain extra concentration on me. It was felt that Moira Shearer was universally known from her film *The Red Shoes*, whereas few had heard of Margot Fonteyn, who was the official Prima Ballerina of the company. Not only was I unpractised in giving interviews, I was about as frightened as a mouse confronting a cobra. I must have been an exasperating subject for the journalists. I had nothing to say about anything. I thought of the old maxim, 'Children should be seen and not heard,' and wished it could be applied to ballet dancers.

For some reason I worried a lot about having the right dressing room. First inspection revealed that they were all small, windowless, hot and rather pleasantly old-fashioned, with a minimum of ventilation. It was easy to imagine the breath of the Divine Melba or the Godly Chaliapin still hung somewhere in a corner of the room allotted to me. I was certainly very conscious of the ghosts of great personages from the past. As I was musing thus before the morning rehearsal, the doorman announced Mr Joseph Stuhl from Philadelphia. It was the ex-G.I. who had visited me in London. I thought, 'Oh, dear, now he is going to be a nuisance, wanting to impose on my time with invitations which I can't refuse.' He came in and, before I could speak, said, 'I know you are nervous and busy. I just want to welcome you, and I am not coming near again until after the first night.' Then he was gone, leaving a large bunch of roses and more proof of his superb manners.

When the long-awaited night was upon me I became unnaturally calm, which worried Pamela May terribly.

'Are you all right?' she asked. 'You're always so nervous before the performance. I've never seen you like this.' In fact, I was completely numb. But everyone else was on edge, from Hurok down to the last corps de ballet dancer. De Valois came to wish me luck, so did Leslie Edwards. It has long been a tradition that he comes to my dressing room before every performance. Such little acts bring me a disproportionate amount of comforts in moments of deep anxiety.

It was a sweltering hot October night, an Indian summer. The atmosphere inside the Opera House was like a jungle minutes before a tropical storm. As the curtain rose, applause greeted the Oliver Messel decor before anyone danced a step. When I ran out on to the stage there was a burst of sound. It drowned out the music and also some part of my mind, for I have never been able to remember anything between those first minutes of deafening applause on my entrance and the incredible reception after the third-act pas de deux with Bobby. It must have been the sheer unexpectedness of it that induced that trance-like state. Unimaginable success! It was unlike anything we had ever experienced before.

The storm had broken. There were flowers everywhere. De Valois made a speech from the stage. Everyone was hysterical. Crowds tried to reach the dressing rooms; the doormen panicked and held distinguished visitors at bay in the street. I felt like a person reprieved from the gallows. With the weight of fear removed, I could have risen straight up through the ceiling. An overriding thirst made me almost inarticulate. 'Thank you, thank you, thank you' was all I could mumble as a stream of people proffered their congratulations.

The excitement wasn't over. I put on the tiered, black brocade ballgown given me by Bianca Mosca and, with my arms full of roses, boarded the chartered bus in which the company was rushed, with wailing siren police escort, to Gracie Mansion for the Mayor's reception. Later, in the small hours of the morning, a sizeable group of us was to be found at Reuben's, fearlessly reading the critics in the early editions.

For two days I was stunned by what had happened. Not really believing it, I cabled my mother a low-key message: 'I think we made it.' I couldn't relax because the rest of the season was still ahead and there were other bridges to cross. But I realized that for the rest of my life I would never again be so nervous for any performance. Some small part of me had actually burned out.

I wonder what it was that I did that opening performance in New York. I really don't know the answer.

When I go out on to the stage, I am the character I portray. I believe that I am Princess Aurora full of happiness on my sixteenth birthday, intrigued by the four suitors come from afar to request my hand. I feel grown-up for the first time as I receive them with appropriate dignity and unpractised charm.

Simultaneously on another plane in my mind I am trying to accomplish the steps perfectly. Since perfection doesn't exist, I conceal the shortcomings as best I can with small spontaneous adjustments – the mistakes are different each time.

In addition, an almost automatic device like a tape recording of the music runs through my mind, dictating my movements. When I succeed in sychronizing this tape exactly with the sound of the orchestra, I – Princess Aurora – am dancing more or less to my satisfaction. Of course a lot of other indefinable things go into it too, but that is the best explanation I can give of how I dance.

A short visit to Washington after the triumphant New York season brought us all down to earth, or at least stage level. The slippery floor of Constitution Hall caught each of us in turn. Dancers in the first ballet returned to the dressing room in tears, saying, 'It's impossible. I just couldn't stand up.' Out I went, thinking 'that won't happen to *me*', and the next moment I was flat on my face in the middle of the stage, with President Truman and his family in the audience. Bobby, I remember, was standing quite still on both feet when, just stretching out his hand towards me, he all but fell over. As a performance it was one big flop.

Back in London we expected a hero's welcome. Instead the curtain rose on *Cinderella* to chilly silence. Perhaps it was not a good performance, perhaps we were spoiled by the volleys of applause that had punctuated every ballet in New York. Whatever the reason, it was an uphill fight until the end of the evening, when our faithful public expressed their usual enthusiasm.

In retrospect, I think I won New York by smiling. The ballerina image at that time was of the tragic swan, or the betrayed Giselle, pale, humourless of mien. A serious classical ballet with a happy heroine must have been a welcome novelty. But it was the Sadler's Wells Ballet that conquered; one cannot separate any one part of the success from the whole, and that was the way in which I viewed my contribution. I was an integral part of the company, and the company was in part my life and my family. Many of the others felt as I did.

Without that camaraderie I do not know how I would have fared through the following years, which brought me enormous successes on the one hand and inner despair on the other.

In New York the rich or successful visitor is overwhelmed by generosity, often from strangers who throw their houses open and go out of their way to be hospitable. Even taxi drivers are liable to be aspiring opera singers who recognize one, and sometimes people in the street greet one out of sheer friendliness. But I think it must be a terrible place to arrive in poor and alone. Paris, with its tree-lined boulevards and sidewalk cafés, seems to welcome even the poorest visitor. But Paris is apt to regard the success of one season as *passé* the next. New York makes its friends and sticks to them.

It was my good luck to have a magical success in Paris under the chestnut trees in May, and the next year to take New York by storm in the fall. Part of the fairy-tale quality of all this was that it occurred in the post-war recovery years and so took on a double sweetness because of the gloomy times before. The beauty of the Champs Elysées and the glamour of Fifth Avenue, at a time when London was distinctly drab, intensified the excitement of our artistic triumphs.

At long last I found some self-confidence. I was heaped with compliments and praise until I concluded it was ridiculous, if not grotesque, to remain so shy at the age of thirty. Katharine Hepburn, unbeknown to herself, helped give me the necessary boost. Bobby and I stood on the doorstep of the goddess's house in New York. She opened the door herself and said, 'Oh, I am so excited to meet you!' I thought the position quite the reverse. It was extraordinary to find this great star thinking me interesting. Shortly after that I was on the cover of *Time* magazine. Perhaps these two ocurrences helped to bring about my identification with the Margot Fonteyn who is always something of a mystery to me. At least I decided to enjoy the benefits of my ambiguous relationship with her.

We were to make several winter tours of the U.S.A. and Canada, some lasting so long that all told I reckon four years of my life went simply in moving from city to city, hotel to hotel, packing and unpacking, on the American continent alone. What an amount of coming out in the footlights and going home in the rain! So much glitter on the stage and flattery over supper followed by so much returning alone to the impersonal hotel room. It is an odd way to live, yet brings a richness of rewards.

On the first of these long tours, *Newsweek* put me on its cover. The article inside gave me the surprising information that everyone questioned, even my mother, found me secretive about myself. I had imagined that I could be read like the proverbial open book. Perhaps it was that apart from my identity in each ballet, and my identity as the ballerina arriving at rehearsal, leaving the stage door, being entertained and so on, there was little else. Perhaps the person they thought secretive spent most of her time projected into some other character and hardly existed on her own.

The ballet company toured North America by train. It was a funny life aboard that chain of sleeping cars and freight wagons, chugging its way along in its own time. Some cars were reserved for the ballet, others for the orchestra and one for the crew. Very soon romances, serious and fickle, erupted and evolved in complicated patterns. Dramatic eternal triangles inevitably formed, bringing bliss to one compartment and tears to the next.

The train was classed as a freight train because there were five wagons of scenery, and it jolted and bumped so violently as it was shunted about in the night that once when we had a derailment hardly anyone noticed the difference. Boarding the train was a special problem, as it had no fixed time of departure. It could not leave until all the scenery and equipment were loaded, but no one could tell exactly how long that would take. Meanwhile, the passengers dispersed in all directions to eat, drink and make merry. There was no way anyone could be sure that all the hundred and forty-odd people were aboard, so the train just took off somewhere between two and three in the morning with the organizers hoping for the best.

Once, in a small town, neither Moira Shearer nor I happened to be dancing in the last night's programme. We went off to dinner together, and then on to the railway station.

'Excuse me, where is the special train, please?' we asked a ticket collector.

'What special train?'

'The Ballet train.'

'The *what*? Show me your tickets.'

'We don't have tickets, it's a special.'

'Well what time does it leave?'

'It doesn't have a departure time; it goes when everything is on.' He scratched his head and said slowly, 'I see.' Pause. 'So you are looking for a train for which you don't have tickets.' Pause. 'And you don't know when it leaves.' Then a longer pause for effect. 'I don't suppose you happen to know your destination?' Shamefacedly, we had to admit that we didn't.

Sol Hurok came across from the East Coast to give a big reception at the Ambassador Hotel for the Los Angeles opening. He insisted that everyone be present. Bobby, however, knowing the theatre world so well, had been invited by the British acting community in Beverly Hills to take me to a supper in our honour. Bobby said, 'Don't worry, we'll go to Hurok's reception and then slip out again. There'll be two hundred people there, so just watch me and leave when I do.' Sol was a bit of an old fox when he wasn't being a Russian bear, and he knew perfectly well what we planned. So when the guests were all inside the dining room, he shut the door, drew up a chair in front of it and sat down. Bobby was stymied; I think for the first time in his life.

One night Charles Chaplin gave a dinner to which Ninette de Valois, Frederick Ashton, Sol Hurok, Bobby, Michael Somes, Pamela Leslie Edwards and I were invited. It was a quite extraordinary evening. No sooner were we seated at table than fierce arguments, political and confused, broke out all around. De Valois's Irish blood was up and she was hammering away at her neighbour, while Bobby's voice was raised angrily in another conflict with the lady on Sol's left. Sol was subdued for a bit then turned to the lady and said, loud and clear, 'You're a sthupid woman. I've met some sthupid women in my life, but you're the *sthupidest*!' Mrs Chaplin, who was pregnant, put her hand to her forehead and excused herself from the table, feeling unwell. Charlie Chaplin, meanwhile, was explaining to someone that there was less liberty for individuals in the U.S.A. than in the Soviet Union.

In San Francisco a lady visited Michael Somes in his dressing room and opened the conversation by saying, 'I want to thank you for carrying my husband.' He gazed at her, not knowing how to reply or to what she referred. She continued, 'I am Romola Nijinsky; thank you for being a pallbearer at my husband's funeral.' We also met Nijinsky's daughter, Kyra, who is fascinating. Sturdily built and full of exuberance, she has the most engaging smile and what must be her father's eyes, of an unusual grey-green, or is it green-brown? She is an artist and uses bright colours. Her father is a frequent subject, but I noticed all her paintings show him in ballet roles, never as himself. When she was describing a Russian dance she made a momentary gesture of her right arm across her brow, and I could see Nijinsky exactly. There was something in her movement and her face that expressed all there is to say about dancing in that one instant, and I can never forget it. Like many people who are heavily built, she has a soft and generous sense of movement. The very thin ones are always in danger of looking brittle. I think the trend these days is for young dancers to be unnecessarily thin, and so to lack something in warmth.

In Philadelphia, of course, Joe Stuhl and his friends looked after me like a princess. He once asked a taxi driver to take us to the theatre, a very short distance away. When the man remonstrated, Joe said, 'The lady is a ballerina. Ballerinas don't walk.' 'Well, what do they do? Fly?' cracked the driver, and drove off without us. I liked best the cab driver who asked me if I was the 'big cheese' in the company. I said I supposed I was, so he asked, 'Tell me, how do you get to be the big cheese?' I said I thought the only way was by being a little cheese first.

During the same North American tour my left foot began giving me some pain, and I consulted a doctor. He did not give me a specific diagnosis, but afterwards spoke to the lady who had given me his name. He said it was very sad that I would not be able to dance for more than another two years. That was in 1951.

At the end of the tour we returned to New York, where

a rich admirer insisted on giving me a mink coat. I had always thought that this was exactly the way ballerinas should be treated, but he had a slightly strange manner, which frightened me, and I asked him to invite Michael Somes as well when we lunched or dined at Le Pavillon. Michael and I had a mind-bending afternoon when the admirer took us to Harry Winston's, the jeweller, and got Mr Winston to take his largest diamonds out of the safe. There was the Hope diamond, which is supposed to bring bad luck to its owner, and a beautiful drop-shaped stone called the Star of the East, of which he casually asked the price. 'One million, one,' replied Mr Winston, and the man mumbled something about selling a city block. Michael and I got very nervous and rapidly escaped.

There had been one odd incident back in Atlanta, where we had stayed only two days. A long-distance telephone call was put through to me in the theatre manager's office. I couldn't think who might be calling. The soft voice on the line said, 'Hello, this is Tito.' 'Tito!' I said. 'Wherever are you?' 'I'm in New York, darling. I just arrived and saw that I missed you here. I called all over the place to find you.' I couldn't believe it was Tito. He was talking as though we had seen each other last week, when it was twelve years since I had heard a word. He continued, 'I have to go to Panama tomorrow. I will take a plane that stops in Atlanta if you will come out to see me at the airport.' I was cautious, thinking of the playboy image I bore of him. Anyway, the whole thing sounded so improbable. I said, 'Well, if you telephone me before you leave to say that you are really getting that plane, I will go out to meet you.' I told Pamela and Leslie. Pamela said, 'I wonder what he looks like now?' I remembered the handsome head on a well-built neck, and something about the visual image made me say, 'I expect he is very fat by now, and has a wife and three children, too.' Next day there was no phone call, so that was the end of that.

*

My mother and father

(*Above*) Shanghai 1931

(*Left*) Dancing

(*Right*) Dancing

(*Left*) Rehearsing 'The Sleeping Beauty' with Robert Helpmann and Nicholai Sergueev

(*Below*) Michael Somes in 'Dante Sonata', 1940

(*Right*) With Leonide Massine in 'Le Tricorne', 1947

(*Top left*) Driving to our reception at the
Plaza-Athenée hotel
(*Bottom left*) With Ashton during
the filming of 'Ondine'
(*Above*) 'Marguerite and Armand' – performance

With Ninette de Valois and Nureyev after our
first 'Giselle'. London 1962

The Sadler's Wells (and later Royal Ballet) tours of the U.S.A. and Canada settled into a pattern repeated every second year. An autumn opening season at the 'Met' Opera House in New York was followed by a three- or four-months' tour across the continent and back. As we set off on the third such tour my heart was heavy, though I now had tremendous success everywhere I went. I had for long imagined that I would retire at the age of thirty-five, taking it for granted that I would be married by that age. Now I had reached thirty-four without encountering the love that would put my life in perspective. I so much wanted to love, and it seemed so difficult for me to love. I decided it was unsuitable for a woman of thirty-five to remain single and I would marry at that age, willy-nilly, whether I loved or not. My reasoning was based on the theory that having those things considered most desirable in life, such as money, fame, success, adulation and in particular most cherished friends, I could hardly expect in addition that which I craved more than all else.

I think some women are necessarily easily influenced because they must adapt to the man they will marry, and until they find him they are indeterminate people. It is not easy to live in that condition. My career offered a splendid shelter, into which I could escape from myself. I had, in fact, reached the point where my own identity was completely eclipsed by my idea of the image I should project to others: a glamorous, chic personage; gracious and a little aloof; but effervescent with gaiety after the performance – this last bit, at least, came naturally. I even thought I ought to have a string of lovers, as many people believed I did. In truth, I never had much aptitude for that life.

Probably my technical accomplishment as a ballerina was now at its peak, for I had been working very hard to eradicate faults acquired during the crowded war years. If anything I gave too much attention to that aspect, and several critics found me cold. I am sure they were right, because there was so little of myself left in the Margot Fonteyn they saw. The created image was in danger of taking over. In retrospect, I can see that I had reached the farthest point in the great arc of my life, and was out in the emotional wastelands of some fallacious person who was yet, in some ways, also me.

BOOK TWO

ONE

I have danced with many partners in my career, though there have been only three major partnerships. The first, of course, was with Robert Helpmann. Bobby, uniquely perhaps in theatre history, planned his career simultaneously as a dancer and an actor. In 1951 he decided to leave the ballet, or rather our ballet, entirely. Before that I had rarely danced with anyone else. In the major ballets he alone gave me confidence. We had danced together all over the world, but one of the most amusing of our engagements was at La Scala, Milan.

The director of La Scala, Dr Antonio Ghiringhelli, came to London personally to invite me to dance in his theatre, a gesture I found immensely flattering. With Bobby as the Prince and Pamela May as the Lilac Fairy I set off to conquer Italy with *The Sleeping Beauty*. Dr Ghiringhelli warned us that the people of Milan held Tchaikovsky in very low esteem; nevertheless we thought that *Sleeping Beauty* on the magnificent stage of La Scala would be invincible. So does pride come before a fall.

We were welcomed to Milan with all possible courtesy, installed in the best hotel and fussed over by journalists and photographers. The rehearsals were more chaotic than at home, but after all we were among the fiery Latins. When it came to orchestral rehearsals we found the conductor more temperamental than any prima donna, but even so it was surprising to hear the ballet director shouting at him, 'All you think about is your long hair and your profile!' At the same rehearsal, in the middle of our pas de deux, just as Bobby had me lifted up in the air, the musicians stopped playing and rapidly left the pit. I thought there must be a fire alarm or something, but no one even blinked on stage. '*Che cosa?*' asked Bobby. 'Oh, just the orchestral break,' replied a dancer.

I sat among a mass of flowers in my dressing room preparing for the first night. I thought, if the so-called phlegmatic Anglo-Saxons are such a demonstrative audience, what will it be like with the volatile Italians? At that moment there was a knock on the door and in came a large gentleman with a big smile. 'Io Parmigiani,' he said in a voice like black molasses. 'Parmigiani,' he repeated. Then he clasped his big hands together and waved them in front of his head in the manner of someone promoting applause for a boxing match. 'Publico molto caldo,' he said several times, beaming from ear to ear. I thought him enchanting. It was so warm and kind of him to bring encouragement just before I went on. I wondered who he was.

I made my first entrance to mild applause and completed the show-stopping Rose Adagio, the dance that always brought the house down in London and New York. Normally I had to run back three or four times to bow, but suddenly the applause died as I reached the wings. My big number had certainly gone flat. (In subsequent performances I decided to run faster to the wings to be able to come back at least once in the same amount of applause. However, this trick failed because the quicker I ran, the sooner they stopped.) The pas de deux with Bobby was much better received, so I took heart for the final curtain, which was foolish because I did not know that with the last chord of music most of the Milan audience would rush for the public transport barely stopping to give a single hand-clap on their way out. Dr Ghiringhelli was waiting to congratulate us, which seemed like a hollow joke. 'It went very well,' he said. 'The public here never applaud much for the ballet and they hate Tchaikovsky. Tonight was an unusually warm reception.'

Dr Ghiringhelli became a dear friend, whose company I cherished for his worldly wisdom combined with the deep love he bore for La Scala, which I could understand so well. It is a theatre of awe-inspiring proportions, where one can find stagehands whose fathers and grandfathers were stagehands before them. Some are now my friends of twenty-five years' standing, and the dressers too.

At supper he talked about building up the ballet, which was then so inferior to the opera. Over the years we had the same discussion many times, and when he retired twenty years later the ballet and the ballet public were a very different story. He is the only person permitted to call me by my childhood nickname, which he pronounces 'Pidgy'.

That first year, however, I am afraid that Bobby, Pamela and I, realizing we were never going to shake Milan with our dancing, decided to have a good time ourselves. We visited museums and made trips to Venice and to Santa Margarita, laughing, eating and drinking heartily all the way. As Bobby and I were dancing in a crowded night club, the orchestra leader thought it would be a nice tribute to move into a version of the Dying Swan. We began to do it as a hilariously corny ballroom exhibition number, and the other dancers retired from the floor. It turned out to be one of our most moving performances. Several people were to be seen wiping tears from their eyes.

An Italian friend complained that my performance looked too effortless. I said, 'That's how it's supposed to look. In ballet one should make the difficult steps appear easy.' 'But,' she replied, 'the Italian public want to *know* that it's difficult, then they get excited.' 'Well, that's not my way of dancing. I can't change it.'

In fact, by the last performance there was much more enthusiasm and a lot of 'Bravos'. Mr Parmigiani reappeared in my dressing room, saying, 'Brava! Brava!' His smile was even broader than before and his impersonation of the cheering public more fervent. In a sudden flash I got it. He was the leader of the claque! What a marvellous relic of the nineteenth century. I did not know a claque of people distributed about the theatre and paid to cheer on order still existed anywhere. I was fascinated and quickly got out some money for him. He bowed deeply several times and left saying, 'Brava, brava, signorina, brava!'

Another charming custom still prevails in some European opera houses. A man came once to my dressing room after I had danced the first act of a ballet. He brought my salary in cash, the idea being that artists are not paid before they have performed at least one act, but they won't complete the performance until the management has fulfilled its obligation. This arrangement might be quite satisfactory for heavily dressed opera singers – I presume they pin the bank notes to a garter – but it is difficult to conceal a wad of lire about one's person while wearing a tutu, and it is notoriously unsafe to leave valuables lying about in theatre dressing rooms.

That summer I was telling Preobrajenska that I had been at La Scala. A wistful look, one of her most touching expressions, came into her eyes as she said, 'Ah yes, Milano. When I danced there I had the biggest success of my life. The public went absolutely wild with enthusiasm.' I suppose that was in the 1890s, when Italian ballet was still at its height, and Russia called on the great Italian ballerinas Legnani and Brianza to dance the first performances of *Swan Lake* and *The Sleeping Beauty*. The Italians were very strong technicians then, and responsible for inventing quite a few of the most difficult steps, including the fouetté turns which Legnani incorporated into *Swan Lake*. I remember, too, Karsavina telling me that, when she was a young ballerina, she went to study in Milan, just as thirty years later I went to Paris to study with Russians. The centre of ballet constantly shifts.

After Bobby's departure I danced almost exclusively with Michael Somes. These were my prime years. In rehearsing the classical ballets with Michael, I reworked my own roles completely under the guidance of Harijs Plučis. What hours the three of us spent with the indefatigable Plučis going over and over the same details. 'No, my dear. Once more again, please ... You must understand. *Schwain* is.' For a long time I thought he had got hold of the old English word 'swain' for a young gentleman, and was referring to Michael. Then I realized that he meant me, the 'swan'.

Nearly ten years had passed since I had worked on the classical ballets in detail with Vera Volkova, and, on a few occasions, with Tamara Karsavina, who gave me marvellous insights into the playing of Giselle. The emotion had always been there within me, and no doubt I expressed it to some effect in small theatres, using the traditional mime gestures – but in a hasty mechanical manner which would not have projected in a big opera house. However, I still had much to learn.

Karsavina never demonstrated the mime scenes exactly the same way twice. She eliminated superfluous actions and followed her line of thought spontaneously, improvising upon a set framework and ground plan. Her gestures were broad and unhurried. From Michael I gained a new, more careful approach to technicalities, and this I needed. I had many faults which I had never had the time to put right and, as Plučis had noticed, it took me two years to break a bad habit and retrain my muscles to work correctly.

A long-held wish was fulfilled when Fred decided to choreograph Ravel's *Daphnis and Chloë*. From the time I first heard the music, when I was about seventeen, I had wanted the ballet desperately. It was well worth waiting for. Fred made of it something so personal to Michael and me that I danced it very little after Michael retired. Perhaps I was foolish to identify the dancer so closely with the roles, and with my own interpretation; but I think I was right to feel so strongly about them: *Nocturne*, *Apparitions*, *Hamlet* and *Giselle* with Bobby; then *Symphonic Variations*, *Daphnis*, *Firebird* and *Ondine* with Michael; *Demoiselles de la Nuit* with Roland; and, later, a new-found *Giselle*, *Marguerite and Armand* and *Romeo and Juliet* with Nureyev. These partnerships held a special significance for me, like love affairs, and I was inflexible in my fidelity. It is only in recent years that I have learnt to be unfaithful in one or two of these roles. My infidelity, however, must be excused on the grounds of irresistible charm, for surely it is an extraordinary chance for a woman no longer young to dance not only with Nureyev but with Attilio Labis, Egon Madsen and Richard Cragun; with Anthony Dowell, David Wall, Donald McLeary; with Desmond Kelly, Ivan Nagy, Heinz Bosl, Christopher Gable, Garth Welch and Karl Musil – all handsome and gallant men. And I must not forget Mikifumo Nagata, twenty-two years old and adorable. It is a sensational array of partnerships for a ballerina who scores her highest marks in pas de deux. I have never much enjoyed dancing solos, with the exception of some lovely Ashton variations made to measure for me. I really like depending on my partner for inspiration and passion.

Soon after the creation of *Daphnis and Chloë*, Ruth Page, the American dancer-choreographer, and her husband, Tom Fisher, invited Fred and me to holiday with them. We were to cruise the Greek Islands, about which none of us knew a thing. I made a point of reading several books, of which the most illuminating was Henry Miller's *The Colossus of Maroussi*. He captures the immensity of sky and sea, and the power of antiquity over one's imagination, and he talks of the light which is unlike the light anywhere else. But he does not write of the strange conjunction of land and sea, of how the one stops and the other takes over, neither encroaching on the other, so that the café owner can set up his little wooden tables and chairs within three feet of the water's edge on the bare earth. Sitting there in the moments just before dusk, and sensing that the lapping water has respected the rights of that little piece of land for centuries gone by, one could be in any moment of time one chooses. The Aegean sea of mythological times is there for one to reach out and touch. The storm clouds gather and one knows the gods on Mount Olympus are angry as Apollo's chariot of fire crosses the black horizon.

I have a romantic character that enables me to be readily transported into other ages. It happens often, suddenly, and at no special prompting – though landscape is the most likely trigger, and Greece is the country above all others where I can float in time. The holiday with Ruth and Tom was almost surreal. From the moment we set sail on the chartered yacht *Elikki*, with several cases of the best champagne and a cook who had never been to sea, it was what would now be called a 'happening'. The first morning I was woken up by a large wave, which crashed in the porthole just above my upper berth and left me lying in six inches of cold salt water. Before lunch the cook, who was an old man, was bitten by a fish and thereafter refused to get up for several days, saying that he was reading about Geisha girls. As we sailed the islands, dolphins escorted us by day and in the waterside cafés at night we watched sailors performing amazing dances during which they somehow picked up the wooden tables in their teeth, and danced with them, balancing meanwhile all the paraphernalia of bottles and glasses atop. The islands were untouched by tourism; we rode donkeys to whitewashed villages, looked in the little churches and found marble statues half-buried in a ploughed field. The cruise ended prematurely in an *Ondine*-like storm, in which it seems that I rode the prow of the ship laughing at the waves while Fred and Ruth clung to the mast. When the captain rushed up on deck waving his charts and shouting hysterically, it was decided to abandon ship at a near-by island.

The next year Fred and I were again invited by the Fishers, this time to the Villa Cimbrone high above Amalfi, and again Fred and Ruth were caught in an appalling storm down on the beach and watched another ship founder. But what a marvellous time we had through those many summer adventures! They were the most enjoyable holidays I ever spent.

Fortune-tellers have no appeal for me. If the future is bad, I don't want to know it in advance, and if it is good, I prefer it to come as a surprise. Nonetheless, on four or five occasions a friend, or someone at a party, has looked at my hand and made forecasts – some of which have come true;

others are maybe yet to come. The first foretold, when I was fifteen, that I would travel a lot, and of that there can be no question. The second said that the year 1952 would be bad for me, and that there was also a very bad time much later, about 1964. The third said I would never be as rich as I deserved, but I would always be comfortable, and that the last half of my life would be happier than the first.

These predictions are fixed in my mind, and in the autumn of 1952 I thought, 'We are nearly at the end of the year. If nothing worse happens to me now, it is not so bad.' Thereupon I developed a very sore throat on tour in Southampton. I had a fever and had to say I could not dance. De Valois visited me in the hotel, and the doctor came with penicillin. The next day, when de Valois came in she looked at the hearty meal on my lunch tray, which I was swallowing with only a little difficulty. 'If you can eat all that,' she said, 'there's not much wrong with you.' A few minutes later the doctor arrived to say the tests showed diphtheria, and an ambulance was on its way to fetch me.

By now I was feeling quite well, and put up some useless opposition to being carried out on a stretcher. I was very angry in the hospital when I was refused a pillow. Later a friend who had been in a Japanese prison camp in Burma told me that there, only the diphtheria patients who were tied down to their beds survived the spread of infection by moving in a vertical position. In my case, it was the penicillin that cleared the infection so quickly, leaving me feeling to all intents and purposes recovered after only two days. It was lucky for me that this new drug had been discovered a few years earlier.

The last of the great London fogs came down while I was convalescent. It continued for five days, making it the longest and most impressive I ever saw, a sort of grand farewell appearance. A slight tingling started in the soles of my feet. 'Ah,' said the doctor, 'I am afraid that means your recovery is going to take a long time. The nerves will die in your feet and grow back again. Do you notice anything about your tongue?' I said something was odd, I couldn't describe it exactly. For three weeks the paralysis in my feet and tongue increased, then receded at the same speed. It reached its peak just about Christmas, provoking a lot of extra laughter as I tried to pronounce words against the hazard of what felt like a plum in my mouth. Giving my name over the telephone was a riot, with the wrong consonants coming out: 'Biss Honheyn' was naturally incomprehensible. My feet felt no contact with the ground, so I walked as though I wore heavy boots, and even started ballet training looking in the mirror to see where my feet were.

Although I never doubted that I would recover in six weeks, as the doctor had said, I found out that many people thought otherwise. I was away from the stage for five months. When I returned in a hesitant performance of my favourite *Apparitions*, the reception was beyond anything I could describe. Flowers spread across the sixty-foot width of the stage. Clearly the welcome was by way of a special message of affection for me, not related to my dancing ability that night. It was a strange, almost weird, feeling to realize that I, or Margot Fonteyn – or perhaps both – was – or were – the object of that flood-tide of emotion.

The next morning, on board a ship sailing into Le Havre, a lonely figure in a black overcoat stood on the deck gazing long and intently through the early morning mists. He had just read an account of my performance in the morning papers. I only knew of it later. It was Tito.

Spain had long been the country of my dreams. I imagined that when I was old and retired I would end up in a little whitewashed villa in a burnt-ochre landscape overlooking the Mediterranean. There would be grapevines shading the terrace, and fig trees, olives and orange trees in the sun. All this came to mind when Fred was asked to direct a performance for the Granada Festival to take place in the open air. Fred, too, was excited at the idea of being in Spain.

'Oh dear, the terrible thing is that I've forgotten all my Spanish. When I was a boy in Lima, I spoke it better than English, but it has all gone.'

That was what he thought until the haughty customs official in white gloves turned his luggage inside out and left Fred to put it back together again. His indignation aroused, Fred let fly at the official in well-turned Spanish, putting himself in very good spirits at realizing he could still communicate effectively in Spanish after all.

The welcome as we stepped off the plane had delighted him. 'Madame Fonteyn! All Spain awaits you!' said Mr Aznar, who was a tremendous balletomane and friend of the critic Alfonso Puig, both of them kindness personified. Fred thought ballerinas and choreographers, too, should always be greeted like that, and I certainly enjoyed the moment fully. It prefaced a week of delight atop the hill chosen long ago by Moorish conquerors for their opulent palace and the beautiful Generalife Gardens where we were to perform.

The stage, built among fountains and cyprus trees under an indigo sky, was a region of enchantment where music and dance reigned far into the night. In the small hours we discarded our ballet slippers to sit in the little house once owned by Manuel de Falla, and watch the gypsies, who came from caves on a neighbouring hillside to dance their flamencos until dawn. In those hours of song and guitar, of dancing and wine and of wandering the rough road to our hotel overlooking the misty plains in the early morning, time had no meaning or value. Ages long past merged with the present, as the sun crept up gently, the farmhouse cockerels crowed, a faint wind stirred the ancient trees and another day, just like thousands gone by and to come, took life. I closed the shutters of my window and slept profoundly in a state of peace, conscious of the long roots of my ancestry stretching back into time and to

I knew not what places, but into the earth over which the sun rises and sets each day as it has for ever and will for ever more.

TWO

The New York season of 1953 opened in September with the traditional *Sleeping Beauty*. I was, as ever, nervous as a cat, knowing that it is even more difficult to repeat a success than to establish it in the first place. The occasion had turned into an established event like the opening of the opera season, and various famous eccentrics made their entries into the 'Diamond Horseshoe' dressed to catch the eyes of the columnists and the photographers' lenses. The stakes that year were won hands down by a bald gentleman wearing a tiara.

On 18 September, just before my second performance, the stage doorman brought a visiting card to my dressing room. It read, *Roberto E. Arias, Delegate of Panama to the United Nations*.

'The gentleman says he will come back at the end of the show,' the doorman said. I ran on to the stage to tell Pamela, who was preparing to dance the Lilac Fairy, and Leslie Edwards, who was dressed for Catalabutte. It was Leslie, standing alone on the stage as the master of ceremonies, who would in a few moments receive the burst of applause with which New York always anticipates the performance about to unfold as the heavy curtain rises on *Sleeping Beauty*.

Curiosity was uppermost in my mind. How would Tito look after so long? Fatter, for sure, but beyond that I didn't know what to expect. I supposed he might remember our flirtation, however unimportant it had been for him as a boy, but obviously he must now be fixed in the web of his adult life. Well, I would find out at the end of the performance.

I was changing my headdress for the second act when the doorman came back. 'The gentleman is here. He has a lady with him.' I was surprised to realize with a tiny heart thump that I had expected him to be alone. He ushered in a man, very fat, very round-faced with thin-rimmed spectacles and a casual, diffident smile spreading lazily across his chubby cheeks. 'This is Miss Gussie Chang. I decided not to wait till the end to see you.' His voice was softer than butter and lazy, like his smile. They sat on the settee. The fact that Gussie was Chinese made me like her instantly; she had that warmth of Chinese people which put me at ease as she chattered, and I chatttered, and Tito said not a word. He sat staring, half-absently, in my direction. 'I would like you to join us for supper at the 21 Club,' he said as 'Act Two Beginners' was called outside my door. 'But I'm afraid I can't come, I have another invitation I can't cancel.' 'Then I will telephone you in the morning,' he said, and off they went.

I was barely awake when the phone rang.

'Darling, I have to leave for Panama at noon, so I want to have breakfast with you.'

'I'm not up, I can't see you so soon.'

'It doesn't matter. Order me some coffee and I will be right over.'

He came into my room and sat cross-legged on the floor as he had done in my dressing room at Cambridge. I was trying unsuccessfully to superimpose this person on the memory of a very slender boy of no more than seven stone. It was hard to know what to say. Each wanted to know the other's position. Just as I had said to Pamela, half-jokingly, Tito was married and had three children. No, I hadn't married. I had tried to fall in love many times but some-how it didn't quite work out. There was someone I thought I might marry next year. 'Why don't you marry me?' he asked. It seemed a strange kind of joke, yet he could hardly be serious. 'You just told me you are married and have three children.' 'My wife will divorce me,' he said in the same lazy voice. I really couldn't take any of it seriously. I laughed and said I was glad to see him again, but it was an empty conventional phrase because I did not succeed in dove-tailing the old Tito with the new, nor was I any longer the girl of Cambridge days. As far as I was concerned, we were almost like two people meeting for the first time.

Next morning one hundred red roses were delivered to my rather small room. A resonant voice on the telephone said, 'Is that Miss Fonteyn? This is Roosevelt Zanders speaking. Did you receive one hundred red roses?' 'Well, I haven't counted them but there is an enormous basket here. Who are they from?' 'They're from Dr Arias. He told me to be sure to send one hundred, not one less. I sure hope you have one hundred there, otherwise I'll be in trouble.' I reassured him. 'Dr Arias says I am to drive you anywhere you want to go. Just let me know the time and I'll be there.'

The next minute it was a call from Panama. 'My wife has agreed to a divorce. I will be in New York tomorrow.' 'But don't! You can't do that. Don't be crazy. I hardly know you. I don't love you.' I was frantic. The whole thing was preposterous. He repeated, 'I will see you to-morrow,' and hung up. I was bewildered, dismayed and unable to believe or understand anything.

I found the attention, the suppers at El Morocco, the enormous limousine driven by the incomparable Roosevelt, all thoroughly enjoyable. But nowhere could I find a trace of my feeling for the old Tito in this new juxta-position of two people bearing the same names. How ironic that the casual playboy was now the ardent wooer, whereas the formerly love-sick girl felt nothing.

'You are going to marry me, and be very happy,' Tito said as he nonchalantly handed me a little packet contain-ing a beautifully simple diamond bracelet. Margot Fon-teyn, ballerina, thought: 'How marvellous! This is the way ballerinas should live!' But I was quite upset. I don't like divorce and I believe it sinful to take another woman's

159

husband. I remonstrated with Tito, begging him to go away, to stay with his family. He went to Panama but was back in a week, noticeably thinner and happier.

Meanwhile, Margot Fonteyn had kept the diamond bracelet.

Tito remembered Fred, Leslie and Pamela well from Cambridge days. He wined and dined us, the perfect host, relaxed and considerate, carefully aware of what everyone would be most likely to want and never letting it be noticed that he paid the bill. He decided to give a party, ostensibly for the visit of President Remón of Panama, but simultaneously for me and the ballet. This double stratagem pleased him tremendously. Fred was horrified by the extravagance of the invitations, in the form of thirty-word telegrams to every guest. The party was after a performance attended by Mrs Remón, founder of the Panama National Ballet, while the President whiled away the time over numerous drinks. Seeing how things were when the President arrived for supper, Tito thoughtfully wedged him in between two people on a banquette, and pushed a table in front of him so he might hold up with dignity. Later, when he had been steered out of the room and sent on his way home, the party really warmed up and Fred did the most sensational series of impersonations I have ever seen at one sitting. He showed us to the very life Pavlova, Isadora Duncan, Lopokova, Carmen Amaya, Pastor Imperia and I don't know who else. He was brilliant. He finds the very essence of people, just as he hears what is hidden most deeply in music. His dancing between the restaurant tables was more pliant and supple than ever before, his body completely flexible and his soul ablaze. This firework display was climaxed by a flying leap into the arms of the headwaiter, who happened to be placed appropriately as Novikoff or Nijinsky. He entered into the following pas de deux with the perfect sang-froid that befits a maître d'hôtel. Several waiters fled in terror through the swing doors to the kitchen.

Tito returned to Panama next day on the Presidential flight. The ballet company moved on to Philadelphia. In no time at all Tito was back, looking once again thinner, his suits by now being quite baggy. Before he arrived, Joe Stuhl, who is definitely psychic, met me at the station and said at once, 'I have been feeling so happy the last few days, I know something marvellous is going to happen for you.' I remained as someone looking in on a scene from outside the window, involved but not actually in the room.

One crisp early autumn day Tito drove me to Milford, in the Pocono Mountains, to the house of Mrs Pinchot, an imposing and very intelligent lady who was the widow of a Pennsylvania Governor, Gifford Pinchot. She looked like Queen Elizabeth I, with handsome features and red hair. Fred Ashton later had some Elizabethan ruffs made at Covent Garden and sent them for her to wear. Tito and I swam in an icy mountain stream on her estate and, in these natural wild surroundings, some tiny part of my true nature began to surface through my layers of ballet artificiality.

Tito kept disappearing and reappearing like the cuckoo in a clock. In Boston he arrived late one evening and the taxi driver, mis-hearing his soft voice, took him to a funeral parlour, where Tito spent some time absent-mindedly trying to check in for the night. Next morning he was at my hotel with a pair of diamond earclips for me and a whole tray of gold cufflinks, borrowed from Cartier, so that I could choose the ones he had already decided I was going to give him for his birthday. In the afternoon a furrier came up from New York with a mink coat in a huge box. The coat hung about me like a tent, so the furrier got out pins to mark the alterations while I protested that I didn't need another mink coat. 'I want you to have *my* mink coat,' said Tito quite firmly. 'It is much too long,' I said. 'You will have to shorten it by several inches.' The furrier looked stricken. 'Ohhh,' he said, and with a heavy Bronx accent, went on, 'don't shorten it; it looks so rich!' I saw my way out and quickly told Tito it was no good. But I took a rain check on a sable. The furrier regretfully packed up his mink tent and returned to New York, while we celebrated Tito's birthday with much champagne.

By now his clothes were hanging about him in folds, like the mink.

Every three or four days I danced *Swan Lake* or *Sleeping Beauty* in a new city, with easier ballets in between, plus the journeys, packing, unpacking and all the to-do of ballet tours. So I never could stop to think. I kept begging Tito to go away for a few weeks, to give me time. But he had no such intention.

In late November he summed up our position in a twenty-three-page letter, written on a plane journey, which said in part:

Wednesday Nov. 24th 4 p.m.

Mujer de mi vida,

Do not despair, my dear child. Do not be too terribly sad (for in the quality of your sadness is that same exquisite sensitiveness that makes you so unmeasurably lovable)....

I have been thinking and reflecting very seriously since this plane left Portland at 8.30 a.m., and am writing these thoughts almost as much for myself as for you.

Only two things seem to be outstandingly clear at this time

(A) There is no question in my mind – nor in yours I believe – that I love you to and possibly beyond the limits of capacity.

(B) I must be patient, and at this time can love you best with patience.

(C) I believe I will always love you and I also feel sure that deep in my heart I have always loved you very seriously. During my early years I thought of you often and felt that the obvious obstacles to our being married and having reasonable opportunity to live in harmonious permanent (as relative as the term can be) happiness were at the time insurmountable. I knew you first loved me, darling, (– I also knew you were destined to be the best dancer in the world –) I was terrified that you might be carried away towards an unobtainable Utopia by an impulsive act of mine.

After I returned to Panama to settle down to work there I realized fully that the little girl I knew would live permanently in a safe niche in my heart. As the years went by and I had to compose to the idea of an impossible love, I could sit for hours trying to remember all the details about you, and feel so very sorry that I hadn't more things of yours with me; (and would comfort myself with the feeling that after I died if people examined my heart they would find the word Margot carved on it, and if an ethereal girl walked in a dream through tropical graveyards she would easily find that heart marked for her and would gently move her fingers on the grooves of her name written into them long ago).

When I began to go to Europe after the war, I was almost frightened to see you.

One day at Le Havre, I believe it was Feb. 23rd 1953, at dawn, I picked up the overseas edition of the London *Times* and read that you had just danced for the first time after your illness. I went up to the bow of the ship where I could only feel the early morning air on my face and probably stood there for hours feeling terribly sorry for myself. I so much wanted to love and it seemed so difficult for me to love. And I knew that if I gave up to that urge that had just seized me to go to Southampton and London I might never want to return home again.

The more recent chronology you know. . . .

Oct. 5th at this point you began more earnestly than ever to beg me to slow down – slow down from where to where? My heart and my mind had already travelled the whole route from Alpha to Omega.

(B) I must be patient – the first fourteen years are the worst!

During the course of the last year, the last of the

obstacles closest to me – the obstacles that *I* could see – have been geometrically reduced in their relative importance. When I was the young boy who kissed you with trembling lips and tightly shut eyes, I was crushed by what I believed then to be insurmountable odds, lack of confidence in myself, sense of insecurity, geography, careers, and financial considerations.

Standing on the bow of the *United States*, steaming into Le Havre with the London *Times* in my overcoat pocket I was overwhelmed by the impulse to new appraisals: the factors that had seemed impossibly difficult in Panama ten years before had been in great measure dissolved by the growth of a firmer, stronger personality (what modesty!).

Careers – you have one – and destiny has given me a surprising multiplicity and flexibility in semi-careers. They, or a combination of whatever they are, can happily intermesh with the life of my love and her adorable one-track tastes, examples: the ballet, Dior, the Mediterranean, Cartier's and the best.

Geography – no need to discuss that, certainly no problem.

Financial – not as hopelessly difficult as it appeared in 1937. We may never have enough to suit Freddie, but I believe that in the foreseeable future we are not likely to be too shackled by fiscal stringency.

The apparent problem was my wife and children. I had felt when in Panama that as long as neither she nor I were emotionally interested in other individuals we should try to keep the house running as best we could, for the children, and perhaps to a certain degree for the public. She often said she didn't agree....

I have written at such length to confess to you that I was to a great extent ready to come to you at the end of September and still deliberately decided that I was willing to take more time to make matters of my life appear as tidy as possible.

You say only 'darling Tito, I am not ready, be patient' and it is clearly indispensable for your good and mine that I *be* patient. And so I will.

There is no valid reason to expect of you – much less demand – that you be suddenly ready. If I had never left you would not have found time to develop complications. Also the psychological climate in which *I* lived was more propitious when I returned to Panama. I *knew* that you loved me, but had been careful in extreme not to tell you that I loved you. It is quite natural that you should have given up all hope long ago. It is just as natural that my vanity should have repeated to me from time to time 'deep in her heart is love for me and some day I will be with her again.' ...

This letter seems to be more for me than for you – yes, it is a need to confess that I have not recently allowed my better nature to guide my love. Unfortunately I do not always act as I write, but today my better nature needs to dialogue with you, without seeking promises by innuendo and without recoursing to shallow heroics. But all of Tito, the gentle and the violent, the good and the bad, the relaxedly serene and the emotionally tense, loves you most dearly.

The letter was very much in the 1930s spirit of our first love; the days when we sang, 'Someday we'll meet again', and a love affair was called a romance. Our attitudes had been appropriate to the period of our adolescence, but had been held over in a kind of deep-frozen state while unnatural violence overtook our world. If Tito was hurt by any reference to my life in the intervening years he would say, 'There are some birds in Panama that run through the mud, but when they come out their feathers are clean and white.'

No one, not even an ice-cool ballerina, could fail to be touched by Tito's letter. But my real difficulty was to find the unused heart crated up and stored away, forgotten, inside the personage of a ballet star. For so long I had felt nothing; now I had to beg Tito to wait while I searched for it, looking initially in the wrong place, among the tissues of the heart belonging to the Margot Fonteyn whose feelings for William Chappell, Fred, Bobby, Michael and Roland Petit were on a different plane, interwoven with the unrealities of art.

When we faced a three-day train journey to the West Coast, I thought, 'Thank God. He won't even be able to telephone. I shall just sleep all the way and try to think later.' Barely a day had gone by when the train broke down for several hours, and walking along the tracks came a guard from some unheard-of junction a couple of miles distant and bearing a telegram: 'See you in Seattle! Love, Tito.' I felt hunted and desperate.

In svelte new suits he came to Seattle, bringing a 'three-piece suite' of earclips and a brooch. I had not been able to find out how one returns jewellery one doesn't want to accept. Understanding me so well, he took me out of the theatre at every opportunity, often to cruise on the misty Puget Sound.

Ten days later he rejoined us in Los Angeles. John Wayne had for long been a close friend of Tito's; we went to his house and he was understanding, fatherly, kind, wise, all these things at once, without saying a word about what he thought of the situation between Tito and me. By now I realized there was no hope for Tito's marriage. I found him serious, unusual, responsible, kind, amusing, determined; in short, I liked him very much. I wished I loved him. An odd thing was that the boy I always remembered dancing impromptu rumbas told me he didn't dance because he wasn't very good. On the other hand, he was unusually agile, and once literally dived from the front to the back seat of Roosevelt Zanders's limousine instead of climbing over or using the doors.

Classes, rehearsals and the inevitable *Swan Lake* ate up whole days of my life in nervous tension, the latter making me unspeakably edgy until the third act was over. The rest of the time I enjoyed Tito's company, if not his driving. He crossed six red lights before I dared to comment on it, then he said, 'Oh, please do tell me; I thought they were green.' After that I assumed the position of navigator for our visits to Tito's friends, including Red Skelton, Merle Oberon, Jules Stein and Danny Kaye and his wife, Sylvia. Suddenly, I was beginning to feel at ease with people I had not met before.

John Wayne lent us his boat, and a whole party of dancers went to Catalina Island on our free day. It was sunny but not hot, a little fresh on deck, but that didn't discourage some of the girls from sunbathing. At the island we were taken as sightseers to some famous bar, which was closed at the time. The manager himself poured a 'Chimborazo' for Tito, consisting of seven different kinds of spirit. He obediently drank it, then put the glass on the table, fell flat on his back, got up, shook his head, put his glasses back on and was quite all right the rest of the day. It was an astonishing sight. I asked whatever had happened. He said, 'I don't know; I just found myself on the floor, so I got up.'

In one of the booths we found an old man who'd obviously been overlooked at closing time. He was in a stupor. The manager said, 'Hey, Joe, this is Dr Roberto Arias from Panama.' The man stirred slightly, turned a bleary eye in our direction and suddenly pronounced, in an unexpectedly loud voice, 'Panama! I was there on 4 May 1923.' Then he went back into his torpor and nothing would rouse him again.

The day had taken on a surrealist quality. My spirits freed themselves from normal preoccupations and floated at random in space. Returning in the boat I stood on deck with a light breeze blowing my hair. The sun was sinking in the sky. I gazed at the sea for a long time, as I had done so often as a child. It is eternal and profound. Some people gaze at the starry night sky to recover their sense of man's insignificance in relation to the universe. I find it is the sea that restores my sense of values more effectively. By now, refreshed and at peace, I understood that I did love Tito, but that my love was not at all what I had expected. In my search for some wild passion I had not thought of the simplicity of the union of two souls. In Tito's company I felt neither alone nor with another person, just fundamentally complete.

At last I knew that I should be his wife.

At Christmas we were in Chicago, still on the same pro-tracted tour, but now in sub-zero weather. Since the day on the boat I had been very calm. Tito and I discussed plans to marry, and I told my family. My heart had been dead too long for it instantly to assume normal living. But even troubled with doubts I was sure of one thing: whatever might happen to us in the future, I would never be bored living with Tito. And how right I was!

Ninette de Valois came out to spend Christmas with the company. Our relationship was not just that of the artist and the director of the company; she had reared me, guided me, given me the background without which I could have done nothing and she was my benefactor, al-most Godmother. I told her over lunch that I had now decided definitely to marry. That evening in the theatre she saw Tito in the foyer and said, 'I am so happy to hear the news. Margot needs an anchor.' 'Damn it, Madame, I'm not an anchor,' he replied with reasonably good humour, wondering if it was wise to marry a ballerina after all.

Knowing that so many people felt I belonged to them was not agreeable to Tito. I doubt whether many men would have allowed me to continue my career. When questioned on this point he would say laconically, 'It's difficult to retire a good racehorse.' He had noticed early on that there are many similarities between dancers and racehorses. Both need careful exercising, they eat a lot, have trouble with their ankles and both were painted by Degas. Later Tito tried to expound this theory to a par-ticularly dense journalist, who ended up writing: 'Dr Arias says his wife resembles the backside of a horse.' *Touché!*

One of the group of friends at Cambridge in the old days, Paul Kramer of Washington, told me that President Roosevelt had shown a very warm affection for Tito, who had worked for a time in the White House press office. I asked Tito if this affection stemmed from the Roosevelts' state visit to Panama before the war, when Tito's father was President and Tito was fifteen. He said that he came to know two of the sons, Franklin, Jr., and John, very well at that time, but that President Roosevelt's attitude towards him really dated from one of those incidents of pure chance that can bring unexpected favours to a man's life. In the last week of August 1939, the summer when I had seen very little of Tito, he was in Paris and had gone to the station with John Roosevelt and his wife to see them off to America. John had asked Tito to finish closing up the apartment they had occupied during their stay, so Tito went straight back there from the station. The telephone rang insistently. He picked it up and said, 'This is Tito Arias speaking from John Roosevelt's apartment.' A lady's voice came on the line, 'This is Missie Lehand, the President's secretary. The President wants to speak to John.' 'They are already on the boat train to Le Havre,' Tito replied. 'I wonder if you can tell me if the President's mother is with them?' Miss Lehand asked. 'No, she is here in Paris.' After a pause, the voice came back, 'Just a moment, Mr Arias, the President wants to talk to you.' He came on the line and asked, 'Tito, are you anywhere near the American Embassy? It is difficult to get calls through quickly now, and I am very worried that my mother is still in Paris. War might break out any day. Please run over and tell Ambassador Bill Bullitt to see that she gets on the next boat.' Knowing that all the boats were absolutely packed, Tito immediately alerted Bill Anderson, manager of the United States Lines, to find accommodation for Mrs Roosevelt, and then went to put Ambassador Bullitt in the picture. The sequel to this brief episode was unprecedented kindness from the President and his mother, Mrs Sara Delano Roosevelt, and Tito cites a story illustrating his point. Mrs Roosevelt invited Tito to lunch in New York and asked if there was anybody he particularly wanted to meet. 'I would like to meet the President of IBM,' he said. 'Good, I'll invite him.' 'How fortunate for me that you know Mr Watson,' said Tito.

Mrs Roosevelt replied, 'Oh, I don't know him. But I think he might come to lunch if the President's mother invites him.'

As soon as the U.S. tour finished I left with Fred and Leslie Edwards for Nassau, where Tito had a yacht, the *Edmar*, which he and his brother, Tony, had recently bought. There was even a piano on board, which delighted Jean Gilbert, the ballet's concert pianist who came with us. Tito had brought the old black butler from his father's house, Milton Garvey, a darling man who was poetic by nature and had written several books and plays. His charm was so great that one could easily understand how he came to have twenty-seven children 'by five beddings,' as he expressed it.

It was glorious to sail in these clear waters, and to go ashore to pearly beaches and lazy little towns. It was a real holiday, and a time when I began to get used to the idea of marriage.

THREE

A year was to pass before our wedding, however. De Valois, ever planning the best for her 'family,' had decided with Fred that *The Firebird* would be a marvellous ballet for the company and for me. It was to open at the Edinburgh Festival in August 1954, and we prepared during early summer. Serge Grigorieff, Diaghilev's régisseur, who was renowned for his retentive memory of every step in every ballet, and his wife, Lubov Tchernicheva, came to reconstruct the ballet for us. In addition, Tamara Karsavina, the original Firebird, agreed to rehearse me in the part. As usual, I was apprehensive before we even started, and more so with Karsavina's first words: 'This is the most tiring ballet you will ever dance.' There is indeed one moment in the pas de deux when the Firebird, struggling in the grasp of Ivan Czarevitch, kneels at his feet in a back-bend and, unbeknown to the audience, almost dies there and then. I have heard of ballerinas being literally sick in the wings shortly after this moment. Nevertheless, the ballet has many compensatory moments that are gloriously satisfying to dance. I welcomed the strong, unromantic character, so different from most of my repertoire.

Serge Grigorieff was known as a stern disciplinarian for Diaghilev, and his wife I had seen dancing Zobeïde in *Schéhérazade*, in which she takes the Golden Slave as a lover and kills herself when her husband returns early from a hunting trip to catch her out. I had also seen her dance Tamar, who lures travellers to her remote mountain castle and drops them through an oubliette into the gorge below after a night of revelling and love. She was magnificent in both ballets, and not unnaturally I was expecting a very majestic lady whose commands must be instantly obeyed. What a surprise to find two adorable elderly people, utterly devoted to each other, Grigorieff tall and gentle of expression, Tchernicheva with the beak nose but docile eyes. They were humble and beautifully old-world in their manners. They never raised their voices, and prefaced every instruction with 'Please,' or 'Would you mind?'

The rehearsals were unusually complicated because Tchernicheva taught me the steps, then Karsavina came to the next rehearsal and altered everything. Two days later Tchernicheva said, 'I love Madame Karsavina. She is greatest ballerina. When she danced I watch her every minute. I stand almost on stage, here like this, and I watch everything. I tell you she say she do like this, but she not do like this. She a little forget. She do like *this*.' So I changed back, but next time Karsavina saw me she would insist on her version, which she had now remembered more fully and altered a bit more. I learned in total two or three different arrangements, and in the end I had to settle on the best amalgam I could and pray that neither of them would be too upset. Karsavina's words in rehearsal were pure gold. Fokine had told her, 'Forget your graces. The Firebird is powerful, hard to manage, rebellious.' And there was one most revealing sentence. 'Here is no human emotion.' That little phrase illuminated the character of the bird so skilfully that I saw it all as she spoke. 'Firebird is proud, arrogant,' she said. 'She gives the feather only to buy her freedom, not to help the Prince. She returns because she has made a promise which she fulfils.'

She said, too, that Fokine arranged his choreography in the most uncomfortable way he could. 'If you liked to turn to the right, he made you turn to the left.' I thought perhaps he had no human emotion either, and I remembered the rather formidable figure of his wife, Vera Fokine, as I used to see her before the war in a box at Covent Garden. She was all white face powder, black tight-drawn hair and black eye makeup, dressed in velvet and old white furs. Once, when I was about seventeen, I was presented to her. She scarcely smiled as she acknowledged the introduction with one courteous sentence. Not that there was any reason for her to do otherwise.

Ernest Ansermet conducted *The Firebird* for Diaghilev, and he came as guest conductor for our performances. He was a man to revere. It was funny to find that he, too, was nervous as we stood on the stage before the ballet. He kept repeating to me, 'The adagio should be not too slow or it will become sentimental. Adagio, of course, but it must not be sugary.' Then he would hum a bit of the music, waving his arms in conducting movements as he adjusted the tempo. 'Is that all right for you? Like that?' he asked. I said that it would be perfect, for he was so rhythmical I could have followed him in whatever time he took the music. It was an honour for me to be consulted at all.

uite like *The Firebird* music. The
mysterious, generating an atmosphere
pelling that in my corner of the darkened
for the curtain to rise, I was already lost,
nvolved in the spirit of the proud arrogant
ure. It was at the first costume rehearsal, when I put
on the golden coxcomb crown pouring forth brilliant red
and orange plumage, that I had a revelation of how the
head movements had to be abrupt like a bird's. It moves
the head in a series of quick jerks, remaining motionless
in between. This feeling, as soon as I caught it, was the
solution to Karsavina's cipher, 'Here is no human emotion.'

Michael Somes looked magnificent and danced superbly
as Ivan Czarevitch. His stance, his walk and every gesture
were all perfect. Tchernicheva had rehearsed the kiss between him and the princess, which was her original role,
over and over to get it just right.

Michael was extremely handsome. We danced together
in many countries, and platoons of corps de ballet girls
lost their hearts to him. Whole companies would cry their
eyes out as they waved our planes off from Brazil, Japan,
Australia and Yugoslavia. Michael smiled down benevo-
lently on them, but maintained a reserve. Only once did
I see him break down in the face of overwhelming acclaim. We danced *Swan Lake* in Belgrade shortly after
The Firebird production. The reception was phenomenal
by any standard, before or since. After Act III we went
before the curtain countless times before retiring to our
rooms to change for the last act. Outside I could hear
shouts and bravos frome enthusiasts who had come round
from the auditorium, and I ran into Michael's room to
share the excitement. To my amazement, instead of finding him as expected, sitting coolly at his table, he was
standing in a silk robe at his window, throwing carnations
down to the ecstatic crowd below. He was actually beaming whole-heartedly. It was my great good fortune to
dance for ten years with so unusually musical and so considerate a partner.

Nowadays, Michael is as jolly a̶ [text obscured]
expectedly warm and lovable. His life [text obscured]
Royal Ballet. It is marvellous to work [text obscured]
where I can still find Jill Gregory, who took c̶ [text obscured]
when I went to Sadler's Wells aged fourteen, an̶ [text obscured]
Edwards, who was in the corps de ballet at that time, [text obscured]
Michael, all of them an integral part of the company,
passing on their knowledge to younger generations. In
this way a real tradition is built and preserved. The people
who love the company are the core of its success. For
many years I was equally devoted and, if things are not
the same now, it is only that circumstances have directed
me to dance elsewhere. But my heart and home, balleti-
cally, are forever with the Royal Ballet, which I believe to
be the best in the world. With that pride do I look on it
now, remembering those immature beginnings but appre-
ciating, nevertheless, that some performances, such as
those given by Mary Honer and Elizabeth Miller in *Les
Patineurs*, have never been bettered by their successors.

Preparations for my marriage brought, for the first time, a
multiplicity of interests into my life. I found it confusing
and exhausting to be engaged in my dancing, which is a
full-time occupation, while decorating and setting up a
home, which is another full-time occupation. I also had to
give attention to affairs of the Royal Academy of Dancing.
It was in 1954 that Ninette de Valois summoned me to
her office and said outright, 'Dame Adeline Genée is retiring from the RAD, and it has been decided that you
will be the new President.' I hated the idea. I said, 'I
don't want to do it at all. The Academy is boring, and it is
absolutely not the sort of thing I am good at.' 'Never
mind,' she said. 'It's all arranged. There is a Chairman
of the Executive Committee and a Chairman of the Technical Committee. Miss Gordon is the Director, and Miss
Lehmann the General Secretary. They will look after
everything; you only have to appear once or twice a year.'
I said I definitely did not want to accept, to which she

replied that it was all settled. I left the office knowing that I was about to be President of the Royal Academy of Dancing whether I liked it or not. I talked to Miss Gordon, Miss Lehmann and Dame Adeline, and found that it was a fascinating institution, one of the four British Royal Academies. Many things needed straightening out, but we could never get them quite under control. So, far from only attending functions twice a year, I spent hours each week engrossed in discussions that baffled Tito. He once said, 'I have been trying for two years to understand exactly what the Academy does, but I am none the wiser.'

I had been so single-minded about my career that I could scarcely boil an egg. It was overwhelming for me to think of house-keeping, particularly since Tito was going to be appointed Ambassador to the Court of St James's and would take up his post on return from our honeymoon.

The London press were frantic to be told when and where we would be married. They were unable to believe I didn't know myself. Even when I did, I considered it bad taste to announce my wedding before Tito's divorce was absolute. Those sorts of things don't enter the minds of journalists. David Lewin, who had gleaned a good deal of information, would agree not to print a big advance story only on condition that I told him twelve hours before making a general announcement. When it broke, two days before the wedding, a furious columnist rang me at 2 : oo a.m. to abuse me for having given the story first to Lewin. I told him sharply that I certainly would not deliver any such rude message to Miss Fonteyn, who was asleep in another room.

At the general press conference held at Covent Garden, someone asked if I planned to have children. I said no, but that when I was young I had thought it would be marvellous to have six sons. I didn't add that when I was even younger I had wanted to have a little black baby because I think they are so much more beautiful than white ones.

We were to be married on 6 February 1955. *Daphnis*

and Chloë was in the programme on Saturday, 5 February, and nothing could have been more felicitous than to dance that very personal ballet on the eve of my marriage. The ballet company concealed streamers and confetti in their hands for the finale and suddenly released them as Michael ran on stage carrying me on his shoulder. It was an exultant performance, and a wonderful send-off.

No doubt we are all nervous of committing ourselves irrevocably in marriage, no matter how sure we are. That night I felt some tremors of anxiety, but on Sunday morning I was all happiness as I set off for Paris with my family and friends. At that time I frequently suffered travel sickness on planes, so I took an antidote. Thinking the antidote might make me drowsy, I had champagne to keep awake. Thinking the champagne might go to my head, I had black coffee to counteract the champagne. All of which made the journey pass in an instant, and in no time we arrived at the Hôtel Plaza-Athénée. It would have been unlucky to see Tito before the ceremony, so we were careful to prevent our paths crossing as I went to dress. My Dior friends, Suzanne Luling and Yvonne Minassian, were ready with my clothes; there was panic when the hat looked ghastly, but evidently it belonged to another client and had been sent in error. I had another bad moment wondering if the shoes would fit. As soon as I was dressed, Tito's witness, Tipi Vaillarino, Panamanian Ambassador to Italy, came to my room with lots of papers in Spanish. After I had signed them all, I inquired uneasily if I was now married.

The ceremony itself was a shambles. The Panamanian Consulate was a small, irregular-shaped room, and we had regretfully decided that only ten guests could be present. Everyone else would come to the reception. When I arrived at the door with Tipi I couldn't believe my eyes. At least fifty people were crammed in, and I couldn't recognize one face. Forcing my way through the crowd, I eventually came across my mother and Lord Gladwyn, then Sir Gladwyn Jebb, British Ambassador in Paris, who was to be my witness. A stranger broke into an explanation that he was Brazilian, I was Brazilian, and that he brought flowery messages of homage, etc., etc. I was in no mood to listen to that sort of thing.

Squeezing through more jabbering strangers with Gladwyn and Tipi, we got to the Consul's desk, where Tito was waiting – looking, I thought, very fine in the hurly-burly. Behind the Consul, squashed up in the corner against the wall, an array of press photographers had somehow mounted themselves in tiers and were no more than six feet from my nose. There were about twenty of them, each with a camera whose shutter made a deafening racket. Some had movie apparatus.

We allowed them some moments to take their pictures, and then the Consul-General, Jorge Tulio Royo, began reading in Spanish. To my horror the noise of cameras redoubled, I couldn't hear Jorge Tulio, and couldn't understand Spanish anyway. This was supposed to be the most beautiful and most moving moment in my life, and it was worse than a prize fight. I whispered to Tito, 'Couldn't you stop the ceremony, get rid of the photographers and start again?' He whispered back, 'It is nearly over.' He put the wedding ring on my finger, asked me to sign a document, and that was it. Turning to where my mother and father were supposed to be, I found the Brazilian again. My parents were out of sight, jostled and frustrated. I remembered June Brae's wartime wedding in the simplicity of an empty church – that was how mine should have been.

After a reception agreeable enough to soothe everyone's feelings, Tito and I boarded the New York flight. I said, 'Now let's get married again properly.' He laughed and held my hand as the stewardess offered Mrs Arias some champagne. For a moment I wondered to whom she was talking.

On our honeymoon in the Bahamas, again aboard the yacht *Edmar*, we visited one tiny township which remains for ever in my memory. The schoolteacher came to welcome us as we landed, saying 'My! You-all are the first visitors we seen heah since last June.' All the village wanted to look at us. They withheld their curiosity as long as possible, out of politeness, so we explained that we were honeymooning. Obviously our age was puzzling. Not wishing to question us too directly, they asked where we were from. 'Well, my wife is from England, but we came from Paris, where we were married,' said Tito. The schoolteacher thought for a moment. 'My goodness!' she said, 'You-ah not that couple I heard on the radio – was it Tuesday or Wednesday? I heard about that couple that married in Paris, England?' We said, yes. She turned excitedly to another lady. 'Did you hear on the radio – I think it was Wednesday – no, it was Tuesday – did you hear about the couple that go married in England and all?' Mabel thought she *had* heard it – she thought it was Monday. 'Well, here they are right here. They came all the way from England right to us!' What a welcome we got then. We were taken to call on the priest and spent the happiest of hours in the company of those simple people of impressive sensibility.

From the start our life together was unusual. Tito called it 'Ballet Bouffe.' Not every man, for example, asks his future wife to look for a combined home, Embassy and ballet studio – with a side entrance in another street. As it happened, we found the ideal place in all respects except there was no studio. But this was not a necessity. The house was charming, in the style Tito described as 'Early Valentino with Georgian overtones,' and it had an excellent escape route by means of a back door several streets away from the front. Few people knew of its existence, and no journalists ever detected it, so we were able to come and go freely in times of siege.

I faced the responsibilities of life as an Ambassador's wife with trepidation. The Vice-Marshal of the Diplomatic Corps, having received us at the airport, wished to pay a formal call the next afternoon. Tito, thinking quickly, made the appointment early enough to obliviate the necessity for artificial light. We had no lamps yet. The furnishing went slowly, but our system of having the pieces we needed sent on trial on the days we entertained, and returning them later if they were unsuitable, meant we could usually put on a reasonable show to guests.

I loved the house, but had no idea how to run it. It was the question of telling servants what to do that worried me most. I found I sat at the dinner table dreading what dish they would bring through the pantry door. One day I realized that at other Embassies I never minded about the imperfection of service or cuisine. I decided that, instead of being a nervous hostess and making my guests uneasy on that account, I would tell myself I was a guest, too. It worked very well, because there is really nothing you can do if the dinner is wrong, and it is better to be relaxed about it.

Mme Pandit, Ambassador for India, was immensely assured, and I tried to emulate her. She recounted how she had had forty people to a very important dinner at which the butler and footmen handed a surprising number of pre-dinner drinks. She signaled to the butler to ask when dinner would be served, but he was too distressed to give a coherent answer, so she descended to the kitchen to upbraid the chef. She found him dead drunk on the floor with the meal half-prepared. This did catch her momentarily off balance, but then she said to herself, 'Well, there's nothing I can do,' and she took her guests to a Chinese restaurant opposite 'millionaires' row" in Kensington.

My life was so totally different from what I was used to that I might have been living in another city. This was not the London I had known during my enclosed ballet life. Still, if one is an Ambassadress, one is usually in a foreign country, and this was certainly foreign to me. But it was fascinating.

When the day came for Tito to present his credentials, the Marshal of the Diplomatic Corps arrived in a royal carriage and Tito went off to the Palace – wives go separately by car. In modern traffic conditions it is hazardous riding in a horse-drawn vehicle, and there have been one or two near spills, but Tito got through without mishap. The choreography for the new Ambassador to meet the

Queen is quite intricate, consisting of three steps forward flanked by the Marshal and the Comptroller of the Lord Chamberlain's office; a bow, another step; another bow; then the flanking officials withdraw backwards. The wife waits behind closed doors until the signal is received. Then the doors are opened, and she performs her own little dance, ending in a deep curtsy. Next she takes a step back to stand beside her husband. The Queen has such unexpectedly beautiful skin and delicate colouring that one is caught off-guard, staring at her without a word. Several of the other Ambassadors' wives had had the same reaction. Luckily, the Queen is ready for tongue-tied emissaries and knows how to put them at ease.

I always found big, formal state functions exciting. The ceremony of the Opening of Parliament is magnificent to witness, once one has got over the shock of arriving at the House of Lords in full formal evening dress at ten in the morning. The protocol of seating is so strict that the French Ambassador, even though suffering from claustrophobia, was not permitted to change his place.

The ceremonial Trooping the Colour to celebrate the Queen's official birthday was another spectacle I had not seen before. I remembered Fred saying the Secretary of State for War had asked for his opinion in rechoreographing the parade, but that Fred thought it could not be improved. All the state ceremonials are beautifully organized, with a thoroughness that overlooks nothing. The 'Royals' themselves plan everything in great detail. Tito once sat next to a royal Princess at a charity performance. She told him that she could not see the stage clearly from the Royal Box and, as she did not wear her glasses on formal appearances, she had become interested in studying the hands of people sitting nearby. It is quite true that you do not expect to see royalty wearing spectacles, any more than you would expect a ballerina or a tenor to wear them on stage. There are prima donnas so nearsighted that they cannot see the conductor, which is an appalling disadvantage. Nevertheless, they adapt themselves and royalty are every bit as professional about their appearances in public. Princess Margaret said to me after a ballet gala, 'I must be careful what I say about the programme while the TV cameras are running. Deaf people can often lip-read from the screen.'

Ambassadors look their best in evening regalia, with full decorations including the splendid coloured sashes worn across one shoulder. Panama decided to invest Tito with some Orders befitting his position as envoy to the Court of St James's and, in due course, on the very morning that I was struggling to rise early and dress in my best to receive my D.B.E. (Dame Commander of the British Empire) at Buckingham Palace, I found Tito lolling over breakfast in his bathrobe having just received by mail a stash of decorations with stars and multicoloured sashes. I was a little irritated that he should get his without bestirring himself in the least, and I laughed wickedly a few days later when he discovered he had the ribbon across the wrong shoulder on arrival at the Lord Mayor's Banquet. He said that he remembered how his father wore it, but had forgotten that his father, as a Head of State, wore certain sashes the opposite way round than lesser beings did.

To be truthful I loved the investiture at Buckingham Palace. The precision with which the ceremony is organized amazed me. From the moment one arrives one is watched over and coached so that there can be no possibility of a hitch during the investing of several hundred people with different honours. An elderly courtier had the duty of pinning on to my dress a little hook, upon which my order would be hung. I had to help him, because evidently my bosom was not as ample as expected and he had difficulty in finding where to position the hook.

Tito was calm and patient with me when I bothered him about housekeeping problems that I should have known how to control. I was mortified to be so inefficient when he always seemed to know what should be done. He took trouble over the menus and choice of wines, and even knew better than I which clothes I should buy.

Most important of all, he knew who everybody was, whereas I found endless scope for confusion among the one hundred ambassadors, their wives and their countries. Three times in the same week I failed to recognize a charming white-haired gentleman. 'You sat next to him at lunch yesterday,' said Tito. 'You asked me who he was on Tuesday, too.' He was one of the most distinguished ambassadors.

Gradually I became more assured, and loved meeting so many new people from all over the world. The protocol of calling on the other ambassadors' wives is designed just for this purpose. The first time I was dreadfully nervous, which was imbecilic, but then I became so interested in the ladies and the varied refreshments they offered that it was fun to visit two or three in the same afternoon. The Polish Ambassadress cooked delicious sweets, which she served with honey wine. Half an hour later I was at the Indonesian Embassy, enjoying something described as 'ironed beef', and from there went straight on to have irresistible oriental cakes with the Ambassadress from Iran. By the time Tito and I sat down at a formal dinner that night my appetite was in poor condition. I was placed next to the Philippine Ambassador, who was graciously forbearing with my fauxpas. 'When were the Philippines discovered?' I asked. 'Actually,' he replied in kindly tones, 'we were always there.'

But my worst moment was at tea in the Royal Tent at a Buckingham Palace garden party. A tall, handsome gentleman, dark-haired and aged perhaps fifty, smiled at me, and said how glad he was to see me again. I knew his face, but had no idea who he was. I smiled nervously, 'Er-yes. It is so nice to see you.' After a little while he asked, 'Have you been in Italy lately?' I noticed that he slightly accented the word 'Italy'. That meant it was a clue. I racked my brains to remember. Had we met in Rome – or Milan – or could it have been Venice? 'No, not very recently,' I replied. I was getting really nervous and searched my memory frantically. He smiled a bit more and said slowly, 'I have just come from Cascais,' with a marked accent on the 'Cascais'. By this time my mind had frozen up with embarrassment and I was almost ready to cry. He gave up the attempt and moved away casually with an amused look on his handsome face. I sought out Tito and said, 'I have done something terrible. He seemed to know me quite well and I cannot think where I met him.' Cascais should have enlightened me easily enough, for ex-King Umberto of Italy had received us at his home there. I had also sat next to him once at supper in a Lisbon night club after a performance. It was unforgivable of me not to realize who he was. Ninette de Valois told me that she is also unable to recognize people, and I hugged her with delight to know that such an intelligent woman could have the same failing. On the other hand, I can excuse her because of her brilliant mind, a sort of absentminded professor, whereas mine is a paralysis of the memory brought on by a silly kind of social fright.

When John Wayne visited London we gave him a large party. Among the people in his entourage was Bö Roos, his agent in Hollywood, a man of outsize personality and zest. It happened that Lord and Lady Attlee honoured us by accepting our invitation for that night, and they stayed until quite late. As we were seeing them off, Lady Attlee said to her husband, 'Is that your hat, dear? I don't think it looks quite like yours.' He said, 'No, it seems too big,' and took it off to look inside. There in large letters was written, *To hell it's yours, put it back!* The hat, Bö Roos and three of the guests were all in the hall next morning as I was hurrying out to ballet class. I was startled to see them sitting there, and ran back to call Tito on the house phone. 'They're still here, whatever shall I do?' Tito was taken aback, too, and said I had better order them some breakfast and go on out to my class.

Another time, King Hussein of Jordan came to the house with a small party of friends. Long before I met him I had thought him marvellously brave and handsome, so I was as delighted as a teenage fan when the next morning I found his beautiful astrakhan hat in the hall. I thought it suited me perfectly, but had to admit that Tito looked imposing in it too. We cherished it for two days until an equerry came to take it away. I was never sadder to part with anything.

Our admirable Italian butler was impressed by some of our guest lists, and we rose even higher in his estimation when he welcomed Vivien Leigh, Joan Collins and Ann Todd. However, there was one star he was still dying to meet – and so were we for that matter. One day the Hon. Mrs Mulholland, Lady-in-Waiting to Queen Elizabeth the Queen Mother, telephoned regarding a presentation at a gala performance. I came home to find a perplexing message written hopefully on the note pad. It said, *Marilyn Monroe telephoned from Clarence House.* Unfortunately we were not able to inveigle her to our embassy, but Tito and I did meet her at a big reception. She was astoundingly beautiful, without the trace of a line or wrinkle on her beguiling face. What fascinated me most was her evident inability to remain motionless. Whereas people normally move their arms and head in conversation, these gestures in Marilyn Monroe were reflected throughout her body, producing a delicately undulating effect like the movement of an almost calm sea. It seemed clear to me that it was something of which she was not conscious; it was as natural as breathing, and in no way an affected 'wriggle', as some writers have suggested. Her beauty was so fresh and her personality so compounded of the childlike and the vulnerable that, although her early death was a tragedy, I can't help thinking it fitting that she never had to contend with the erosions that time brings to the rest of us.

Some Panamanian journalists arrived at the time of a Royal Gala performance at Covent Garden. Tito had fun outfitting them in white-tie attire rented from Moss Bros. The first one said, 'It's eerie; just think that the dead fellow who owned this suit must have been exactly my size.' The second one got all dressed up in the stiff shirt, collar and waistcoat and came to Tito's room, saying, 'It looks all right to me, but I have this handful of nuts and bolts left over.' And he held out several front and back studs. The third one said, 'They'll never believe it when I tell them at home; I must be photographed in it.' Tito got out his camera and grouped them against a white wall, but one of them said, 'That won't do; people will think we just stuck our heads through one of those pictures like they have at fun fairs.' At supper after the Gala two British peeresses joined us. This threw the first journalist into such a nervous state that, as the party broke up, I heard him saying to one of them, 'Goodnight, Lady Chatterly.'

Every day there was some new confusion, and I was enchanted by one Panamanian delegate to a conference in London who went to Buckingham Palace at noon, insisting that his Ambassador had invited him to lunch there. The Palace officials, with their usual tact, politely rerouted him to the pub called 'The Buckingham', and phoned Tito's secretary to inform her the delegate would be only a few minutes late.

Being an Ambassador did not mean that Tito stayed in one place. He was constantly on the long-distance phone or dashing to the airport. He hated to arrive early for a flight. Roosevelt Zanders, his chauffeur in New York, had referred to him as 'The Globemaster', and used to say of planes that Tito liked to 'give them a sporting chance. Let them take off and then catch them.' One morning Tito was reading *The Times* over a leisurely breakfast. He was in his dressing gown. In the time it took me to have a shower he had decided to take the morning flight to New York and Panama, and he was dressed and packed, ready to leave the house. He could really move quickly when he wanted. I noticed that these sudden departures towards the tropical climate of his birth usually happened in the winter months, when London is at its most melancholy. I knew that he felt as I used to do when riding home from Sadler's Wells Theatre in the bus on a cold wet evening before the war.

FOUR

In 1956 the Bolshoi Ballet finally appeared in London. The visit had been expected for several years. Sir David Webster, the General Administrator of Covent Garden, had issued an invitation ten years earlier, when Convent Garden Opera House had reopened, and he told me that he had a recurring nightmare: just as a cycle of *The Ring* was under way, he would receive a telephone call from the Russian Embassy saying, 'Two hundred and eighty dancers have arrived this morning. They are ready to perform tomorrow night.'

When they did come there was fog at London Airport, and they were diverted to a little-used field where no immigration officers were immediately available. They were held on the plane for two hours. The press office phoned me to go to Covent Garden, since the dancers were due to arrive in half an hour, and when I arrived they were just coming into the foyer, a whole crowd of people milling about confusedly. I found an interpreter and asked if she knew where Mme Ulanova was. 'She is over in that far corner. I will come with you to interpret.' So I ran ahead, and when I saw Ulanova herself, looking a little bewildered, I was so emotional that I threw my arms round her and gave her a big hug, and put into her hand a little Victorian locket that I had picked up as I left the house. I had the impression that people were not usually so forward when they met her, but I think she understood that it was a spontaneous action on my part.

Their opening performance was of *Romeo and Juliet*. Since that night I have danced a different version of the ballet many times, but no moment of the Bolshoi performance on 5 June 1956 has been dislodged from my memory. There was great excitement as the audience took their seats. People up in the gallery had actually queued for tickets for three days and four nights. In the tiers and in the stalls were women in long evening gowns, their jewels gleaming across the house as the dimming lights caught heads turning towards the heavy velvet curtains. The conductor raised his baton, there was an instant of bated breath and then, with the first bars, the velvets swung open and we were transported into that incredible evocation of rich, Renaissance, provincial life; of stupid family feuds and bawdy servants; of hot-tempered youths and hapless young lovers, enmeshed, like innocent birds, in their tragedy.

The very weight of the production, criticized by some as old-fashioned, was what impressed me. No doubt it was just such realism that Diaghilev had discarded when he presented his innovations early in the century, taking Europe by storm. Now it burst on me as new and completely valid, in the same way that the young today are thrilled by the fashions of the thirties that so appall me. Taste and fashion bring everything back into favour except that which is too near to us in time.

The first view of the Bolshoi was glorious. Every dancer presented a complete, full-blooded character, but we were stunned by the revelation that was Ulanova. Her dancing had exactly the smooth perfection of thick cream poured from a jug, with never a harsh movement anywhere. Her beautiful legs were steely and lithe. The most breath-taking moment came when, despairing, Juliet threw her cloak round her shoulders and ran to Friar Laurence's cell. Fred had told me a thousand times he wished I had seen the way Pavlova ran across the stage, 'leaving everything behind'. I never could understand, even from his impersonations, how it was achieved. Curiously enough, running and walking are more difficult to master in ballet than many of the complicated steps. Now at last I saw. A few moments later, Ulanova left Friar Laurence with swift steps depicting glowing hope. The contrast was striking, and Tito was deeply impressed. By way of a great compliment, he later told Rex Harrison in his dressing room after *My Fair Lady* that he was marvellous and very like Ulanova. Rex was a bit nonplussed, but of course Tito was right about the perfectly relaxed and coordinated way Rex could walk across the stage and sink into a chair. It had the ease of great art. The unforgettable Margaret Rutherford also had this gift of expression through total mobility of the body.

Each performance in *Romeo and Juliet* was on the grand scale. Yuri Zhdanov was a noble Romeo, Konstantine Rikhter an odious, arrogant Tybalt, Sergei Koren the lively, cynical Mercutio, and the Lady Capulet of Elena Iliushenko literally tore a passion to tatters at the end of Act II. Yuri Faier conducted with love and care for every note and every step. In our three brief meetings, admiration and warm affection flourished between us. He was such a dear old man, stockily built and with gravely failing eyesight. He had come to London in advance of the Bolshoi dancers to rehearse the orchestra, so had been able to see a performance of *Birthday Offering*, for which he expressed great enthusiasm.

The second time I saw him was in a hotel lobby in Brussels, where the Bolshoi was dancing. I noticed the familiar badger-like figure retreating towards a quiet lounge, so I ran after him and said, 'Mr Faier. I am Margot. I was at the performance last night; it was wonderful.' He turned and hugged me warmly, saying, 'Come and talk to me.' And he sat me down while he explained, 'I can scarcely see the stage any more, but I know every step they are dancing. I know each dancer. I love the ballet like my life.' The last time I saw him was when we danced in Moscow in 1961. His sight was almost gone, and he was sad. I believe his death came from a broken heart – after he had in the end to give in and live in retirement.

We gave a party for the Bolshoi at which Tito got annoyed with a severe lady member of the group, who was overzealously guarding the dancers. Some of them wanted to stay later than others, but she objected. Tito invited her upstairs to show her the box of Russian perfumes presented to me by Mr Khrushchev and Mr Bulganin when they had attended a ballet at Covent Garden. The lady could hardly refuse such an invitation, and went like a lamb to the bedroom. Tito locked the door when he got her inside, and forthwith persuaded her to trust her dancers and leave them in peace. We had arranged a small flamenco cabaret in the hall, but the Spanish dancers were so *mañana* about getting started that Ulanova and a lot of others were sitting on the staircase for hours waiting for the show. I was reminded of my second visit to the open-air theatre in Granada. Tito had come along, and overheard two policemen commenting on our warming-up exercises. One said, 'These people really work hard. I can't see our dancers doing that. They just wave their arms around catching a few flies until they get in the mood, and then they dance.'

Soon after the Bolshoi visit I was invited, with Michael Somes, to dance in Australia. It was a place I had no wish to visit. My preconceived notion was of a thoroughly dull place full of stodgy people. Goodness knows how I acquired such fantasies! It took a lot of persuading before I agreed to go, for two weeks each in Sydney and Melbourne. We danced with the Australian company, directed by Borovansky – a rare character left over from a tour made by Colonel de Basil's Ballet. He was a smallish, bald-headed man who had been a character dancer and sometimes confused the names of ballet steps, saying 'port de bras' when he meant 'pas de bourrée'. He tried to keep discipline by shouting all through rehearsals in his cracked voice and Russian accent. He even, to our surprise, gave instructions to the corps de ballet from a down-stage wing during performances. Dancers in Ninette de Valois's company knew what they were doing by the time they got on stage, and didn't need coaching as they went along. We asked him to go away from the corner while we were dancing, as he distracted us.

From Sydney to Melbourne the ballet company had a

long overnight train journey but, without taking this into consideration, Borovansky ordered a full dress rehearsal of the programme we had danced for the past twelve performances. Michael and I were indignant and, to show our disapproval of his methods, refused to participate. But de Valois's discipline was so ingrained in us that it was a daring thing to disobey the director. It must be said, too, that for all his cranky ways of running a ballet he did a marvellous job for Australia by maintaining a very good company with an enthusiastic public for many years. Without him some excellent dancers would have been lost in the sands of a ballet desert. As it was we encountered incredible acclaim from audiences well-versed in the classical repertoire. As had happened in New York, one of the critics complained that my 'fouetté' turns were not performed on one spot the size of a sixpence, as Australian ballerinas were able to do them. He was quite right to point it out. The American critic had expressed it more colourfully, saying, '... she took a Cook's tour of the stage'. As I have said before, this particular step always gave me trouble.

During this tour Michael suffered a lot from a painful knee. He marked up the number of performances on his dressing room mirror, and ticked one off with glee each evening. Meanwhile, I was looking into the mirror in my room as I made up my face, and composing farewell speeches to make on the occasion of what I expected to be my imminent retirement from the stage! Tito was unable to join me in Australia, and I was finding the long separations unbearable. Before leaving London I told Plučis I did not think I could dance much longer. He threw his big hands up in the air. 'Margott! Vot you say?' he exclaimed. 'You vill dance more fifteen years, my dear. Your legs are straight, you are in good strong.' I really laughed in his face. 'Never! never!' I said 'Why, by then I shall be fifty-five. I don't intend to be an old ballerina.' I can vividly remember Bobby Helpmann at Sadler's Wells saying, 'There is an old Chinese proverb that goes, "Never name the well from which you will not drink."'

Sure enough, I have time and again found myself thoughtlessly naming the well; and in due course, as I am now at the age of fifty-five drinking from it.

In Australia I was treated like royalty. A department store came to a standstill when I attended a function there; I was expected to patronize the races on Melbourne Cup day, and several ladies involuntarily dropped into curtsies on meeting me unexpectedly. The experience was extraordinary because of my inability to see myself as a great celebrity. Nevertheless, I found it very gratifying. I don't think that was the only reason I loved Australia. I loved the country, the space, the trees, the colours, the sense of everything yet to come instead of having all been achieved in the past, as in England; and I loved the Australians, with their much maligned accent, which I find very attractive. 'Dime Fontyne' has a sort of Elizabethan charm and, of course, the 'Dame' or 'Dime' was much used in Australia. I seldom use it at all, preferring to describe myself as Mrs Arias, or professionally as Miss Fonteyn, but with encroaching years it begins to fit more comfortably. There is an august ring about the title which was not ideal for the image of a young ballerina. Now I rather appreciate it. I have had a lot of fun collecting incorrect versions of my title, such as Dome Margot Fonteyn; Jane Largo Fonteyn; Miss Dame Fonteyn; and eventually the one I had been hoping for, which arrived at the head of an international cable: Lame Margot Fonteyn. Mrs Dearies was an unusual rendering of de Arias, too, while a lady from the Deep South in America recently addressed me repeatedly as Dumb Fonteyn, which, I think, wins the prize.

Back in London I was able to accompany Tito on short trips to Europe in between my ballet performances. We were invited to a house party for the Swedish Derby, which is run in Malmö. The races got off to a zany start when the Swedish Royal Family stepped out of a Rolls-Royce on to the course directly in front of the grandstand. After reviewing a line of the Royal Guards, they mounted to the box, and the Rolls was supposed to drive away. As luck would have it, the car stalled hopelessly and had to be pushed some considerable distance by red-faced attendants before the horses could come galloping down the turf. It was an episode worthy of a Jacques Tati film.

That night our host at the château made a welcoming speech over a sumptuous dinner of several courses, in the middle of which he offered the Swedish 'sköl' to his guests and hoped that 'after dinner ... you will all enjoy each other'. As an afterthought, he added, 'In the best possible manner.' Of the twenty-odd guests at the table, those who spoke the best English looked the most surprised, and I did not dare to catch Tito's eye across the table for fear I would get a fit of the giggles.

We went several times to Belgium, and once were entertained to lunch by the Governor of Flanders and his wife, two exceptionally charming people who were uncertain of what protocol to adopt in the face of an unexpected guest who made thirteen at table. This supposedly unlucky omen was observed only as we were gathered in the dining room to be seated. The atmosphere was terribly strained because the host and hostess were anxious for everything to go with perfect propriety, so Tito decided to put them at their ease. He removed his glasses, handed them to me, turned a neat somersault on the dining-room floor, then carefully replaced his glasses. The sight of the Panamanian Ambassador behaving in such an original manner broke the tension very successfully.

The extra guest was an ardent admirer of Michael Somes, who was with us that weekend. On their return to London, the lady suggested Michael drop her at her home on his way, which he did. Then she suggested he should go in to meet her husband. As Michael recounts the story, they went in the front door and the husband came forward saying, 'Hello, darling. How did the trip go?' To which the wife replied, 'Nothing went as planned.' The husband raised his eyebrows and said. 'What, my dear? Nothing went as planned?' And he turned inquiringly to Michael, who got very nervous indeed and said vehemently. 'No, no. *Nothing* went as planned,' then fled the house as fast as he could.

Tito was – and still is – a lawyer engaged in international law. He specialized in marine law, and one of his clients before we were married was Anders Jahre, the Norwegian owner of the biggest whaling fleet in the world. He and his wife, Bess, were dear and marvellous friends to us. Aristotle Onassis was building up his own whaling fleet, and Jahre recommended Tito to him. Onassis by now had big interests in Monte Carlo, where he set up his office. It was the most agreeable place to have a client. Tito and I went often, sometimes staying on the yacht *Christina*, then brand new and fitted out in exquisite taste. The interior was almost like a perfect house. Conversely, Onassis's house in New York gave the impression of being a luxurious yacht on the East River, which could be seen from every window.

Onassis had extraordinary charm and was a perfect host, always relaxed and unhurried. I thought he lived in a very intelligent and civilized manner. His preferred hour for discussing business was about two in the morning in a night club, so Tito sometimes slept for a couple of hours after dinner in order to have a fresh mind later on. As Onassis never went to the theatre or ballet, I was surprised to find he knew a bit about entrechats-six. He said he had greatly admired Anna Pavlova when he was a very young man in Buenos Aires, and his eye had been caught by one of the dancers in her company.

Tito enjoyed uniting his and my business 'geographically', so it was ideal that I had frequent chances to dance at the theatre in the Monte Carlo Casino. It is a tiny theatre, built in the same elaborate style as the Paris Opéra, and by the same architect, Garnier. It is full of ghosts from the Diaghilev Ballet, many of whose works were created on that very stage. Michael Somes and I danced at a gala commemorating Diaghilev. Serge Lifar arrived from Paris carrying the death mask of his former friend and patron under his arm. He set it down on the dressing table beside his makeup as he prepared to dance, as a solo, *L'Après-Midi d'un Faune*. Sadly, he no longer had a suitable waistline for this, and some stagehands laughed in the wings as the thick figure, slightly short of breath, pursued imaginary nymphs.

It was in Monte Carlo that Jaime Ortiz-Patino, grandson of the Bolivian tin millionaire, Simón Patino, started to laugh for the first time in several years. We had met him shortly before in London, where he was engaged in litigation against a newspaper as the result of inaccurate reporting of his unhappy first marriage. He is one of those people who incline easily towards overweight but are noticeably quick and light in their movements. His features are attractively indicative of his Andean origin and he has the most engaging personality, but in London he was depressed, worried and even mournful. In that state of mind he joined us in Monte Carlo and, having strong gourmet instincts, he took us to lunch at a restaurant where his troubles fell from him quite suddenly, without rhyme or reason. As the hot hors d'oeuvres trolley was wheeled up to us, he began to laugh. He laughed and laughed till the accumulated emotional stresses had all broken down. He nearly fell off his chair with mirth. It was astonishing to watch, and he has been the most ebullient companion ever since.

To increase our pleasure in Monte Carlo, two cherished New York friends, Trumbull Barton (Tug) and John McHugh, arrived the following day. They are two people of exceptional generosity to those they love, not only in the giving of presents and parties, but to the extent of crossing the Atlantic to help a friend in distress, and inconveniencing themselves in any other way that will be useful to others. I have always longed to be benevolent on their scale. But, alas, I have a mean streak lurking deep inside, and when occasionally it surfaces it leaves me quite shocked at myself. It must be inherited from distant ancestors; it is certainly not from my immediate ones.

Tug and John had a poodle called Nicky, who habitually wore a gold chain collar from Cartier. We were telling them about our new friend Jimmy Ortiz-Patino. Tug said, 'Oh, is that the Bolivian tin millionaire Patino?

Well, for heaven's sake, tell him the dog's collar is made of tin.'

Since my marriage I had felt as much at home in New York as in London. I looked forward to the ballet seasons there, and to the time we spent with friends. Elizabeth Taylor, whom Tito had met in Honolulu as he was returning from a two-day visit to Japan (which he described as an economical way to buy me some pearls), invited us to dinner. She and Mike Todd had been married for less than a year. We went to the apartment at 6: 30 p.m. one Wednesday, as requested, and a manservant ushered us into the living room to wait for our hosts. Before us was a perfect theatrical setting for the opening of a play, each detail putting the viewer as it were in the picture. There was a corner-angle settee, with a large coffee table in front of it. On the coffee table, half in and half out of its presentation box, was a magnificent diamond tiara. Beside the tiara were two half-finished martinis, and on the floor by the settee was one lady's high-heeled sandal. After about half an hour, the spell-binding Elizabeth emerged with Mike, who was the ideal complement to her. He was dynamic, amusing, generous and attractive. Each Wednesday he gave her a present, because that was the day of the week on which they had met. Elizabeth was wearing a 'sack' dress, the latest fashion, which Mike found very sexy. It was a development of Christian Dior's 'trapeze' line, which had been mass produced and worn by so many wrong-shaped ladies that Christian Dior confided to a friend, shortly before his death, 'My God, what have I started?'

Mike and Elizabeth invited us to stay at their country house, where they gave up their own room to Tito and me. I could not imagine putting myself to such inconvenience for guests, but Elizabeth is generosity itself.

They both came to see me at the 'Met'. The programme included *Petrouchka*, in which I danced the role created by Karsavina. I wasn't very good in it, but I don't think

that influenced Mike Todd. He came backstage at the
end and said, 'Why are you dancing that ballet? It's
called *Petrouchka*, isn't it? Are you Petrouchka? No!
Well, get out of it then. And another thing,' he continued,
'have you seen this souvenir programme? You must be
crazy! It says here "Margot Fonteyn made her debut as a
Snowflake in *Nutcracker* in *1934*!' You can't have that
in the programme. Tell them to take out the date!' I
heeded the great showman; he knew what he was talking
about.

But in truth I have never bothered about my age. I
don't care who knows it, as long as they get it more or less
right. A Dr Felici, as quoted in a New York paper, was a
bit too far out when he said, '... ballet dancers have better
conditioned legs than athletes', adding that Dame Margot
Fonteyn '... was dancing flawlessly when she was with
Nijinsky'.

Flawlessly?

FIVE

It must have been early in 1958 when Sr Don Francisco
Assis de Châteaubriand Bandeiro de Melho was appointed Brazilian Ambassador to London. A more vigorous, imaginative, restless little man it would be hard to
find. Of tremendous charm, though neither handsome nor
well-built, he had a funny, animated face. He was always
talking excitedly, but was rarely understood, for his pro-
nunciation was so contorted that no one could make head
or tail of the words. I was told that even Brazilians found
him hard to comprehend. When he referred to our friend
Fleur Cowles, for example, he said, 'I saw Floccles.' I
once heard him make a long speech to open the Antique
Dealers' Fair. It was quite unintelligible, so no one knew

when he was nearing the end. The poor Mayoress, sitting on the dais beside him in the stuffy atmosphere, nodded off for a few moments. Suddenly a large bouquet of roses was crammed into her lap. She jumped up quite startled, as the Ambassador, a good head shorter than herself, reached up on his toes to embrace her.

We met one day at a diplomatic reception. '*Mar*gott!' he said, 'you are – Bra*zh*ilian. You – must *come* to – Bra*zh*il. *You*. And *Mama*. And *A*rias!' I said how fantastic that would be. He asked what day we could go, so I hastily thought ahead to the end of the ballet season and gave a date which would just allow time to pack and be off. Château, as he was called for short, said, 'My *sec*retary will call you *tomor*row.' I thought, that's the last I will hear of the matter. But Château was as good as his invitation, so when my holiday came round my mother and I flew off to Rio. Tito was to join us from Panama.

Neither of us had ever been to Brazil. We arrived to find the city gone wild because the Brazilian football team had just won the World Cup. Pele was the current super-god, and an off-season Carnival was in progress. Château owned twenty-seven newspapers and several television stations, so he was wealthy and powerful. His newspapers proclaimed our presence, and we were received by President Kubitschek, who lent his private plane to take us on a quick tour of his immense country. Travelling with Château was hilarious. He invited along a Polish prince, who immediately bought a map on arrival in each city so that he could escape in the event of an uprising. He also believed that pilots were incapable of landing their craft after dark. He was reassured about this by the Panamanian Ambassador, Julio Briceño, who arranged with the captain to open the flight-deck window and shine a flashlight on to the tarmac as we walked out to board the plane. 'You see,' said the Ambassador, 'I told you it is quite safe. They land by the flashlight; there is no danger at all.' Though greatly reassured, the prince wanted to sit with the pilots during landing. This unnerved my mother. 'Stop him, someone,' she demanded. 'He will distract them with his silly nonsense.'

Château hated to waste time sleeping, so he had perfected a technique of losing consciousness for a few seconds at a time throughout the day and going to bed for a bare three hours at night. These catnaps overtook him in mid-speech, or in the middle of the soup. This did not faze him in the least. He awoke and continued the sentence or the meal without hesitation. Since he slept so little at night he improvised hectic schedules for each day's progress through Brazil. As we tottered up to our hotel rooms around midnight he would say, 'Mummy *uppy* five-o'clockee. Plane leaves *six*sh-o'clockee.' 'Did he say five o'clock? He's crazy,' said my mother. But she would be up on time, only to wait two or three hours at the airport because our pilot had overslept, or because Château was at a meeting, or they had filled the tanks with the wrong fuel and had to empty and refill them.

Nevertheless, it was a sensational trip. From Ouro Prêto, the tiny eighteenth-century capital buried among hills, we flew to the site of Brasília, the newest capital, high on a plateau. As the plane approached, we looked down on an empty expanse of red earth, marked out in a giant bow-and-arrow formation. It was as though someone had scraped a stick on the sand. 'Where the central line intercepts the curve will be the buildings of the executive and the justice. At the point of the arrow is the presidential palace, which is almost completed. All this area will be a lake. Here will be the ministries, along the curves will be the embassies and here in the centre the business section. Over there the residential areas.' After landing we were driven across the plain that was to become a city, raising clouds of red dust as we went. A small chapel, a hotel and the palace were the only buildings. As we looked at the architect's futuristic plans for the cathedral and the principal buildings, and as we walked through the beautiful Palace of the Dawn, I was overcome by the experience. It was a unique sense of standing on the very ground upon which a great city would one day rise, on which there would be streets and homes, shops, banks and theatres. People would be born there and would die and love and weep, and trees would grow. I thought of how I had visited the remains of ancient cities, and had tried in my imagination to reconstruct them bustling with people who went about their lives unaware that their homes in later centuries were to become the desolate habitat of gawping tourists – like me. I had the knowledge to visualize myself as a citizen of ancient Greece, or of Pompeii at the time of its destruction. Brasília, by contrast, belonged to the future. It was the only time in my life that I would knowingly stand on the bare earth of a great capital as yet unborn.

We flew on to Manaus, the legendary ghost city a thousand miles up the Amazon, where a waiting journalist asked about my impressions of Brasília. I tried to explain my sensation of awe at standing on the threshold of a city's life instead of in the ruins of its demise, as was the usual way of things. The newspaper carried an item the next morning which was succinct if not perhaps immediately comprehensible. It said, 'Miss Fonteyn thinks Brasília is like Pompeii in reverse.'

At the mouth of the Amazon near the Equator lies Belém, and not far down the coast is the island of São Luis, whence my mother's father set forth to make his fortune in England at a time when many Europeans were travelling in the opposite direction to get rich quick in South America. I caught the heel of my shoe on the last step as I descended from the President's plane and, appropriately enough, landed on both knees on the soil of my grandfather's birthplace. This steamy, tropical little town, cooled by a breeze from the sea, is so like what Panama must have been fifty years ago that I understood my affinity with Tito. I thought again of my father's two years spent as a little English boy in the sun by the sea at Imbituba, farther south, and of how he had sought out a dark-eyed, half-Brazilian wife. The imprint of Brazil can be very strong.

Château took us to the old house, tiled in the Portuguese manner, where my grandfather's family had lived

and where an old, old lady who had been in their service
from childhood cried with joy as she embraced my mother
and me. She was ninety-eight, and had risen before dawn
to be ready for our visit. It was terrible to leave her so
quickly in order to rush on with our frantic tour. I
longed to spend more time in São Luis, but we had to see
the fabulous baroque churches of Bahia, one of them
decorated throughout in elaborate carvings coated in gold
leaf – a veritable Aladdin's cave in the middle of desperate
poverty. We saw the voodoo ceremonies and Caphueira
dancing, the dancers wearing razor-like spurs with which
they fight each other as they leap in the air. We had to
taste, and pretend to enjoy, the alarming cuisine of the
northeast region, based on eggs, coconut and oil of den-
den, which is so strong that it could be used in Rolls-
Royce motors. I pecked at the banquet as politely as I
could until I was offered some little apricots swimming in
syrup, which looked delicious. Alas, far from being the
fruit I had expected, they turned out to be yolks of hated
eggs in – guess what – oil. The liver attack, or jaundice,
which I suffered as a three-day-old baby was probably
hereditary if my ancestors lived on such a diet – no wonder I could never stand eggs. Tito said the cuisine was
evolved from the mixture of the native Indians and the
rough Portuguese sailors, the earliest settlers. It was not
surprising that it should be so coarse and rich.

Château explained how the Indian women had seduced
the invading sailors with food and love, and later – at his
Embassy in London – he gave a party in memory of the first
Portuguese landing in Brazil. His high-society guests sat on
luxurious rugs on the floor, surrounded by thousands of
fresh orchids, tasting the lighter delicacies of Bahian food.
They were undoubtedly seduced by food, but not, so far
as I know, by love.

Château told a story, apocryphal I'm sure, of going as a
very young man to ask my late Brazilian uncle, who was a
millionaire, for money to back him in his first enterprise.
According to Château my uncle looked through a little
grille in his front door and asked, 'What do you want?'

Château explained, my uncle refused, and clicked shut the little window behind the grille. What made me laugh most about the story was the picture of my uncle, who was a marvellously elegant and handsome man, but very small, and Château, who was even smaller, standing tip-toe on either side of the door in order to conduct the conversation. Furthermore, Château was incomprehensible in any language, and my uncle spoke English with a heavy Lancashire accent, quite incongruous, although lovable, in a South American millionaire.

One result of that whirlwind tour of my father's native land was that Michael Somes and I returned a little later to dance at a gala for the Red Cross under the patronage of Mrs Kubitschek, the First Lady. We followed it with a tour, quickly improvised by our young friend Dalal Achcar, during which we performed *Giselle* accompanied by a group of twelve dancers and enjoying many amusing incidents. It was the kind of tour that is marvellous to do when one is young, though, come to think of it, Michael and I weren't as young as all that. But age is relative, and adventure gets into the blood.

Time slides by in the most deceptive fashion, and super-imposed upon those days in Brazil I can see the visit of the Royal Ballet in 1973, organized by Dalal together with Marcia de Barbará, who was eleven years old when her father, President Kubitschek, received us at his Palace with Château. Instead of twelve dancers there were eighty-five, but dancing in some of the same theatres and finishing up with an audience of nineteen thousand wildly enthusiastic people, plus three thousand who rioted outside the hall because they could not get tickets – in, incredible as it may seem, Brasília! Where did all those people come from so suddenly in that city that had so recently been an empty, sunbaked plain?

SIX

I had twenty-nine linen-covered books, filled with fairly repetitious clippings, when I decided to cancel my subscription to the press cutting service. Shortly thereafter my life took a new and venturesome turn.

It is said that events cast their shadow before them. In odd little ways and insignificant occurrences, I can see that it is often so. For instance, some aspects of Tito's and my visit to Cuba gave a foreshadowing of his revolution in Panama, although the two were not connected in any way and there was no actual resemblance between them. We were on our way to Acapulco for a short holiday, for I was free for a little over a week from the daily ballet routine. I loved to lie lazily with Tito on a sandy beach without a care in the world; I had never been to Mexico; and the trip promised to be heaven. We had got as far as New York when news came of Fidel Castro's victory in Cuba. Tito said, 'I think it would be interesting to go to Havana,' so we rerouted our tickets. Tito had many friends among the Cuban exiles from the regime of Batista, who were now overjoyed to return and help in the reorganization of their government. We arrived in Havana three days after Batista's downfall, and only a few hours after Castro's return. Castro had been in Oriente province at the time of his triumph, and insisted on marching with his rebel troops all the way to the capital. It wasn't the march that took them so long, but Castro's compulsion to address the people of every village on the way and to speak for never less than three or four hours at a time.

The airport was somewhat disordered when we arrived, with people trying to get in and people trying to get out. All had equal difficulty with the new officials. To our surprise, a representative from the Mayor, who was one of

Tito's friends, greeted us and asked us to wait a moment while he arranged our formalities. He assigned us to one of Castro's 'barbudos', the 'bearded ones', as a guard. The boy looked all of eighteen, with olive skin and black hair and a splendid bushy beard. He was not tall, but wiry; a country boy, as they all were, who was trying to appear very professional in his new responsibilities but still had the reflection of the cane-fields in his eye. He wore green cotton battle dress, and the soft army cap so familiar now in photographs of Castro. Several hand grenades and a knife decorated his trim waistline, and he held a menacing firearm, which he looked much too young to control. I was enchanted by the idea of this picturesque youth guarding my baggage and helping me into the taxi. Of course, he was not the only one. The airport was littered with them. But that was nothing to the scene at the Hilton Hotel, where Castro was installed on the top floor.

The lobby was crowded with militia and civilians, moving in all directions and talking excitedly as though at a giant cocktail party. Going up in the hotel lift was nerve-wracking. Most of the passengers were barbudos, fresh from the mountain spaces, and with little idea of how to carry their rifles indoors. They aimed them vaguely at the floor, but in the confined space I found it difficult to keep my feet and ankles out of the line of fire, and I was very conscious of the threat to my career if the boys didn't have the safety catches on – which seemed unlikely. Apart from this there were enough hand grenades about to blow up the whole hotel, and I watched anxiously to see if there was a danger of the pins coming loose. Many barbudos were seeing city life for the first time, and they filled the lifts night and day, joy-riding up and down for the fun of it. They were always armed to the teeth, but never aggressive. They had the simple manners of country youths, with candid soft eyes looking out from their would-be ferocious faces.

We were barely settled into our room when a knock at the door announced a man with a curious-looking piece of equipment, obviously not a vacuum cleaner or a fire extinguisher – we didn't need either of those, anyway. He spoke only Spanish, so I repeated to Tito the word he said, and got the English translation that he was the exterminator. 'The exterminator!' I said, my hair standing on end. 'It's only for the cockroaches,' said Tito.

Antonio de la Carrera, another of Tito's friends, was secretary to the new President, Urrutia, who wished to receive us. Inside the palace in the centre of Havana it was obvious that the newest tenants had moved in very recently. There was none of the formal hush and unhurried walking down carpeted corridors that I associated with visits to heads of state. Antonio welcomed us warmly, and darted about in and out of the office. 'The President is in a meeting at the moment; would you mind waiting here a short time?' he said. It was one of the main rooms on the second floor, decorated in the usual French style. Antonio hurried back to us. 'The President won't be free for a bit. Would you like to see the other rooms?' He led us through a door to a private study, or living room. It was neat, though it hadn't been dusted that morning. The next room was much the same. Another door took us right into the bedrooms, with unmade beds and the kind of untidiness I knew so well from hotel suites when one hasn't had time to unpack. The President's wife graciously apologized and led us to the dressing room, where she and a group of friends were discussing what to do about the mass of clothes that filled every closet and left no space for the newcomers. They had belonged to Mme Batista, who had left home in a hurry. One cupboard had nothing but shoes, in all styles and colours, enough to stock a small boutique.

After we had seen the President, Antonio said we must meet Castro. There was no way of knowing when the meeting would take place. We arrived back at the hotel in the lunch hour. The crowd in the lobby had swelled considerably, with everyone hoping for a glimpse of the hero. The lift doors opened and out he stepped, dressed exactly like the other barbudos but without the more cumbersome hardware. Exceptionally tall for a Cuban, he had a magnificent biblical face with long straight nose and lofty expression. It was easy to see his head above the crowd as he made his way slowly through the people, listening to their homage and talking easily with them. He was a man with a mission, dedicated and unsmiling, but not necessarily humourless. His eyes seemed to be more used to scanning the horizon in remote provincial regions than focusing on jostling city workers; or perhaps it was the distant look of the visionary who has spent years imagining the ideal world he would build if he should ever gain power. He did not shift his gaze rapidly, as do city dwellers anxious to stay alive when they cross the roads.

Two days later we met him personally. Having braved the hurly-burly of the lift, we found ourselves waiting on the top floor outside the big double doors to the V.I.P. suite. After establishing that we were who we said we were, the guard admitted us. The scene inside was fascinating. The large hallway was partly obstructed by two or three room-service tables on wheels, carrying the remains of several meals and a litter of unfinished food and dirty crockery. In one of the five or six rooms a small group of top officers was gathered round Castro. Documents lay about, and another trolley, pushed away against a wall, bore the remnants of the most recent meal. Castro stood up to greet us. I was again impressed by his height. His voice was attractively deep and melodious. He had a long discussion with Tito in Spanish. Towards the end he noticed that I could not follow what was being said. Hesitantly he brought out the words, 'I am sorry I cannot speak English; I would like to speak very much.' I apologized for being too stupid to learn Spanish, thinking that would be the end of a polite exchange between us. But his compulsion to communicate pushed him to try further. He said haltingly, 'I need to learn English; it is very important.' Gradually he gained speed, saying, 'I *must* learn. I *will* learn; next time I will be able to talk to you in English.' By the time he had finished that was exactly what he was doing. I never saw anyone learn a language so quickly. It was instant English.

On our return to London I was amazed to read a story cooked up by a journalist who had spoken briefly to us on the phone to our Havana hotel. He said that I admitted helping Castro secretly for more than a year, by informing the British Government that they were underestimating the Cuban situation. I could just imagine the British Government taking advice from a prima ballerina on any subject! The newspaper concerned is now defunct, and no wonder.

All these years since my marriage I was dancing as hard as before – in fact more so, with the extra tours to Australia and Brazil. This makes me wonder about 'Margot Fonteyn' and why she was still dancing, now that I was so happily married to Tito. I think she could not just disappear, for she had become too real to everyone, including Tito and me. Also, I could no longer extricate myself from her. But gradually I could put more of my newly understood self into 'Margot Fonteyn' in a slow merger so that, little by little, she became, I hope, a real human being.

All this time I supposed that I would not dance for more than another year. Having spent all my career in the Royal Ballet, without the need for an agent or manager, it seemed hardly worthwhile to alter things for only a last few months. In this manner, with one brief exception, I have been working for about fifteen years: making my own contracts, dates and arrangements without help. It is perhaps a stupid way to work, but the managers talk as though the only thing one cares about is money. This annoys me. I completely disdained money until my first tour in America, where people said things like, 'Do you realize your value? I hope they are paying you enough.' After that I occasionally rearranged my salary with Sir David Webster, General Administrator of the Royal Opera House. Once it was agreed, I put the whole thing out of my mind. Now, with each engagement, I do the same. As soon as I have accepted the contract I forget the terms and get on with the job. Only one journalist ever asked me to what extent I continue dancing for the sake of money. I really didn't know the answer. On reflection I said I thought about half. But if it had been only for the money I could have found other ways to earn it, by teaching for instance. However, I think people must do what they are able to do, even at cost to themselves – and occasionally the cost to spirit and body has been heavy. The secret of my lasting so long is probably a simple one: it lies in my well-balanced proportions, which distribute the stresses evenly over the whole skeletal structure.

SEVEN

Tito was normally pensive, having the capacity to think coherently and with total concentration. This trait often made it difficult to get messages through to him, so that I felt I wanted to climb inside his head. My undisciplined brain flits about like a gadfly, expecting instant replies to irrelevant questions; thoughts rush into my head and out of my mouth without due consideration. In fact, I am incapable of attending to one matter for more than a very short time, and have to wait until it comes back into my mind to proceed with the thought. It is fortunate that Tito has such an exceptionally well-ordered brain, for it has been virtually his only resource in the last years.

From the second year of our marriage he was more and more absorbed in his idea for a revolution, his sixth, in Panama. Now, rumours of murkiness in high places of Panamanian government once again led him to thoughts of plotting. This time the rumours involved a supposed Colombian 'Jungle Connection' for smuggling drugs through Panama. As the pilot mentioned in this affair was a distant relative of Tito's, called Pastor, Tito sought him out with a request to accompany him secretly on a mysterious, predawn mission.

Pastor picked Tito up at 5 o'clock one morning and drove him to Paitilla, a small airport well inside Panama city limits, telling him, at the last minute, the name of the person Tito was supposed to be. He named a relatively unknown copilot. Tito was to wait in the car, in an unlit area, until Pastor called for him, and then go straight to the little aircraft and climb in.

They made a perfect getaway at dawn, just before the airport opened. There had been no cargo manifesto. Pastor broke the silence by saying, 'Just because their consciences are overloaded they always try to overload the plane, too.' There was never any other hint from him as to the impropriety of the expedition. As they headed towards Colombia, Pastor said: 'We will make a technical stop in Darien and get the timing of arrival at our destination just right.'

After crossing the Bayano River, which is exceptionally wide and dirty, they began to lose altitude in mid-jungle, preparatory to landing on a tiny airstrip. The plane taxied directly to a single grass-roofed hut, just beyond the apron, where a weedy, dark-skinned man with a rifle came out to greet them. Pastor said that he was the local policeman. Two youths, wearing old, sunbleached cotton trousers, dragged a barrel up to the aircraft on a primitive trolley, and Pastor himself did the refueling. When it was accomplished, they waited a good half-hour on the ground, so as to reach their destination as near as possible to the hour of the appointment. As Pastor remarked drily, it would be unhealthy to dillydally in Colombia.

The motive for all this? In Panama, the Chief of Police held legal custody and control of explosives and arms; designated persons were permitted to re-export the surplus goods. As the story went, the weapons and explosives were sold to the notorious jungle bandits of Colombia – the 'bandoleros'. The bandits soon ran out of cash, but a few installations for refining drugs were conveniently situated in the inaccessible areas they frequented.

The birth of the 'Jungle Connection' had been some-what Solomonic, for the Commandante in Panama would not actually dirty his hands with drugs. But the agents of the bandits were allowed to smuggle the stuff into the country in order to raise cash for their lethal purchases.

Trade was brisk and murderous: guns and explosives one way, drugs the other.

Tito and Pastor took off, and soon after crossing the Colombian border they saw the dense jungles of Coto, and the muddy Jurado River, which flows into the Pacific.

This time their landing strip was not even a strip, simply an open place on the mountainside. Here activity was brisk and highly skilled. Pastor gave a signal as he jumped out of the plane, and immediately wooden crates were unloaded from the luggage compartment at the rear of the cabin.

Three men, each carrying an American-type briefcase, got quickly into the back seat and away they went, back to Darien. The men were clean-shaven and wore neat sports shirts and dark trousers. None of them was overtalkative.

The stop at the airstrip was somewhat longer than before, so that the plane landed at Paitilla just after dusk, when the airport happens to close. A car was waiting for the passengers. They were not even bothered with the usual formalities of immigration, but got straight into the vehicle with their perhaps deadly briefcases, and dis-appeared anonymously towards the lights of the bustling city centre.

Tito found it impossible not to notice that they were veterans in the mysterious 'connection', and this re-affirmed his belief that his country needed a revolution. He observed that this episode was not the only overripe portion of the tropical Camembert, and so it was he set about plotting.

Tito's favourite plot, never alas carried out, was the idea of a masked ball at which all the male guests would be invited to go dressed as the President – who had a distinctive small moustache and smoothed hair style. When the party reached full swing the real President would be unobtrusively hustled away, and taken out of the country aboard a yacht, preferably Errol Flynn's to add colour to the coup.

Tito discussed the revolution openly and amusingly with many people in London. It came to be a sort of romantic jaunt in my mind, an idea that we lived with rather cosily for quite a long time. In due course, Tito resigned his position as Ambassador in order to plot. The two assignments were clearly incompatible. He was away when one day I received a phone call from a friend in Panama. Unguardedly, I said, 'Tito is in Spain. He is leaving tomorrow for Zurich and will be here in the evening.' I told Tito when he returned and saw him angry with me for the first and only time. He said, 'That's ruined everything. That person will know who I went to see in Zurich, and his wife is a terrible gossip. The government will soon be aware of what I am doing.'

The next time Tito went abroad I received another phone call late at night. 'Chicago calling for Dr Arias.' I replied, 'Dr Arias is away.' 'Do you know where he can be reached?' 'No, I don't know where he is.' 'You don't know what country he is in?' I said, 'No, I don't; who is calling? Can I help you?' I thought I was protecting Tito very efficiently this time. The caller said, 'This is the Chicago *Tribune*. I wanted to speak to Dr Arias about a report I have here of a pending separation between him and his wife.' Well, I gave up! I was hardly now in a position to convince the man that I knew perfectly well where Tito was, and that the report was false. After I had thought over the conversation a few times, I decided that some journalists probably ring people up at random with that story, and just occasionally strike a lucky response. There could really be no other explanation, and I never heard any more about it.

Tito had said his revolution would have to take place early in the year, 'before the rainy season'. This amused me because it reminded me of my days in Shanghai when

China was beset by little local wars between Chinese war-lords, and I was told they did not fight each other while it was raining. How sensible of them!

Our friends, by now very intrigued with Tito's plotting, were never sure what to believe as he made it so laugh-able. When it was over, so many were upset not to have been invited to take part that I was able to compile a very distinguished international list of volunteers for the next time. So far the need hasn't arisen.

Typically, our complex personal geography took me on a distant tour to Japan and New Zealand – which I will describe later – during the spring of 1959. Communication by telephone with Tito in Panama was nearly impossible, and I received few letters because the things he was doing were highly secret. As soon as I was free I flew to San Francisco, and phoned Tito at once to know where I should meet him for my two weeks' holiday. He sounded diffident about seeing me. He said, 'Things are a bit strained here. I don't know whether you still want to come down or not.' How absurd to imagine I might not want to spend my vacation beside him! I said, 'But of course I do.' Still he was doubtful. 'Darling,' he said, 'I'm afraid it might be rather uncomfortable for you.' For eight weeks I had been dreaming only of being reunited with him, so I said, 'Don't be silly. Of course I want to be with you; I don't care about comfort. I will leave by the first flight tomorrow.' 'Good,' he replied and said no more.

I put through a call to Judy, a friend in New York. She was an English girl who I knew was doing some liason work for Tito. I recounted my curious conversation with him.

'Oh, how lucky you are!' she said eagerly. 'It must be going to happen any minute. I do wish I could be there too.' 'What is going to happen?' I asked. Judy launched into a long, confusing story. She had been in Panama on some mysterious mission and, back in New York, she had got herself a jungle-green revolution suit. The armbands had been sent concealed inside a Teddy bear. The whole thing sounded like Modesty Blaise, and about as believable. Judy and I are both incurable romantics, so I asked no more questions, being too exhausted by the long flight from Auckland to sort the story out further. I just went to sleep, not wanting to look terrible when I saw Tito the next day. It was fortunate that I got up early and went to the hairdresser and beauty salon before I caught the plane to Panama. Ten days later, facing a barrage of cameras and newsreels, I was glad I had taken that last opportunity to be groomed.

Tito was not on the tarmac, nor in the airport lounge, when I arrived in Panama. Friends led me from the customs hall to where he was waiting in a car outside. He seemed pleased that I had decided to join him, but more than ever preoccupied. In answer to my questions he gave noncommittal replies, or a quiet laugh. I was content to be sitting beside him with my hand in his as we drove into town. It was always a relief to be free of the worries about preparing pointe shoes and practice clothes and getting to the theatre on time, and all those little chores associated with my everyday life. I put everything out of my mind and felt utterly carefree.

We had recently taken an apartment high up in a building that overlooked the bay, with its picturesque shrimp boats lying at anchor or fishing in the local waters – the word Panama means 'abundance of fish' in the Indian dialect. Farther out we could see the ocean liners waiting to pass through the Canal. The apartment, like our Embassy four years earlier, was almost devoid of furniture, so I was not too surprised that we drove instead to the El Panama Hotel. Later in the evening Tito said that the hotel manager, a close friend, had changed our room to one next to the service staircase. 'I might have to leave quickly' was all the explanation Tito gave. At midnight, however, instead of going to our new room in the hotel, we went to an apartment I had never seen before. A visitor came to confer secretly with Tito. I could not follow their conversation in Spanish, so I looked anxiously through the slatted window at a Guardia Nacional patrolman in the street below. We were on the second floor and had turned off all the lights. Some illumination seeped in from shop signs on nearby buildings, from street lamps and from a half-moon that was occasionally screened by thin cloud. At about one-thirty in the morning I saw a police car drive up, and two more Guardias stepped out before the entrance to our block. I was really panicky, and interrupted Tito to whisper that the police were at our door. 'Oh, don't worry, darling, it's quite all right,' he said. 'They are only changing guard on the next house. That's why I chose this place. They would never think of looking for me so close to the home of the Assistant Chief of Police.'

Before dawn we sneaked out by the back way and went to our own apartment, where I spent most of the next few days. At night, we never stayed twice in the same place. Once it was a disused retreat in a tower above the family's newspaper office – Tito's father was publisher of the *Panama-American*, and Tito ran a tabloid called *La Hora*; his brother had a third paper. We spent the best part of one night sitting in the car in a country lane waiting to make a secret rendezvous, and another time calming some young rebels who were getting impatient in their hideout.

During the day Tito went to the newspaper and the law office, following his normal routine. I was at our apartment when he telephoned me very briefly around ten in the morning, sounding vague, as though he had forgotten what he meant to say. An hour later he called again. 'I think we might go on a fishing trip, darling. Put some things in a bag and come down to the office.' I tried to sound unconcerned as I asked if I should hurry very much. 'No, not too much,' he replied in a casual sort of way that made me feel he meant just the opposite.

At the newspaper building I took the elevator to the little hideout on the top floor of the tower, but he was not there. I left the overnight bag with our things and went two floors down to the office. His brother was there. 'Where is Tito?' I asked. 'Upstairs in the apartment,' he said. 'No, I just came from there. There was no sign of him.' His brother got very excited, saying, 'Whatever Tito does he mustn't leave the building, there's an order out for his arrest.' Their eldest brother, Modi, rushed in at that moment saying he had just passed Tito running down the stairs. They got into a heated discussion about where Tito was, and what he should do or shouldn't do. 'They won't dare to come in and arrest him here. He must stay.' But by that time no one could find him anywhere. Modi remembered to tell me that, as Tito was running down the stairs, he called out a message for me to meet him at the Yacht Club. The confusion and raised voices in the office were almost comical, since the object of the argument had vanished into thin air. I reasoned the best thing for me to do would be to follow Tito's instructions. Modi's assistant, Gloria, was the only one to stay calm. Against contrary advice, she said, 'I have the car right outside. I'll drive you to the Yacht Club.' I fetched the bag from upstairs and hurried off with Gloria, anxious not to keep Tito waiting. Not unreasonably, I had the impression that whatever the situation might be it was urgent.

At the Yacht Club, which is in the Canal Zone and therefore out of Panamanian jurisdiction, all was tranquil. We waited a good half-hour in the sun at the end of a long pier. Then we heard a car in the distance. As it pulled up, Tito stepped out, giving last-minute instructions to a friend, Moreno Gongora, as they approached us at a leisurely pace. After a while he told us where he had been. He had gone to the basement of the newspaper building and jumped inside one of the vans as it was rushing out the noon edition. Amid the noise and flurry of little newsboys grabbing the batches of papers, he had leaped out close to the Canal Zone boundary and, once safely inside, Moreno Gongora, who was following in his car, had picked him up.

So we boarded the little launch *Nola* for all the world

as if we were setting off for a weekend's fishing, and indeed much of the time we spent on board during the next five days was idyllic.

Most of the business in hand took place after dark, so we slept little at night but made up with some long snoozes as we sat out the daytime hours, hiding in deserted island coves and tiny bays. The problem was to assemble in one place the eight impatient rebels who had been transferred from their city hideout to a shrimp boat called *Elaine*, and the guns that had been smuggled into the country in the false bottom of a speedboat. We sought out the right shrimp boat and clambered aboard to confer with the itchy-fingered but unarmed boys. One bore the exotic name of Heliodoro Portugal. Another, called Floyd Britten, spoke English, as did an older, rather shy man called Baquero. One man with an expressionless face was called Alfredo Jimenez. I liked Baquero, who was much the most sympathetic, and I liked Floyd, although his outlook was rather mulish – however, I suppose that is what you need in a revolution. All discussions took place in Spanish, so I never had any idea what was going on.

The little speedboat with the false bottom was success-fully located, but being unnaturally heavy it sank while being towed in shallow waters. At dusk we returned on the *Elaine* to find it. Bill Sruta, a splendidly fearless character who had captained our honeymoon yacht, and who was resourceful if sometimes erratic – en route to pick us up in Nassau he had missed Jamaica and landed in Haiti by mistake – dived into the shark-infested waters of Panama without hesitation to tether the little speedboat. Bill was a Panamanian of Czech origin. He had knocked around the world in freighters, and talked volubly about his exploits, including the time he dived overboard at Suez and was swimming happily in the refreshing waters when his companions yelled at him to get out quickly. He said, 'These a-big-a-fish bump into me all around, but I not a-know they are sharks. They never touch me, not a-once.' Bill is fair and blue-eyed, with a tanned weather-beaten skin and the rough good looks of a sailor. He has a lot of charm.

The speedboat was hauled aboard after dark and pried open by the light of a single lamp. There was no moon that night. As the little boat gave up its secret hoard, the men fell excitedly upon the guns and ammunition, arming themselves to the teeth like schoolboys until, suddenly, they fell asleep, as children will. Some sprawled uncomfortably over a mountain of loose cartridges on deck; others clutched their guns in their arms as they slept on their bunks.

Meantime the *Elaine* had damaged her steering gear and veered constantly to the right. She could only proceed in a series of circles – not very practical for a ship trying to avoid attention. Near dawn she dropped anchor while Tito and I went back to our launch to spend the day alone, swimming in a little bay on the tiny island of Bona. Apart from Dawkins, our captain, the only other person we saw was a wizened little man who came in a canoe to gather some pineapples that he grew there.

As night fell, activities recommenced. We made rendezvous with another shrimp boat, into which the men and arms were transferred in the dark. The *Elaine* circled off back to harbour, and we went with *Nola* and the new boat to the Pearl Islands. It was still dark when we arrived. As dawn broke I could see a wide bay with a long sweep of golden beach and palm trees edging the thick vegetation of an uninhabited island. It was perfect; a slight breeze kept the temperature ideal.

Tito's theory of revolution was that actual fighting should be avoided. Indeed, an unsuccessful revolt was the best way to create the necessary state of tension for changes to be wrought in government. The war of nerves had to be kept up as long as possible.

By evening, the tension had started to cut both ways. After the crew of the *Elaine* reached harbour in Panama, they were arrested and interrogated. The Government had already made some of the political concessions Tito wanted, but they were now out searching for us. Our two boats moved to a small inlet to shelter for the night. At two in the morning we sighted a craft without lights out to sea. Perhaps it was a police boat. Tito sailed out on the darkened shrimp boat, leaving me on *Nola* as a decoy. I watched and waited in the warm night air. Summer lightning flashed among thick clouds, momentarily illuminating the jungle-covered coastline, and the moon broke through now and then. Everything was peaceful. Dawkins slept on the deck. As nothing happened I went down to my bunk. Tito came back and slept for an hour or so.

Suddenly it was dawn, and there were shouts from the shrimp boat alongside. A light plane was circling the island. It carried the Guardia Nacional, and it swooped low over our two boats nestling together in the early morning haze. Tito climbed across to the shrimp boat for an emergency conference. He was back in a few minutes to tell me the boys had the whole place rigged up like a man-of-war. They were trigger-happy, and were planning to commandeer an island and fight all who came near. Obviously, the concept of bloodless revolution did not appeal to any of them except Baquero, who was outnumbered. The question was whether Tito should stay with me on the *Nola* and return to Panama, or go with the boys and control them. I asked, 'What will happen if you come with me?' 'They will arrest me and put me in jail.' At that moment the plane swooped past again, very low, then swept off towards Panama.

I saw the whole escapade in *Boys' Own Paper* terms. Of course, it was unthinkable to give in to the enemy! I said immediately, 'You can't do that, you have to go with the others.' He thought they might get to Costa Rica, if only their fuel would last out. I did not ask if I could go too. A woman would be too much of a liability. I took my things out of the overnight bag and gave it to Tito. He put a revolver inside it. It was the only time I ever saw him with a gun.

He asked me to cruise about the islands all day as a decoy, and to reach Panama as late as possible so as to give them more time to escape. Then he kissed me good-bye, jumped over to the shrimp boat and sailed off at once. It had all happened so quickly that the sun was still barely up.

In what seemed like no time at all a little speck was vanishing in the mists towards the horizon, while our launch pulled away in the opposite direction. Bravery had been easy while Tito was there; in telling him to escape rather than give himself up, there had been no time to think of the implications. Now it was not so simple.

I stared and stared until the last trace of his boat was lost. Then emptiness, loss, reality, a deadening of the spirit – or the heart? I don't know how to describe the state I fell into at that moment. Only once afterwards did I experience anything to match that despair. But despair is only an emotion of the whole being. This was a half-dead sensation, as though only a part of me remained to suffer. The other half had disappeared into the unknown. The idea that he could be killed hit me unexpectedly, and I realized I might never see him again. How could I send him off like that, so stupidly, so thoughtlessly even, in my idiotic bravado, encouraging him to go? I cried, but as unobtrusively as I could, for I didn't want Dawkins, the only other person on the boat, to see me. But Dawkins, black, poor and compassionate, began to talk of his troubles. I knew it was his way of helping me. He was anxious to return immediately to the city, where he had left his wife with only enough money for three days. We had been put out in the *Nola* five days, so his family would be short of food. On top of that, the police would take him in for questioning as soon as he got back, and they might keep him for days. Yet he dawdled the launch among peaceful islands the whole day long, waiting for nightfall to head back home. His first name, Aguinaldo, means 'Christmas present'.

Once on land, my sister-in-law picked me up, and I expected to make up for the sleep I had lost in five days and nights of wakefulness, but it was not to be.

Tito's mother would rise early for daily Mass. A kindly, imperturbable lady, her features clearly reveal the exceptional beauty of her youth. She had four sons and a daughter, all with fertile imaginations. She had long been conditioned to their exploits. Her husband was twice President of the Republic; her brother-in-law was overthrown three times. Revolutions were somewhat commonplace in her country, which may be one reason why she travelled so extensively. Even allowing for the hazardous life she had led, I felt terribly guilty as I went to confess my negligence in not holding Tito back. I expected to see her agitated by the news, but she took my hand as I sat beside her on the settee, and then, putting her head back a little and half-closing her eyes, as though recalling memories, she said, 'Never mind, never mind. Tito always comes back.'

Our relations advised me to leave Panama, but this was contrary to my every instinct. The British Ambassador kindly offered me the protection of his Embassy, but I would not accept, as his position would not permit him to harbour Tito should he reappear. Instead I made an appointment to see him next morning. It happened that the Duke of Edinburgh was aboard *Britannia*, not far from the Yacht Club, when Dawkins and I returned in the early hours. I had half a mind to go alongside and ask for admittance, but I knew *Britannia* was due to sail almost at once, as Prince Philip had completed his three-day visit to the Republic.

Tito's brother-in-law suggested that I spend the night in the Canal Zone. I didn't see why I should, as it looked like running away, and I had done nothing illegal. I was merely holidaying with my husband, who happened to be plotting a revolt. An emissary arrived at the door asking me to sleep at the house of Mrs Valdez, wife of the Chief of Secret Police. I agreed readily, and went to bed immediately after I got there. At last, I thought, I will get a good night's sleep!

My light had been out about ten minutes when the good lady knocked on my door. Almost in tears, she asked me to get up and dress as I was wanted for questioning. Waiting with a limousine was a gentleman who greeted me with extreme courtesy. He had a look of such formality and strain that I did not recognize Max Heurtematte, who was Ambassador to France when he attended our wedding and was now, as Minister of Government, sent – though I failed to realize it – to arrest me. He asked if I would mind accompanying him to the Fiscal for questioning. Doing as I was told, I got into the car and was driven through the enormous iron gates of the Carcel Modelo; in English, the Model Jail. I walked up the short flight of steps to the main entrance and was ushered into an office. Several Guardias were standing around, jackbooted and battle-helmeted, hung about the waist with guns and truncheons. They were 'the enemy'. They looked at me with curiosity, and I held my head high in disdain.

Max left me in care of the Major on duty, and formally excused himself, trying to hide his distress.

I sat down to wait. The Major spoke some English. He said, 'We are sorry for the delay. The Fiscal is very busy. You must be tired, would you like to rest in a quiet room?' 'No thank you,' I replied. 'I prefer to wait here.' The office had the three-quarter-length louvered swing doors typical of saloon bars in Westerns. Below the doors I could see the jackboots. A voice called for the crew of *Elaine*, the shrimp boat, and after a few minutes some feet shuffled past. My Major said, 'When you walk in here you look quite happy, cheerful. Most people not look like that. They look a bit, er, nervous.' I said coldly, 'Why should I be nervous? I haven't done anything wrong.' It was odd he should have spoken then, for I was thinking about resistance fighters in Europe during the war as they were taken in by the Gestapo. I suppose I am always imagining myself in the place of other people – it is what I do on the stage – and I was imagining myself walking up the steps of the Carcel Modelo, knowing that I had reason to be afraid. I noticed how everything is designed to intimidate. The huge iron gates are closed noisily and definitely behind one; the building is unnaturally active, lights are burning and people are moving everywhere in what should be the dead of night; and uniforms make menacing figures of men who no doubt look benevolent to their families at home. I was fascinated by the scene, wondering how much courage I would muster in other circumstances, and rating it rather low.

Time passed. The Major chatted a bit; the crew of the *Elaine* shuffled back the other way with a noticeably slower gait. Months later I learnt that Demetrio Fabrega, a friend of Tito's who had spent two years with us at the Embassy in London, was knocking unsuccessfully on the big iron gates to find out what had happened to me while, at the same moment, the secret police were at his house trying, also unsuccessfully, to arrest him.

At about three in the morning the Major repeated his apologies for the delay and renewed his offer of a room to rest in. 'There is a bed there; you can lie down. I think you must be tired.' He was right about my being tired; waiting had become very tedious. 'How much longer will it be before the Fiscal is ready?' I asked. 'Is it difficult to find an interpreter,' he explained. It wasn't surprising at that time of the night! 'Maybe in the morning – or in the afternoon,' he added. 'The *afternoon*?' I said. 'In that case, I will lie down. Thank you.'

The room was on the third floor, quite spacious and with a bathroom to the side. It was clearly the V.I.P. suite, furnished with a table, a chair, bedside table and bed. The mattress and pillow felt as though they were straw-filled, but the sheet looked clean if not exactly white. The ever-courteous Major said, 'The Governor apologizes for the room. The roses are from the prison garden. He grew them himself.' I wasn't going to let up on my distant attitude towards the enemy, so I just said, 'Please thank him.' He hesitated as he went towards the door, and looked terribly apologetic. 'You must understand there are bad men in this building. It is not nice for you to be here. You will understand if I lock the door for your protection.' 'Thank you,' I answered. 'How very kind.'

The curtainless window was screened against mosquitoes. Outside I saw the courtyard surrounded by high walls, turreted at each corner. I could see over the wall to other buildings. Being unprepared to spend the night, I could only take off my dress and lie on the bed, hoping to sleep at last.

No sooner had I dozed off than four very shrill whistles brought me smartly back to consciousness. I worried about the forthcoming interrogation. Without telling lies, I was anxious not to give anything away lest I unwittingly jeopardized Tito's escape.

I decided that at all costs I must get some sleep, so as to have my wits about me when the time came. I soon learned that it would have been wiser to have accepted the room when it was first offered, as the piercing whistles were repeated every hour from the four turrets, to prove that the guards were awake. Everyone for miles around must have been awake, too. At 5 : 00 a.m. what sounded like all five thousand National Guardsmen in outsize boots went through heavy drill in the courtyard, followed by the noisy breakfast line-up of prisoners, all clanking their tin mugs and plates. By now it was after six, and all Panama was out and about in the streets.

The Major, whose name I now know to be Araúz, brought me tea. I declined everything else, including a radio they wanted to install so that I would have music to dance to! Araúz soon came back to ask if my family was going to send me food. I said, 'Why should they? Is the food so bad here?'

'No, no. Food very good.'

'Do you eat it?'

'No, my wife send me food.'

'Well there you are! The food must be bad. Why do you work in such a terrible place?'

'It is very interesting.'

'I hope you get well paid, at least?'

'Not too much money. Very interesting work. Three days here, three days stay home.'

'Oh, I see. You get a lot of free time?'

'Only in trouble time no go home. Stay here.'

'But it's always trouble time in Panama. When were you at home last?'

'Oh, two months no go home.'

'Two months! You must be crazy to work in this terrible place.'

'It very interesting. I like.'

He said he ought not stay too long talking. The next time he found reason to unlock the door we embarked on an absurd wrangle about whether I was a prisoner, as I maintained, or 'only a guest', as he patiently insisted.

With interludes for these verbal minuets, and an occasional look outside to see how two goats in the prison yard were passing the hot day, time went by. I was quite settling down to the idea of a week or two of early nights and uneventful days. I was already getting accustomed to the sound of the whistles. My only concern was to have news of Tito's whereabouts and, since I was forbidden newspapers, I hoped Araúz's conscience might bend just enough to tell me when he heard something. In the early afternoon Tito's family, familiar with the routine for revolutions, sent me food and clothing. I had so little appetite I shared the chicken with the Major.

The questioning took place in the evening, and I got the impression that it was designed for me to prove myself innocent of involvement. They asked about Bill, the one who was fearless of sharks, but as they gave his surname and nationality incorrectly I felt justified in denying knowledge of such a person. The British Ambassador was waiting in an office to claim my immediate release from the prison authorities. But they had other ideas. They said my papers required the signature of an official who could not be located because he had gone to a party. While I waited another hour or two, I observed a large red arrow on a wall map indicating a location on the coast near my father-in-law's ranch. I guessed this to mean the shrimp boat had landed there. But what had happened to the rebels? I concluded they had gone into the mountains, and blamed myself terribly for not having packed Tito's boots in anticipation of such an eventuality.

A newspaper lay on the desk. The Government had announced, in defence of my arrest, that there would be no 'sacred cows' in Panama. I admit that they won that round.

Max Heurtematte returned and led me through the women's dormitory to a side entrance. We drove straight to the airport, where I was dumped in a plane with a one-way ticket to the first stop, which happened to be Miami. In short I was deported. It goes without saying that the plane left in the middle of the night, and I didn't get to bed at all.

My brain had gone numb and I was half in a trance by the time I disembarked at Miami. It was as though I saw myself from the outside as I stood in customs waiting to clear my baggage. I heard a 'Psst', by my left ear. I was starting to hear things, I thought. The 'Psst' was repeated, and I turned to see a dark little man who whispered in a thick Spanish accent, 'Captain Perez wants to talk to you.'

'Who is Captain Perez?' I asked.

'Friend of your husband.'

'Where is he?'

'Over there.'

Against the wall, half-sitting on a ledge, was another dark little man, trimmer-looking and with a neat moustache. As I turned towards him he made a slight movement of his head and shoulder as though he had an involuntary twitch. Then he winked. His face showed no expression, and I began to think I was getting hallucinations. Both men were lean and poorly dressed.

'Tell Captain Perez to come over and talk to me here,' I said.

'No, must be private. Very important must talk to you alone.'

I looked at Perez again and he twitched and winked as before. I felt like Alice in Wonderland. Pan Am kindly lent me the use of an office, to which the three of us retired, and the interpreter fellow said: 'Two hundred and thirty Cubans with guns will arrive Panama tomorrow.' I was horrified, and said, 'No, no! Cancel them, don't send them.' 'Yes. Captain Perez want to help your husband. Cubans arriving tomorrow,' he announced, almost smugly. Nothing would shake them so I called Judy in New York. She had never heard of Perez, and the fact that he was asking for $800 cash on the spot made me even more suspicious. (As it turned out, a revolutionary group *did* reach Panama, but had nothing to do with Tito.) Fortunately my flight was called at that moment. I escaped the two Cubans, but never guessed that dozens of pressmen would be waiting to catch me at the other end in New York. There they were, at the foot of the plane steps. After a moment of fright, I thought, this kind of thing only happens to visiting Prime Ministers, so you had better make the most of it; it will never happen to you again. I was relaxed and laughing because I really thought it all incredibly funny. The mob scene from the plane to the newsroom was fantastic, with journalists and photographers fighting for a picture or a quote. At the start of the conference I explained that I could not say anything about my imprisonment. There was a difficult moment when some of the questioners got aggressive, and one of them asked a very pointed question to which, out of the blue, it came into my head to reply: 'You can read the answer to that in the papers.' The others laughed, and with that one heaven-sent phrase the atmosphere changed in my favour. I learned an invaluable lesson about keeping good-humoured relations with the press and, with rare exceptions, they have been nice to me ever since.

What promised to be a good night's sleep at Judy's apartment was disrupted by a phone call at two in the morning from a journalist who informed me that the Panama police had given out the text of a letter from Judy to me describing her participation in the plot. The letter had been left in the overnight bag with Tito. One has to be very careful about details like that in revolutions. Thinking the press, and possibly the New York police, would soon be on Judy's track, we dressed, packed and moved to the house of my friends Tug and John. Judy never saw her apartment again. Some efficient cloak-and-dagger planning over tea and muffins at the home of

Sir Pierson Dixon, the U.K. Ambassador to the United Nations, and Lady Dixon, resulted in Judy and me unobtrusively boarding a plane that night. We were in London next day. We had not, of course, been to bed.

Just five days after I had watched that little boat carrying Tito away into the mists, Eddie Gilmore, Chief of the Associated Press Office in London, telephoned me to say that Tito had taken political asylum in the Brazilian Embassy. Thank God! He was safe! But two months went by before he was allowed to travel to Brazil. I joined him at once, and heard of the adventures that befell some of those on the shrimp boat. As Tito had feared, there was insufficient fuel to reach Costa Rica, so he landed at a beach near his father's property. He had chosen the site because it gave on to the President's ranch, which he thought a sensible place to bury the arms. The seas were high and the landing extremely hazardous. For reasons of discretion the men dispersed in various directions, Tito going with Baquero and two young boys, Luis Raoul Fernandez and Chino Delgado, to the house of a close family friend, Betty Webster, a remarkable woman not likely to be surprised at any capers Tito might get up to. She offered all four men rooms, and went back to sleep while the rebels tried to snatch some rest. Fernandez went off to catch an early bus, hoping to slip back into Panama City. The others stayed in the house, but were on edge. Delgado thought a car or jeep was moving suspiciously about the neighbourhood, so they left and headed for the mountains on foot.

Dawn was just breaking when a voice cried, 'There they are!' followed by a burst of gunfire. Instinctively, Tito followed Baquero; Delgado took a different direction. Baquero crouched behind a big clay anthill on the edge of the llano, with Tito behind him. When gunfire began to demolish the anthill, Baquero said quickly, 'I can't get up. You run for it.' Tito ran, and Baquero was killed. Despite the redoubled firing, Tito had one advantage: he knew the terrain like the back of his hand. Instead of crossing the main highway on its surface, he chose to crawl through a culvert. At the other end he came suddenly nose to nose with an astonished Guardia, who simply threw down his gun and ran.

A number of ladies in the area hid Tito in their homes, until President de la Guardia fortuitously summoned the National Assembly to ratify his emergency powers. This gave Tito an opportunity to get back into Panama in the trunk of an Assemblyman's car. As he was a prominent man and was believed to be a supporter of the President, his car was not searched at the numerous roadblocks they encountered.

A sticky moment occurred at the Colombian Embassy, where Tito hoped to be granted asylum. A little girl, perhaps ten years old, answered the door and, as it was too much to expect her to grasp the immediate and urgent problems of a political refugee, they hastily drove on to the home of the Brazilian Ambassador.

The first night, as Tito sat at dinner with the Ambassador and his guests, there was an unseemly shouting and banging at the door in the middle of the meal. 'Go and see what the trouble is,' the Ambassador told his butler. Outside was an angry group of protesters, led by a woman. The butler came back and whispered something to the Ambassador, who was clearly embarrassed. 'What do they want?' asked Tito. 'They are asking for your head,' replied the Ambassador. Tito looked up from his plate and said to the butler, 'Tell them it is busy – eating.'

Before joining Tito in Brazil, I had a letter from the valiant Bill Sruta, reporting that he had managed to sail unobserved from the Yacht Club in his own little boat and get to Golfito in Costa Rica. There he had to lie very low for fear of extradition, and now he was broke. I sent him something, and he replied with a thank-you note written exactly in his manner of speech, saying: 'To tell you a-truth is a very first time I ever receive a-money from a lady.'

I was lonely in London, unable to communicate with

Tito and not knowing when he would be allowed to leave his political refuge in Panama. Our chauffeur, Leonard Lindley, was a silent sympathizer. Gilbert Mayo, the butler, also worried about me, and I spent several evenings eating in the kitchen listening to his tales of former times. Gilbert was reputedly seventy-four when he came out of retirement to help us, and he was still seventy-four when we closed the house five years later. So far as I know he was the same age when he died not long ago. When he was thirteen he entered service as an apprentice gardener at a house in Sussex. From that position he worked all his life, rising to butler and developing a very keen eye for antiques. Whenever I bought a piece of furniture, Gilbert would give it a rather baleful look-over and say, 'Of course, *I* like Queen Anne myself.' Or, if I said, 'Gilbert, Lady Jellicoe is coming to dinner tonight,' he would answer, half mumbling to himself, 'Oh, Lady Jellicoe. Dinner will be late' – making sure the last word was just audible as he moved off towards the pantry. David Metcalfe merited the comment, 'Mr Metcalfe? Then I had better get some extra greens for dinner.' He liked to lace his sentences with French: 'Shall I serve coffee in the – er – *salle à manger?*'

In his spare time he bought extraordinary bargains, never paying more than a few shillings for items that he sometimes verified as quite rare by reference to museums. As a concluding anecdote about him, it is worth recounting that he was one of the few collectors to get the better of another determined connoisseur, Queen Mary. During the war his employer often stayed at a house in the West Country. Queen Mary (whose eye for antiques was so renowned that it was said her hosts sometimes discreetly removed favourite pieces to the cellar before her arrival, lest she should admire them in conversation) was a frequent guest. Gilbert arranged his connoisseur's collection of silver snuff boxes on a table in the housekeeper's sitting room because ' 'Er Majesty liked to go snooping around the kitchen and the 'ouse-keeper left 'er door a bit ajar so they would catch 'Er Majesty's eye as she passed.' Her

Majesty duly noticed the boxes and admired one in particular. Gilbert didn't budge, despite her enthusiasm.

Back home, he took up the morning mail to his employer's mother. In Gilbert's account of the scene, she said: ' "Oh, 'ere's a parcel with the Royal cipher on it. I wonder what it can be?" And she opened it all excited, like. When she found a message inside asking if she would kindly give the enclosed Georgian snuff box to her butler, she was absolutely furious.' Here Gilbert gave a wicked laugh and shook back the lock of white hair that invariably came down over his forehead and almost into his left eye. 'Well,' he went on, 'I tell you, she sat up in bed and she almost threw it at me!'

And Gilbert would sit there in the kitchen, chuckling away for several minutes, the lock of hair falling back into his eye.

EIGHT

In 1951 my partnership with Michael Somes, which had already taken us to many parts of the world, led us to Japan, where we were invited to dance *Swan Lake* and *The Sleeping Beauty* with a Japanese ballet company.

I was not sure how I felt at the prospect of being with Japanese people, whom I had disliked as a child because of Japan's belligerence towards China, and later because they had held my father interned in a Shanghai camp for two and one-half years. I thought of them as aggressive and humourless. But all these fears evaporated on arrival in Tokyo.

Everything about the country was very different from my memories of China. The people were diffidently, instead of confidently, smiling. The streets were somehow monochrome by comparison with the colourful merchandise in Chinese shop windows and the profusion of banners in crowded business areas. Japanese houses were concealed behind high walls, showing only the paper screen of upper windows and the roofs, which, though in the country were of lovely blue tiles, in Tokyo were more often shingles merging with the colour of the wooden houses; twisted pines added a touch of soft green to the subdued and secretive aspect. The kimonos worn by young women stood out from this background like hummingbirds, flashes of bright colour, whereas in China the majority of people had dressed for the street in shades of dark blue or in black. Everything else, even the sound of voices, seemed more muted in Japan.

At our first rehearsal with Mr Masahide Komaki's company, they danced every step of *Sleeping Beauty* and *Swan Lake* from beginning to end, taking six hours with occasional breaks for delicious soup and cups of tea. The next day, and on succeeding days, we asked to concentrate on our sections of *Sleeping Beauty*, without ever dissuading the other dancers from conscientiously repeating the entire ballet. It was good to live with the company all day long instead of rehearsing our dances in isolation, as we do with the Royal Ballet. With the exception of the conductor, Michael and I were the only foreigners involved in the performances. Few of our colleagues spoke English, apart from Yaki, who had spent some time studying in London. She was an unusually tall Japanese girl, with long legs that served well for her line in classical ballet, and a perfect, very expressive Japanese face. Mostly it was expressing her sense of humour.

The day we took our things to the theatre for the stage rehearsal we were surprised to see, written on the dressing room door, 'Miss Margot Fonteyn, Mr Michael Somes, Miss Ayako Ogawa' – the last was Yaki's full name. It was a big room with a corner curtained off for dressing purposes. Yaki and I settled our makeup on one side of the room, and Michael on the other. On our side stood a very young girl with an impassive face; on Michael's side stood a youth even more impassive; they were our dressers. It was a most unusual arrangement, particularly in view of our habit, when with other companies, of sitting around half-dressed between acts. There was no question of that here, with a swarm of people coming in to congratulate us in the intermissions. It was like dressing in the middle of Piccadilly Circus.

Of course, most of the girls fell in love with Michael, so, in an expansive mood after the last performance, he went down to their room in order to distribute an armful of gladioli among his blushing admirers. He returned in some confusion, for after opening a door he found the whole corps de ballet, boys and girls, in various states of dress in the same room. That was another thing we could not imagine happening at home.

My photographobia had to be abandoned from the day of the dress rehearsal. When Michael and I did the spectacular 'fish' lifts of Aurora, a snapping like hundreds of turtles broke out all over the theatre. I could only laugh at it and stop worrying. At the performance I was tremendously flattered by members of the audience shouting 'Nihon ichi' at the climactic moments of our dancing. Apparently it means 'Best in Japan', and is a sporting term used to encourage favourite footballers. But the nicest of all the delicate compliments, so humbly offered, came from Mogi, the stage manager, who was a shy, poetic young man. He dreamed of prehistoric times before civilization built concrete jungles to stifle the free spirit of man. I nicknamed him Dinosaur, and he came to me as I waited in the wings to say quietly, 'Japanese sun come out for your Aurora. Now Japanese rain come for your *Swan Lake*,' and it was true that the weather had turned bad that day.

A hundred fragile moments to cherish showered on us like apple blossom petals in the spring. Japanese people have such a refinement of manners that Westerners feel gauche and boorish, and tone down their strident ways to mingle better with their hosts. We had gentle fun with Yaki, who found the most humorous ways to explain Japanese customs. The four young men who danced with me in *Sleeping Beauty* were so nervous and unhappy at rehearsal that they giggled each time they proffered me a hand, and that set me off laughing too. Mr Komaki was a magnificent Carabosse, Yaki a benevolent Lilac Fairy, and the scene design, Western in style, had a charming Japanese overtone you couldn't quite point to.

The critic Natsuya Mitsuyoshi was most skilled at an intriguing game of putting Western names into Japanese characters then translating them back into English. There are many possibilities, and the skill lies in choosing characters that can be related in some way to the person. For 'Margot Fonteyn' Mr Mitsuyoshi interpreted, 'Every time you dance you soar up into heaven.' For 'Arias' he made 'There is always tomorrow for you.' Yaki preferred funnier versions and coined, 'Every time you dance – a half turn!' and for 'Michael Somes', 'Crazy dancing horse.'

The banquets were too much for my conservative palate and finicky liver. One evening I decided to brave it out and eat everything. An unrecognizable tidbit was put on my plate. I foolishly asked Lees Mayall, from the British Embassy, now Ambassador to Venezuela, what it was. 'Sea-slugs' entrails,' he replied, popping another delicacy into his mouth. The trouble was, it could easily have been true. Whatever it was, it made me violently ill, spoiling my enjoyment of a night in a real Japanese hotel as I tossed about on the tatami bed on the floor. Sleeping or dining at floor level is difficult enough for Westerners but, for real discomfort, there is nothing like trying to paint your face in front of a dressing table and mirror designed for someone kneeling on the floor, a position very unpropitious for a ballerina about to attempt *Swan Lake*.

I write about all these frivolous incidents in my life because the impressions that sink deep into the soul, producing that accumulation from which an artist manufactures his art, are intangible and insubstantial. They cannot be itemized or explained or pinned down. They exist in the air, in sounds and smells and colours and complex combinations of messages unconsciously received by all the senses and stored away. I can describe only the ripples on the water's surface but nothing of the light rays that penetrate beneath or the convolutions they illumine there. A quotation from Karen Blixen (Isak Dinesen), which I found in her biography by Parmenia Migel, illustrates something of what I am trying to say. That Danish writer said, 'There are in the nature and being of people many things, perhaps the most significant among them, that demand darkness and that need to go unobserved in order to grow soundly.' These things, to my mind, are the essence of ourselves, the secret inner workings of which we are sometimes aware and sometimes unaware. Even if it were possible to lay them bare to the light, it would be wrong to try, because they are the basis of that strange process whereby the impressions and emotions, themselves inexplicable, are received, hoarded, blended and transmuted and given out again in another form. It happens as naturally and unconsciously as breathing. The important thing is to live, laugh, suffer, eat and love and let the rest take care of itself. Inquiring too closely into it endangers the whole system. Probably I am wrong but that is what I believe. The frivolous things of which I write are as much a part of Margot Fonteyn as those deeper things that I often do not know and cannot tell.

My left foot gave me increasing trouble during the 1950s. It was often painful and discouraging. Somewhere about 1959 I gave up dancing *Swan Lake*, feeling my technique too undermined by unconsciously trying to save the bad foot. In October 1958 Fred had presented *Ondine*. It was the ballet I had dreamed of, and worked for, and waited for him to create. It was the perfect character for me, naïve, shy, loyal and loving and a creature of the sea. For the second act Fred drew on his shipwreck experiences with Ruth Page and Tom Fisher so brilliantly that queasy members of the audience actually felt seasick. I was so happy with the ballet that it was no wrench at all to lose *Swan Lake*, which had always frightened me. My only fear was that, once I renounced the most difficult ballets, my strength would decrease and easier roles become difficult in their place.

I knew my mastery of the classical technique would decline. Consequently, I was worried when the long-postponed visit of the Royal Ballet to Russia was announced. We were due to open the tour in June 1961, in Leningrad, the home of Karsavina, Pavlova, Nijinsky, Petipa and the highest traditions of classical ballet. Shortly before the tour I was in despair about my foot. The doctor decided to try a manipulation under anaesthetic, with excellent results. As the Russian tour progressed, I regained confidence and some facility in steps where I had long been forced to cheat because of the pain. The tour itself was a curious experience. I had expected the Soviet Union to be more advanced, and therefore better, because the country had been communist for longer than the other 'Iron Curtain' states I had visited. The first and lasting surprise was to find that, without wishing to be impolite about it, everything concerned with everyday living was worse. Objects were of the commonest functional type, since there was no incentive to make better ones. It looked as though Russian artisans had, over the years, lost their initiative in matters of style. Judging by the glories of the past that were on display in museums, there must be a wealth of creative talent smouldering, but without means of expression. Indeed, one was hard put to find anything of beauty that was not a product of one of the three institutions destroyed by the Revolution; the Czars, the Church or the rich merchants. I well understand that under Czarist rule millions lived in absolute poverty, without education or the bare necessities of life, and that those abominable conditions have now been wiped out, despite the toll taken by World War II. But even so, other countries in the West have changed dramatically in those fifty-odd years, and I couldn't help feeling that a little bit of free enterprise might do wonders. Certainly, in the realm of ballet, there existed a frustration expressed more in a glance of surprise or a shrug of regret than in words. Someone said they were happy we brought Stravinsky's *Firebird* because they had been hoping for years it could be produced in Russia; our showing of the ballet might win approval from the authorities. Unhappily it didn't, and *Firebird* is still not danced there, though I cannot see what harm it would do and it would be a stupendous vehicle for their marvellous ballerinas.

We were greeted on the tarmac at Leningrad by those formal speeches about friendship between countries, which are always superfluous because the people are always ready to be friends; it is only the government officials who have to state it. Those members of the Kirov Ballet who were not dancing in Paris with their company were at the airport to greet us, and as friendly as could be. We all felt the instant understanding that exists between ballet dancers the world over. Perhaps that is why I refuse to take an active part in political activities. If everyone danced, we wouldn't have time for political problems!

The first morning we were there, two of the younger boys in our company were arrested right in front of the Kirov Theatre while trying to photograph the poster, printed in Russian, which announced our appearance. They were soon released, and I felt sure it must have been a routine move to warn us all to behave circumspectly.

The Kirov Theatre is very beautiful and packed with historical memories. How moving it was to stand on that stage and look out into the delicate blue and gold auditorium, or to work in the studios and to walk in the corridors and sit in the dressing rooms. All these places had been inhabited by the greatest Russian and Italian ballerinas. I thought of the journeys made by Legnani and Brianza from Milan to this beautiful but remote northern city. However did they get there in those days? I suppose by train via Warsaw in the 1880s, but what about Taglioni going from Paris in 1837? It must have been a very long and tiring journey by carriage. But then again, it took Pavlova and Genée six weeks by boat to go to Australia. It must have been difficult to keep in training for so long on the high seas. Air travel really has changed life for dancers more than for most. One can go to class in London today and San Francisco tomorrow, hardly missing a step.

For the opening night programme in Leningrad we danced *Ondine*. As I stood, with Michael, on the bulwark of the ship in Act II, I remembered Karsavina writing about her first performance in the ballet *Corsaire*. She described how elated she became in the scene of mutiny and shipwreck with the crescendo of music augmented by storm effects and the firing of cannons. Such moments on the stage are heaven. The evening was very well received, the Russian dancers in particular being excited to see a new three-act ballet that was modern and yet romantic. I felt that the audiences as a whole were very serious in their attitude to new works. Even if there were some things they didn't like, they went home and discussed the choreography, music, conception of the subject and the dancing thoroughly and at length, weighing up the pluses and minuses. They had fewer opportunities to see foreign dance companies than London and New York audiences. It was a public more like that which existed in London before the war.

Normally I am not much of a sightseer, but Leningrad's beautiful architecture tempted me out. There are few modern buildings in the centre of the city to mar the calm grace of the streets, squares, churches and the Winter Palace and the Neva River. The white nights of June cast an eerie glow over Leningrad as one looked out of the hotel window before going to sleep. Couples walked in the square below at two in the morning as though they never rest in the summer months, trying to store up daylight for the long dark winter.

Three days after our opening night, Georgina Parkinson spoke by phone to her husband in London. He told her that a dancer had defected from the Kirov company as they left Paris for London, where they were to dance at Covent Garden in an exchange with our visit to Russia. He was reported to be their best young dancer. Georgina's husband knew no more than that. Of course, nothing was said in Leningrad, but I did notice that a ballerina who had come shyly to my dressing room two or three times appeared no more. Rudolf Nureyev, the defecting dancer, later told me she was the one he had admired the most. She was a very sensitive artist, and he had learned a good deal from watching her.

The Sleeping Beauty had been created in that very theatre, which gave me a terrible complex. I think I gave my worst performance ever the night I danced it at the Kirov. It was not the general public's judgement I feared, but that of the Russian dancers and teachers. There had been a time, when I was dancing in Helsinki, that they told me Maya Plisetskaya was arriving from Moscow in time to see my Giselle. I literally stumbled through the evening, imagining how she was assessing each step, and then, at the end of the terrible performance, they told me her flight had been delayed and she had seen only the last two minutes. I could have kicked myself.

From Leningrad we flew to Moscow. Ulanova was among the dancers waiting at the foot of the plane steps to greet us. She drove me in her car to the hotel and, as she left, she hastily pressed a little box into my hand. Inside was a beautiful antique oval ring, with several rows of little diamonds set in gold. She invited me to her flat overlooking the river in the centre of Moscow near the Kremlin. One of our interpreters took me, and there was another guest, a Russian dancer, and Ulanova's husband, the painter Vadim Rindin. It was a very friendly gathering, and the atmosphere in her home was cosy and simple. Ulanova is a ballerina who had to work and fight to gain her place in Soviet ballet. A product of the more lyrical, and in my opinion much better, Leningrad school, she was transferred to Moscow and had to compete with the flashier dancers there. She had no need to worry. The beauty of her style and interpretations won the day. But she must have felt the way I did in Milan, where the public wanted to *see* that the steps were difficult. Her health was not good when we were in Moscow. She could not eat several of the dishes at her table, not even potatoes, which I always thought so bland and harmless. I wondered if the war-time privations were not the cause. There must have been grim times when people in Russian cities were near the starvation point.

We dined very early, about four-thirty, and afterwards drove in her car, with a chauffeur, into the country. We got out and walked through silver birches to some open rolling fields, gathering wild flowers and talking about this and that, mostly ballet and art. It was a lyrical day, the happiest of the whole tour. She said she was very upset she could not attend the opening, as she had to go to a sanatorium for four days, but would be back the following week by which time she expected to be recovered. In fact, she was ill until the very last performance, when she suddenly came to my dressing room as I was preparing for *The Sleeping Beauty*. She was as simple and friendly as could be, picked up a pair of my ballet shoes with curiosity and examined them carefully. I did the same with Soviet shoes. I felt that the warmth she showed me broke through her natural reserve, and I appreciated it all the more.

Before leaving Moscow I was anxious to send flowers to Ulanova at her flat. It was then I realized there were no flower shops! Somebody must make up the huge presentation baskets that adorn receptions, but it might be done inside the Kremlin for all one could see. I understood why ballet fans go out and pick flowers in the fields to throw down on to the stage for their favourites – I was struck in the chest by a remarkably solid and heavy water lily after *Ondine* in Leningrad! It was an appropriate flower, but I wished they would stick to daisies and cornflowers. (In London, a front-row enthusiast found he could lob his little bunches of flowers over the orchestra pit more successfully if they were weighted; I had to keep a very wary eye on his missiles as I was bowing and smiling graciously in front of the curtain.)

Finally I telephoned a secretary at the British Embassy and asked his advice on how to send the flowers to Ulanova. He had to think hard. Then he said, 'Will you leave it with me for a while, and I will see what I can find out.' He phoned back in the evening. 'Mme Ulanova has the flowers,' he said. 'I thought the best thing would be to go to the market, where I bought some flowers from the peasant women. There was a bit of a problem about wrapping them, but I managed to find some paper and do them up in a nice bouquet. Then there was more trouble about getting them to her. Anyway I was able to trace her address and I got a taxi and took them there myself. I rather enjoyed it all, it took most of the day.'

I heard that Elizabeth Taylor had arrived in Moscow for the film festival, for which a new theatre was completed before our eyes in about ten days, with hundreds of workers on night and day shifts! It was truly impressive to see how quickly the work could be done. I asked the nicest of our very agreeable interpreters to take me to Elizabeth's hotel. We found her in her suite with Eddie Fisher, a male secretary, an assistant and her hairdresser. After the visit, which was altogether enjoyable, the interpreter had a look of wonder on her face. As we rode back in the taxi she said, 'She is beautiful, like a queen. How extraordinary it must be to live like that with all those adoring men around her.'

Although I wouldn't have missed the Russian tour for anything in the world, I did miss certain comforts (though the people who most disliked life in Russia were our stage crew, the British workers). One day, sitting over a very inadequate lunch, I was handed a cable. It was from Venice and read: *Drinking your health in champagne at Harry's Bar stop Wish you were here love Tug and John.*

They could not have guessed how very much more *I* wished I was *there*!

Soon after the Russian tour Michael Somes gave up his strenuous dancing roles. We had such a fine partnership that I think he was almost sad that I continued without him, but just then my left foot was much better than it had been for years, and I began to dance *Swan Lake* again, now partnered by David Blair, who took over most of Michael's roles. *Swan Lake* was in the Royal Ballet programme for their visit to the Baalbek Festival in Lebanon. I decided to dance the ballet in sections, the second act one night and the third act the next, in order to regain my stamina gradually.

The ruins of Baalbek are incredibly imposing by day, and fantastic by night. The inside temple walls are standing and many of the gigantic outside columns too. Some of the columns lay spread across the forecourt like mammoth slices of jelly roll, which is belittling them, but I couldn't help thinking of it when I saw them. The moment when they crashed down, probably in an earthquake, must have been like the end of the world.

At one time the temple was buried in sand to halfway up the walls, and one can now see the iron rings thirty feet up at which camels were tethered before excavation revealed the full magnitude of the beautiful carved doorway. Leading up to the forecourt is a wide flight of steps, where a temporary wooden stage is built for the festival performances. The upper steps form a part of the background scenery, with the illuminated temple resembling a palace from which the dancers emerge. A partly ruined Crusaders' fortress, built on to the side, serves as a dressing room area. The stage is an enchanted place under the bright stars. It is a strange, pagan, Arabian Nights setting, but real, not made of painted canvas. There is a wall at Baalbek, serving as the foundation of the largest temple, which was built before the recording of time. The wall is built of stones so immense that it would be a major engineering feat to assemble them today. No one can say who brought them to that place or by what means. Curiously enough, that most artificial of arts, the ballet, fits into Baalbek with an aptness that can only be explained by the fact that dance itself is also as old as time.

The hot Lebanese sun forced us to rehearse in the early morning, before it was strong enough to fry us. Our hotel was forty minutes away, so we were up at first light to drive across the wide fertile plateau ringed by dark mountains. On our way we passed little villages and an abundance of vines and fruit trees. It was easy to imagine that the Garden of Eden was not far distant from that luxuriant place. Our driver, George Ibrahim Issa, was born and lived all his life in the village of Zahlé, yet he saw the ballet with his soul; he never questioned what it was about, he just understood.

NINE

When I was in Russia I had taken the opportunity to ask Mme Furtseva, then Minister of Culture, if Galina Ulanova could come to dance at the fund-raising gala in aid of the Royal Academy of Dancing that was to take place in November. On returning to London from the Baalbek visit, I received a letter regretting deeply that our date coincided with an important State celebration at which Ulanova would be dancing in Moscow. This news was distressing, because it was the fourth year the Royal Academy had held this special matinée, and we were running out of attractions. Ulanova's presence would have given immense prestige to the occasion – and would have sold the tickets instantly.

Colette Clark organized the galas, with Mary, Duchess of Roxburghe, acting as Chairman. The three of us met in gloom to consider what action to take. Colette said, 'I hear that Rudolf Nureyev, this dancer who defected from the Kirov, is sensational. He's just finished a season in Paris with the de Cuevas Ballet.' 'A brilliant idea,' we said, and Colette spent two weeks chasing after him by phone. By the time she got his number in Nice he had left for Copenhagen. That was perfect because he was working in class with my old friend Vera Volkova. Messages passed endlessly between Vera and Colette, and were relayed at either end to Nureyev and me. In London, they went something like this:

COLETTE: He says he wants to dance with you.
MARGOT: I've never set eyes on him, and anyway I've asked John Gilpin to dance *Spectre of the Rose* with me. Ask Vera if he is a good dancer.
COLETTE, the next day: Vera says he's adamant about dancing with you, and that he's marvellous.
MARGOT: He sounds rather tiresome to me.
COLETTE: No, they say he's extraordinary. They say that he has such a presence he only has to walk on the stage and lift his arm and you can see the swans by the lake. I think it would be wonderful if you danced with Nureyev as well as Gilpin.
MARGOT: The more I hear of him the worse he sounds. I don't mean as a dancer, but why should he decide to dance with me when he's only twenty-three and I've never even met him?
COLETTE: Well, Vera thinks he's a genius. She says he has 'the nostrils', you know what I mean? People of genius have 'nostrils'.

Colette dilated hers to illustrate the point. She is very intelligent, much younger than I, and has watched ballet all her life. She was always sure about Rudolf.

He gave in about dancing with me, and asked for Rosella Hightower instead. Then came another request: would Frederick Ashton choreograph a solo for him? Fred agreed nervously, saying, 'I don't know what kind of solo.' He needn't have worried. Rudolf knew exactly what he wanted. So all was decided, and Vera Volkova, her job completed, said, 'Well, as it were, now I hand you the baby!'

We knew Nureyev was anxious to see London, so we invited him to come over secretly for three days. The press wouldn't know about it and we would give him a false name – even for the ballet world. We chose the name of a Polish dancer, Roman Jasman, who was also engaged to appear in the gala.

On the day he was due to arrive from Paris, Colette lunched with me at home. He was due at 5:30 p.m. I had to go to a cocktail party, but planned to meet them both afterwards. At 3:30 p.m. the telephone rang. 'Here is Nureyev,' said a voice. It was a deeper voice than I had expected, crisp, the accent pronounced. 'Where are you?' I asked. 'In Paris?' 'I am one hour in London airport,' he replied. 'Oh! We expected you later. The car isn't there. Wait where you are and I will send it at once. It will take twenty minutes.' 'I will take taxi,' he said. 'Don't do that. It's complicated. Wait where you are!' Panic! The chauffeur dashed off to the airport.

Forty-five minutes later the telephone rang again. 'Here is Nureyev.' 'Didn't the chauffeur find you?' 'No. I will take taxi.' 'No,' I said, 'ring me again in five minutes. I will try to get hold of the chauffeur there.' But they could not locate each other, so I told Nureyev to take a taxi after all. It was getting late, so I dressed for the cocktail party. I remember the dress very well – it was navy pleated chiffon and had a satin ribbon round the hem and a white camellia at the neck. The reason I remember it so well is because Rudolf saw it again one year later, and immediately noticed that the satin ribbon had lost its true colour from dry cleaning. 'What happened to ribbon? Looks different.' He misses nothing. As he stepped out of the taxi, Nureyev seemed smaller than I had expected, probably because I was standing above him on the doorstep. He had a funny, pinched little face with that curious pallor peculiar to so many dancers from Russia. I noticed the nostrils at once.

The three of us sat over tea – five sugars for Rudolf. As I was summing him up, I could see that he was doing the same to me. He was extremely polite, sitting up rather straight but intending to look relaxed. His sentences, in limited English, were concise and clear. I said something light and silly. Suddenly he laughed and his whole face changed. He lost the 'on guard' look, and his smile was generous and captivating. 'Oh, thank goodness!' I said. 'I didn't know Russians laughed. They were so serious when we were there.' I left Colette to explain the arrangements for his incognito stay in London. Later, when Colette asked me how I had found him, I said, 'I like him nine-tenths, but once or twice I saw a steely look in his eye.' His face had reflected every thought, changing like lightning. Then a very cold look flashed through his eyes, just there long enough for me to catch it. Now I realize it was a manifestation of fear. I haven't seen it for a long time, as he is very self-assured these days. In the beginning, though, it was always just below the surface, ready to show itself at the slightest suspicion of attack.

Fred choreographed the new solo behind closed doors. As the curtain rose on the performance, Rudolf was standing swathed in a long red mantle. He rushed forward and threw it off to dance freely to the passionate music of Scriabin. Many people put a symbolic interpretation on the hampering red cloak, whether correctly or not I never knew, but I think Fred and Billie Chappell, who designed the costume, were more likely to have been thinking of the theatrical effect, which was terrific.

Colette and I had watched the first rehearsal in the theatre. Rudolf was a riot – not intentionally, but his character revealed itself through his dancing and everything was there, including his sense of clowning. He was actually desperately serious; nervous, intense and repeating every step with all his might until he almost knocked himself out with the effort. From time to time he stopped to take off his leg warmers before a very difficult step; after the exertion he stopped again, let out a breath rapidly and forcefully with a sound like a sibilant 'Ho'. On went the woollen tights. After a few more steps he changed his shoes and put the leg warmers back on top of the woollen tights. So it went on for two hours. He was working like a steam engine. Colette and I couldn't help laughing. At the same time, I thought he would never get through the solo if he put so much effort into each movement. Surely he ought to save himself somewhere? But I hadn't counted on Rudolph's strength. I think it was from that morning that we took to him wholeheartedly. Afterwards, when I suggested he should save something in the middle so as to finish the long solo strongly, he said with what sounded like pride, 'In Paris I never once finish variation!' I said, 'Wouldn't it be better if you did?' He considered the point as though it were an original idea.

When it came to the gala, I visited all the dressing rooms beforehand to see if the artists needed anything. Rudolf said, 'They send wrong wig!' He was preparing for the *Swan Lake* pas de deux with Rosella Hightower, and in his hand was a blond wig – a very blond wig. It was too late to change it, just before his first entrance. Colette and I agreed afterwards that if he had the success he did, which was nothing short of tumultuous, while wearing that wig, he was certainly great. I have never changed that opinion. He is great in that he is unique, not only an exceptional dancer but a unique personality, fortified by one of the sharpest brains imaginable.

The gala took place in the afternoon at the Theatre Royal, Drury Lane. At the end, the crowd mobbed Rosella and Rudolf outside the theatre. I could hardly drag her to the car as people pushed this way and that trying to touch them and get autographs. Rosella's costume, which she carried over her arm, was ripped and almost lost in the mêlée.

That evening there was a party at our house for the cast to relax. I admired Rudolf's patience in talking to many strangers as well as the dancers whom he knew, and it was not till the last guests were leaving that he asked to be dropped in the King's Road, which I am sure he had scented out the first day.

Earlier in the evening, Tito had asked him conversationally, 'What were you doing in Copenhagen?' Rudolf replied darkly, 'Is story better not told.' I noticed how quickly he was picking up English.

Like all dancers in Russia, who are cut off from many of the ballet contacts we take for granted, Rudolf had a discerning knowledge of English ballet acquired by a sort of sixth sense before he left home. He knew the first person he wanted to meet was Ninette de Valois, and he invited her to lunch. They got on like a house on fire. The Irish and the Tartar understood each other at sight. Her wit, shrewdness, humanity and intelligence delighted him, and he has revered her ever since. Of course, he was just the kind of rebellious talent and engaging 'enfant terrible' that she loved.

Part of his defence system when he was nervous was a penetrating criticism. We all came in for it in turn, and some of us didn't like it at all. It is quite amusing now to remember how barbed he sometimes was during the first few years. His biting remarks clashed with Fred Ashton's wit a few times, and the sparks flew. But he always acknowledged Fred's genius, and a true affection grew between them. After one such bout, when Fred had parried Rudolf's cutting remark with a lethal reproof, Fred put on his long-nosed Peruvian face, with his eyes half-closed, and said: 'I gave as good as I got, my dear!' Certainly, no one has ever been known to get the better of Fred in a challenging verbal exchange.

De Valois told me that Rudolf would dance *Giselle* at Covent Garden in February, three months ahead. 'Do you want to do it with him?' she asked. My immediate reaction was to say, 'Oh, my goodness! I think it would be like mutton dancing with lamb. Don't you think I'm too old?' I said I would give my answer the next day. I discussed it with Tito, and we came to the conclusion that Rudolf was going to be the big sensation of the next year and I had better get on the bandwagon or else get out. I called de Valois to thank her for asking me, and accepted. I had often expressed my abhorrence of old ballerinas dancing with young men. Once again, however, it was a case of 'Never name the well ...!'

That winter I danced with Michael Somes in Monte Carlo, where a rich English lady, none too sober at a party, expressed her astonishment that Christopher Soames, a British Minister of State, should be appearing in a ballet at the Casino. Rudolf came over from Cannes with Rosella Hightower and Erik Bruhn. He stood in my dressing room, looking like a little boy, and said, 'Tell me. I must be in London long time for rehearsals. I cannot stay so long in hotel. What you think I do?' I said, 'I don't know. I will think about it and tell you tomorrow.' He had stayed in our Embassy on his short incognito visit to London, and I told Tito: 'It's very funny. I'm sure Nureyev really wants to stay with us, but I'm rather suspicious. Supposing the Russians have made a deal allowing him to remain in the West on condition he does some spying or something. What do you think?' Tito thought my imagination was overworking.

Rudolf came to stay and was on his very best behaviour. It was at least two weeks before he tentatively mentioned the fact that he hated cold roast beef. I love it, and often serve it when there are no other guests. It seemed Rudolf had never eaten meat cold in Russia.

By now he no longer looked pinched, and his colour was improving. He liked the house, but I saw he was anxious about something, yet extremely hesitant to speak. 'What's the matter?' I asked. 'I am like dying,' he said. 'Why?' 'Four days I hear no music,' he replied. We rarely play music as both Tito and I, in different ways, find it distracting – he from his thoughts and I because the rhythm calls me. Poor Rudolf literally fed on music, and he was like a starving man in the silence around him.

The first *Giselle* rehearsal found us both edgy. With a new partner there is some carpentry necessary to fit the two different versions together. Usually each does as he or she is accustomed to do, until there comes a section

247

that doesn't match. Then one says, 'What do you do here?' And the other says, 'What do *you* do? I do this.'

Most of the men say, 'I will do it your way, how does it go?' Rudolf, however, said, 'Don't you think this way better?' We entered into some negotiations, and each altered a few steps here and there. What mattered to me most was the intensity of his involvement in the role. Two hours went past in no time at all. I was Giselle and he Albrecht. Often he was Rudolf showing me, with infinite exactitude, how I could better do some step that I was trying to remaster now that my left foot no longer hurt. At other times he was practising his own solos, still like the old steam engine. He literally *became* Albrecht, and there was an extraordinary harmony between our interpretations. I was deeply impressed by the unexpected felicity of working with him, and I forgot my complexes about mutton and lamb. We were happy with each other over *Giselle*.

During those rehearsal weeks I danced the complete *Swan Lake* with David Blair. It was difficult after the two-year break, but I knew the fact of dancing the most taxing of all ballets would give me more strength for the *Giselle*. I was having greater trouble than usual with the fouettés in rehearsal, and Rudolf asked, 'What is your mechanic for fouetté?' I was dumbfounded by the question. I had never thought of the 'mechanic'; I just did them with determination. I faltered in my answer and tried the step again. 'Left arm is too back,' he said, and, with that one simple correction, I recovered my old form easily. I learned a great deal simply from watching him in class. Never had I seen each step practised with such exactitude and thoroughness. It was paradoxical that the young boy everyone thought so wild and spontaneous in his dancing cared desperately about technique, whereas I, the cool English ballerina, was so much more interested in the emotional aspect of the performance.

Indeed, when I fling myself into the rapture of, say, Juliet, and nearly overbalance the two of us, he will say, 'Don't get hysterical.'

Rudolf came to my dressing room after *Swan Lake*. He

seemed genuinely impressed as he said, 'It is very beautiful performance.' But he added that, although he marvelled at the way in which I did the mime scene (dating from the original production and no longer done in Russia), he thought he would not be able to do the scene himself when we danced it in the summer. He thought he would feel silly standing about doing nothing while I told the story in gesture, and added, with a touch of embarrassment, 'I am afraid I will ruin your *Swan Lake*.' I looked him straight in the eye and said amiably, 'Just you try.'

Meanwhile, as we prepared for the first *Giselle*, Rudolf explored London and London life. Although, as I had realized from the day I saw him handling his first press conference for the Royal Academy of Dancing Gala, no one is better able to take care of himself than Rudolf, he nevertheless had a 'little boy lost' quality that made one want to help him. I became what I called 'the London nanny'. He had another in Monte Carlo, one in Paris and gradually acquired them in almost every city in the world.

Sitting down to lunch after four hours of rehearsing, and spending the energy that most men would not use in four weeks, he would be pale, exhausted and prickly. 'I hate weak people,' he would announce, looking ravenous as he waited for a big bowl of soup. 'All should be killed!' It was the Tartar speaking. Then, after a huge steak and several cups of tea, he would regain his lust for living, and say, 'Trouble is, I suppose I do not have courage to be wicked as I want.'

Among his boyish characteristics was an inability to say 'I am sorry' and a difficulty in expressing standard social phrases like 'Thank you for your help.' They apparently struck him as stilted or false. At the end of the first *Giselle* performance, in front of an overwhelmingly enthusiastic audience of shouting and stamping Londoners, emotion brought him on to one knee as he kissed my hand. It was his way of expressing genuine feelings, untainted by conventional words. Thereafter, a strange attachment formed between us which we have never been able to explain satisfactorily, and which, in a way, one could describe as a deep affection, or love, especially if one believes that love has many forms and degrees. But the fact remains that Rudolf was desperately in love with someone else at the time, and, for me, Tito is always the one with the black eyes.

Rudolf one day suffered a personal rebuff. He groaned and said, 'Better to have stone in place of heart.' I tried to comfort him by saying, 'You must think how much you give to other people. Look how marvellous it is for me to dance with you. You have brought new illumination to a ballet I've danced hundreds of times. If you had no heart you couldn't do that.'

Even while we were rehearsing and dancing *Giselle* in February 1962, I was deeply involved in the diplomatic round with Tito, who had once again taken up his post as Ambassador. After the morning dress rehearsal for that first performance, I lunched with Mary Roxburghe, then paid two courtesy calls on Ambassadresses – Belgian and Colombian – and dined at the Japanese Embassy. My days were jigsaw puzzles of rehearsals, visits, interviews, photographs, RAD meetings, receptions and dinners. The daily morning class was, as always, the only constant factor, come hell or high water. In the middle of March I took a long weekend in Panama, getting back Tuesday in time to dance *Ondine* on Thursday. The following week I danced *Ondine* on Tuesday, spent Wednesday in Paris with Tito and danced *Sleeping Beauty* in London on Friday. Five minutes later I was on my way to Australia for a tour which ended in Manila and Hong Kong. It was the end of May before I saw London again, and then I went straight back into the same round.

Tito decided we should live more in Panama, as he felt his father, who was getting on in years, needed him. We were privately discussing whether to sell our London home or not when a remarkably gifted estate agent succeeded in arranging a sale between Tito, who had not put the house on the market, and a purchaser, who was not especially trying to buy. The agent had not even seen the house when he initiated the negotiations. The formalities were soon completed, and I had just two weeks to pack up the accumulated chaos of seven years. In the cellar I found an unopened, unmarked wooden crate. I guessed it was not the kind of thing I should discuss over the telephone with Tito in Panama, so I put it in a tin trunk under some curtains and shipped it off with the furniture, hoping for the best.

By the time the stuff was delivered to our new home in Panama the Government was less friendly to Tito, and the customs inspector was on the lookout. All day long the big containers were being unpacked and our possessions carried into the house. When I saw the tin trunk my heart sank. I directed the unloaders to one room, and Tito directed the inspector's attention in another, while the wooden crate was dispersed innocently among the glass and china already checked. It was a tense moment because Tito had told me it contained hand grenades – a leftover from the revolution days.

In July, Rudolf and I danced *Swan Lake*. We rehearsed Act II, in which he had told me he felt unable to play the mime scene. I did not mind learning his dance version, but I objected to some of the other changes he proposed. I said, 'Rudolf, I have been doing this ballet since 1938.' He giggled a bit, and I quickly added, 'I suppose that was before you were born?' He replied, 'No, just exact year.' It broke us both up completely. As our rehearsal progressed we came to loggerheads. Neither of us was prepared to give an inch. Finally, I said, 'We had better go and have some tea, otherwise this will ruin our friendship.' The same thing happened next day with Act III. We reached hopeless deadlock and tempers were rising. So we broke off to go and laugh at other matters over lunch. Apart from one morning on the stage at the open-air theatre in Nervi, Italy, where the first performance took place, that was the sum total of our rehearsals for *Swan Lake*. The performances came out beautifully.

The RAD Gala came up that year in December. Two weeks before the date Rudolf had some trouble with his ankle and was obliged to rest it for a month, which caused great consternation and some cancellations of gala bookings. I said jokingly to Rudolf, 'This is really too much! We had four very successful galas before you came along, and now everyone is asking for their money back because you can't appear.' He said, 'I have very good friend in Budapest, Viktor Rona, why don't you ask him?' 'Whatever would I dance with him?' I asked. Rudolf, never at a loss for ideas, suggested a pas de deux from *Gayane*, which he could adapt to suit me marvellously.

We got through on the phone to the Opera House in Budapest. Poor Viktor! Apparently he was called out of rehearsal to answer the telephone. When he returned he said, 'Margot Fonteyn just asked me to dance with her in London.' To which the other dancers replied, 'And I suppose the President of the United States invited you to Washington, too! Come off it.' He went to ask the theatre administrator for leave of absence, but he wouldn't believe the story either. Viktor begged me to apply personally to the administrator, who then decided to take it seriously.

Colette and I were at the airport to meet Viktor on his first visit to the West. A tall, good-looking young man with black curly hair and beautiful eyes came through the barrier dressed in a big sheepskin coat with fur collar. The waiting press photographers took aim with their cameras as I advanced to greet him. He saw me and a heart-melting smile spread over his face as he threw open his arms and said, 'You are my heart's desire. Only you for me!' Then he gave me a big bear hug. The press loved it. So did I. It transpired that these were the only two English sentences Viktor knew, having learnt them from the movies.

Rudolf was about to leave for Australia and did not want to jeopardize Viktor's position in Hungary by meeting him publicly. So I organized a cloak-and-dagger rendezvous in the car park – a procedure I had picked up from Sir Pierson Dixon's super-efficient staff in New York after the Panama revolution.

Viktor was as different from Rudolf as chalk from cheese, but he won all the hearts with his warm personality and vigorous dancing. On the stage he was a winning mixture, half agile tiger and half cuddly bear. The gala was a success after all, and Viktor met Queen Elizabeth, the Queen Mother, at the end of the performance.

He was due to return to Budapest immediately, but I had a call from the American Ballet Theater. Lucia Chase wondered if I could dance for her at an important gala in Washington in two days' time. I said there would be no time to rehearse, and I could only manage if Viktor and I went together and repeated *Gayane*. But he was Hungarian; how could they possibly get a U.S. visa for him at a day's notice? Miraculously, the visa was granted in a matter of hours, and Viktor really did dance for the President of the United States in Washington, because Jacqueline Kennedy, who was the guest of honour, telephoned the President fifteen minutes before our entrance, asking him to come over to the theatre to see it.

Tito and I thought Viktor should not go home without seeing New York, so we took him to the top of the Empire State Building at sunset. He stayed for an hour, absolutely enraptured, until I thought we would never get him down and back to Hungary.

Tito and I went to spend a short time together in our new home in Panama. It was a heavenly place, a small quiet house with blue-tiled floors. The terrace opened on to a stretch of lawn that dropped down to the beach. I was happy all day long watching the tide rise and fall as I waited for Tito to come home. There was a big mango tree in the garden, and a shy iguana, who lived under the tiles of the roof. He came out to sun himself in the morning, retreating hurriedly when he saw me, and making a funny clattering sound as his tail swung round and struck the tiles. A friend brought us two puppies, which Tito named Otoque and Bona, after the little islands where we had sheltered so happily in his revolution. Otoque was handsome and thoughtful, like Tito; Bona was silly and impulsive, like me.

Two nights before Christmas, at about three in the morning, Tito let out an odd strangled sound in his sleep and sat up gasping. I awoke and saw him sitting on the edge of the bed. 'What's the matter, did you have a nightmare?' I asked. 'No. I don't know. I don't know what happened.' He got up and walked around for a while, without being able to explain exactly what he had felt. I went back to sleep. At six-thirty his sister telephoned to say that she had just reached Panama from Boston, where she had accompanied their father to the Mayo Clinic. He had died of a heart attack on the return flight, at 3.00 a.m.

The shadows that are cast by coming events more often than not fall unnoticed. By chance, I lately opened a little book to find inside a dedication from Leslie Edwards for the first performance of *The Quest*. The date is April 1943, almost exactly twenty years before the first performance of *Marguerite and Armand*, which took place in March 1963. The title of the book is *La Dame aux Camélias*.

Frederick Ashton had earlier been drawn to the idea of a ballet on the subject of Marguerite Gautier, the heroine of Alexandre Dumas's novel. He studied the story of Marie Duplessis, on whose life the novel was based, and he almost mounted the ballet to music written by Jean Françaix for a version presented at the Paris Opéra. At the last minute he decided to shelve that production, and another two years passed until he heard a piece of music by Liszt that brought the story rushing back to his imagination, all the elements fitting together. In the meantime, Rudolf had burst headlong into our world.

Fred liked the coincidence that Liszt actually had an affair with Marie Duplessis, and he quoted her words beseeching Liszt to take her to Italy with him: 'I will be no trouble to you. I sleep all day, go to the theatre in the evening and at night you may do what you will with me.' The words were particularly touching – I don't know why. I think they contain something of that vulnerability of the feminine woman, like Marilyn Monroe. I fell in love with the character of Marguerite.

Fred cast Michael Somes as the father of Armand, and choreographed our renunciation scene alone. When is was finished, Rudolf joined the rehearsal. As Michael and I played the scene over, an electrical storm built up in the studio. We came to the end, and Rudolf tore into his entrance and the following pas de deux with a passion more real than life itself, generating one of those fantastic moments when a rehearsal becomes a burning performance.

There were more photographs taken during the rehearsals of this ballet than for any other I can remember. Cecil Beaton took his own inimitable pictures; no one has equalled his airy style of photography, evoking mood, period and personality in so masterly and subtle a fashion. The costume fittings did not go at all smoothly – they seldom do. Beaton designed matchless costumes for me, but I had a slight wrangle about the red camellias, which, for reasons of modesty connected with the novel, I was embarrassed to wear. Without liking to explain, I insisted on wearing white flowers. Meanwhile, Rudolf was vehemently refusing to wear the long coat-tails of the original design, saying he didn''t want to look like a waiter. It was no use my pointing out that Bobby had looked elegant and poetic in *Apparitions*. Rudolf chopped the coat-tails to a length that satisfied his keen sensibility to his own proportions, regardless of what might suit anyone else or what the designer thought. He had discarded wigs altogether with the first *Giselle* dress rehearsal, and rapidly developed a strong personal style, with an instinct for forthcoming fashions in his street clothes that anticipated long hair and Nehru collars.

There was a high degree of expectation before *Marguerite and Armand*, generated by Ashton's choreography and Beaton's designs – and by now a web of romantic attachment that had very publicly been spun about Rudolf and myself. Hardly anyone knew where truth ended and fantasy began. But what a plum of a ballet it was for me, and what a success for all of us.

On the day of the first performance Rudolf brought me a little white camellia tree, which seemed to symbolize the basic simplicity of our relationship in the midst of so much furore. It was only for a year that we had been dancing together. As we were taking innumerable curtain calls, with flowers raining down from the gallery slips, I said, 'Well, now do you think you will stay another year, even though you are so unhappy with us?' He replied, 'Margot, you know I will never be happy anywhere.' For he was still defensive and dreadfully critical. It was as if he had expected England to be a veritable paradise and all who dwelt there brilliant creatures of great beauty. Naturally we were a bit of a disappointment. On the other hand, when I apologized for us being so ugly he replied, 'I did not say I not like. Ugly can be charming.'

Soon the Royal Ballet set off yet again on an American tour. *Time* and *Newsweek* gave Rudolf cover stories simultaneously. One of their representatives, interviewing me prior to filing his story, persisted in one particular question, phrased differently each time. Finally I said, 'Tell me what answer you are trying to get and I will tell you if I agree with it.' He was wanting me to say something about the wild Tartar being tamed by my influence. If he had stopped to consider that twenty-three years of brainwashing in Russia hadn't exactly tamed Rudolf, he would have seen how unlikely that was. I told him I thought Rudolf behaved in the West exactly as he would in Tartary.

Little Genghis Khan was in fact growing up like a young lion. I learned that the secret when he snarled was to make him laugh and, thank heaven, he found quite silly things amusing, such as the sign 'Dead Slow', which I suppose is hilarious to someone approaching English with a clean eye. It wasn't long before he could make puns, too. In most pas de deux there are some lifts where the girl's arm is round the back of the boy's neck. If I put my arm too high, Rudolf finds it killingly uncomfortable and says, 'Necrophilia! Necrophilia!' even in the middle of a performance.

In New York we danced the *Corsaire* pas de deux, which we had already done in London. Then it had been programmed like a one-act ballet, with intermissions before and after. I was upset, thinking that people would feel cheated to get only ten minutes of dancing. I went to Ashton in great distress to complain. He simply said, 'Well, it will be all right. Ten minutes of *Corsaire* and twenty minutes of applause. What are you worrying about?' I was full of apprehension until the performance came. Rudolf's *Corsaire* is the stuff of which legends are made. The first step of his variation, when one clearly saw him sitting high in the air with both feet tucked under him, exactly as though he were flying on an invisible magic carpet, was beyond description. One watched with a touch of disbelief. I imagine Nijinsky's famous leap gave just that impression, as I have often heard that he appeared to stand still in the air. I am sure, though, that no one has ever danced *Corsaire* like Rudolf, and it is permissible in this case to use the adjective 'sublime'. It was so exciting to watch him from the wings that I lost all nervousness for myself and danced with a glow of exhilaration and joy. In New York the applause lasted at least twenty minutes – in fact, it only stopped when the curtain rose on the following ballet.

The Royal Ballet tour did not include Washington that year, but Jackie Kennedy invited us to make a special visit. A private plane took Fred, Michael, Rudolf, our conductor, John Lanchbery and me to tea at the White House. Jackie was almost fey, with that breathless voice and those wide-set eyes, except that I found great warmth mingled with her manner of seeming surprised that she should be the First Lady. At the same time, it was a role that suited her beautifully as she had the charm and poise and the easy dignity required for the job. She showed us the public rooms and the guest bedrooms and then, after tea, said, 'I will just see if the President is busy,' as she showed us the Cabinet Room. While she went to the Oval Office, Rudolf took the opportunity to find out what it felt like to sit in the President's chair. The President received us and astonished me by saying, 'I remember your husband, Dr Arias, told me something about sugar that I did not know. I was very grateful for the information.' He was referring to a moment the year before when Tito and I attended a big lunch at the White House. In a conversation of only two or three sentences, while standing in the doorway to the dining room as the party broke up, the President said that he understood the price of sugar was low and likely to go down as there was a world overproduction. Tito replied that he believed, on the contrary, the price was high and that the Russians could well afford to be generous to Fidel Castro because they had contracted the Cuban sugar harvest at below the market rate. Evidently Tito's information was correct, because later, Attorney-General Robert Kennedy, with characteristic candour and sense of reality, said, 'Fortunately, or unfortunately, you were right about the Cuban sugar, and the President's economic experts were wrong. Now they are after your neck.' It was more than flattering to have the incident recalled so clearly by the President without apparent prompting. I couldn't wait to report it to Tito.

Rudolf was naturally the centre of attraction and curiosity wherever he went, and he was not averse to being noticed. Usually people saw him first and then, realizing I was with him, added a nice word of appreciation to me. Not so the lady in New York, who bore down on our table and talked volubly to Rudolf in Russian while I sat by wearing what I thought was a rather becoming, wide-brimmed white hat. In the midst of her gushing, she suddenly noticed me and turned back to Rudolf, saying in English, 'Who is that? Your mother?' Another time, we arrived together at a big social bash, the kind where you have to show your invitation cards at the door. I was presented to the hostess before Rudolf. When she heard his name she was all over him like a tent, waving her arms and effusing for several minutes while I stood to one side. At the end of her fascinating performance she pulled herself together and said, 'And where is Miss Fonteyn?'

Rudolf's talent for brevity is at its peak with hostesses. Once, when he was dancing every night on a long U.S. tour, he explained a truth in four concise words: 'Chicken lunch, chicken performance.' To the lady who gushed, 'Mr Nureyev, I just can't leave without speaking to you,' he said simply, 'Why?' I love, too, his fund of Russian maxims, such as: 'Ask wife three times and do opposite.' Best of all is his quickness with words and phrases. A mutual friend, who saw him during a long tour he undertook with the Canadian ballet, asked, 'Where is Margot now?' And Rudolf, putting on a mock tragic face, replied, 'She is dancing with a younger man.'

It was Rudolf who persuaded me to study with the teacher Valentina Pereyaslavec at Ballet Theater School in New York. Together with several other Royal Ballet dancers, we went to her class every morning, hardly missing a day. One had to be tough to survive it, as the class was really hard. She is not tall, but more than makes up in strength and personality for what she lacks in height.

The pupils assemble before she comes into the studio, and she immediately rearranges some of their places on the barre according to a private system of her own. The Royal Ballet dancers and other distinguished guests are given certain places which no one else may usurp. Everyone stands ready to start pliés. In ringing voice, with clear enunciation, she commands, 'First position! Shoulders down. Head up. Back straight!' Then she claps her hand with astonishing force, her pianist, Valya, launches into the music as though she were playing at Carnegie Hall and away we go. The room is held in a spell, no one dares to slack or miss an exercise as one might with other teachers. Sometimes she speaks quietly: 'Arabesque. Veery beautiful.' Unexpectedly she produces a deafening hand-clap and booms: 'Passé! Attitude!' One cannot help but make a superhuman effort to do as she commands. There is an iron discipline in the room. If there is not, she draws herself up, puts her head slightly back and, with eyes almost closed, not looking at anyone she says cuttingly, 'I not like talk in class.' The culprit always knows at once. At the end of one and a half hours when the last step is done, there is a tremendous round of applause as Valya plays a fanfare and Madame curtsies to right and left, with a radiant smile, before making her exit on a cloud of gratitude and affection. It is the sense of theatre that she brings into the classroom which inspires such total attention. The curtain was rung down ten minutes early in her class one morning because three ballerinas in the front row were dancing in different tempi, one ahead of the music, one behind and one on the beat. She said nothing, put on her most serious face, looked at the floor, paused dramatically and then, with a resounding clap of her hands, announced, 'Class finished!'

She loves Rudolf and, whenever I pass through New York and snatch a class with her, she asks were he is and how he is dancing. Once it was near Christmas and I was in her dressing room when, having just inquired about Rudolf, she asked cryptically, 'You see *Vogue*?' 'No,' I replied. 'What's in it?' She made no answer but took the current issue from a side table and handed it to me. There was no expression on her face and no further conversation. Inside I found two or three pages of Richard Avedon photographs of Rudolf, artistically stark naked.

To this day I have no idea if she approved or was shocked.

Another teacher Rudolf found is Hector Zaraspé, an Argentinian, and a great comedian. When one thinks of approximately three hundred hours of rigorous class each year, for thirty or forty years of one's life, it is easy to appreciate that the teachers' personalities are immensely important. Those who love music, dancing and theatre are easier to work for than those who care most about the placing of the hips but, of course, one cannot have one without the other, and all classes are absorbing. All the same, it is nice to laugh, and Hector has a delightful sense of humour to lighten the difficulties. His English is good now, but he likes to tell of the days when he first travelled in the New York subway. The train was crowded and he was strap-hanging, hemmed in by big tough Americans. Hector is light of build, and when he reached his station he could not push his way out. Timidly he spoke to his neighbour. The huge man glowered down at him: 'What d'yer say?' he growled. Hector, more nervous than ever, repeated his phrase: 'I say, ex-squeeze me please,' and with a desperate thrust got out, somewhat alarmed by the look on the big man's face.

I invited him to Panama one Christmas so that I could holiday without losing my training. Unfortunately, he came tearing down in such a hurry that he forgot to have his American re-entry visa in order and didn't get home again for six months. He was very good-natured about it.

The death of his father had left Tito profoundly at a loss for direction in his life. At such a time of uncertainty he did not want to ask me to retire but, as I continued dancing with Rudolf, who grew stronger daily, the effort required took all my resources, and I had little left over to help Tito. It was a critical period for him, and for me, too, as I struggled to regain a technique that had eroded during the years with the bad foot. Muscles that had grown lazy did not take willingly to coming out of retirement. Subsequently, on tour in Israel, where we danced somewhat unsatisfactorily in football fields, I damaged my left calf muscle but managed to continue for another three weeks, with difficulty and in pain. Tito travelled extensively in South America, and at times it was impossible to locate each other for days on end, which added to our unhappiness. Then Tito developed a serious attack of shingles, but despite this insisted on crossing the Atlantic for a reunion while convalescent. These bleak days in our life were assuaged briefly when we managed to spend ten days together in Honolulu. A kindly doctor there repaired my leg and Tito's health. It was a small oasis in which I could once more hold Tito's hand, but he felt compelled now to involve himself in Panamanian politics, and the Covent Garden season obliged me to spend much time in London, where there was little in the purely social life to occupy a mind like Tito's, only fulfilled by tackling complex business or political problems.

As I was obviously very fond of Rudolf and spent so much time with him, it was food for scandal to those who liked it that way. I decided that there was little I could do but wait for it to pass. The truth will out eventually, I thought. Meanwhile, I worked with Rudolf and often went out with him. But I hardly ever saw him go home. He always walked off into the night, a lonely figure diminishing in perspective down a desolate street. There was something tragic in his departing step after the uproar of laughter and gaiety over supper. It is frequently so with stage people, who pay for coming out in the limelight by going home in the rain. Is it that we are stage people because we can never really live normal, settled lives? And isn't Tito one of us in his inability to settle, which explains why he understands me so well?

In the spring I was able to spend a few days campaigning in Panama with Tito. He was a candidate for the National Assembly, as a Deputy for the Province of Panama. In spite of all I have just said about stage people, my moments of pure happiness are those spent in the sun, enjoying freedom like an uncaged bird.

This time I saw a different side of Panama, the slums,

the villages, front porches, farm houses and the little corners where people came to hear Tito speak. His electioneering personality was so different from his normal contemplative demeanour. I had never heard him talk so much or with such vehemence, and everywhere there were throngs of people, poor people of all shades from café au lait to black, with hundreds of squirming, healthy, black-eyed children with laughing faces. The old ladies doted on Tito, and the young ones worked with fervour for his election. Campaigning with him every day was Alfredo Jimenez, the expressionless one whom I had last seen sailing away on the shrimp boat in the revolution. He was hoping to be at least a substitute deputy, to stand in for Tito during his absences abroad. That position, however, legally depends on the number of votes gained by each candidate in the ballot.

A young friend, Louis Martinez, came with us, not taking an active part, but deeply interested. He translated the Spanish for me as we scrambled along after Tito through the crowds, in and out of cars and helicopters, or sitting down to marvellous village meals of sancocho, a stew of chicken and root vegetables.

These pleasant days were soon over, and I had to go back to work. I left Tito to an accelerating programme of campaign meetings up to election day on 17 May. In April he was travelling to the farthest parts of the interior, addressing three or four meetings a day. By that time I was leaving London with Rudolf for a four-week season with the Australian Ballet in Sydney and Melbourne. On the long journey out, I said, 'Rudolf, you look much happier these days; what happened to you?' He never feels confident on a plane, which may account for his reply: 'I know now I want *not* to die.' At the press conferences we were besieged by questions about the secret of our partnership. We really did not know the answer, but thought it was due to the parallel ideas we held of what we were trying to do on stage. We could spark each other off along the same path, each inspiring the other to excel. For my part I felt that as long as the audience saw Rudolf they got their money's worth, and anything I did was extra, so my sense of obligation was lessened. But the Australian programmes were physically tiring, consisting of either *Giselle* or *Swan Lake* three times a week. It was while putting on my makeup for *Giselle* that I wondered if I would have time to visit the Barrier Reef in my two free days. I asked my dresser if it took long to get there and she said not. 'Approximately how long then?' I asked, to which she replied, 'Only about two days by train.' A similar answer had come from an old Panamanian farmer and his wife to whom we once gave a lift on an uncompleted road. 'When the road is finished, how long will it take from here to Nombre de Dios?' Tito asked, to which the charming and hardy old man replied, 'About four days on foot.' The road was hilly, and his wife was very happy to climb into the car, saying, 'Oh, it does hurt the knees, this road.' They were both in their sixties, at least, and quite prepared for several more hours of walking had we not chanced by.

On the Australian tour I found the competition with Rudolf really stiff. When we first danced together, it had been only his third *Giselle*. He was then still green and dancing with something of an amateur's enthusiasm. He had since gone through the period of losing his natural excitement for each performance, and was now learning to manufacture spontaneity. He did it by getting angry – it is easier to dance in a rage than in cold blood, and I noticed him looking around for an excuse, no matter how flimsy, to shout one or two profanities before an important evening. The system worked well, though at the expense of a few individuals who had to be sacrificed in a good cause. I could understand it because I did much the same thing – I made myself frightened, though, instead of angry.

Dancing every night, Rudolf was happier than I had ever seen him. This was fine, except that I could hardly compete even without the added drawback that this was my third visit to Australia whereas he was an exotic novelty. I was exhausted at the end of the tour and anxious to see Tito, who I hoped would be able to meet me in Miami on my birthday.

After an interminably long flight, I reached Miami and telephoned. But Tito said it was impossible for him to leave, as the votes were still being counted. By the time I got to Panama he was still in deep discussions about the possible outcome of the election. I felt lost in the political jabbering and had a very brief time with him before heading on towards Europe and yet more performances.

TEN

Three weeks after my birthday the election result was still unannounced. That day Alfredo Jiminez asked Tito to register him as his substitute deputy. Tito sent a message saying that he would be happy to do so if Jiminez gained the requisite number of votes, but that if someone else earned that position he must give it to him. Jiminez put a gun in his pocket and drove through town. At the point where Calle 50 and Via Brasil intersect he saw Tito's car ahead of his own. It had stopped at the red light. He got out and shot Tito five times at point-blank range. Tito was instantly paralyzed. He keeled over towards the chauffeur, who courageously got out and tried to remonstrate with Jiminez, but then, realizing it was too late anyway, rushed Tito to the hospital.

Two bullets had smashed through his right arm and into his chest – where they remain to this day. One of them had punctured a lung. A third grazed past his shoulder and lodged against his spine high up near the neck. Surgeons operated within two hours, but the damage was irreparable.

Tito describes the events thus:

I was under the impression that 'Yinyi' Jiminez, the

would-be assassin, was firing an automatic. After deciding he had done the necessary he turned his attention to my driver, Nato Medina. 'I will kill you, too, if you get in my way,' he threatened. Then he tried to finish me off by emptying what was left in his automatic into me.

The first shot had been the most effective. I felt a sharp pain in the back of my neck. It is odd to smell gunpowder and know that you are the victim. I had often wondered what people about to die really think and I did quickly think of my wife and three children. I also realized that most of the bullets went through my arm, and I was smiling or laughing at the thought of what a bum shot Jiminez must be. Then I was lying on the front seat of the car feeling rather helpless as it was manoeuvred violently to turn left towards the hospital. After that I lost consciousness.

The next impression was that some people were pulling me by the arm – the left arm luckily. I hoped they were friends. Then I came to again in the dispensary or emergency room.

It is difficult to recall exactly what happened in the dispensary because I was only semi-aware. In any event service was excellent and an adequate amount of blood flowed. There was some ripping and cutting of clothes. A little later there developed some of the usual arguments about overtime, but suddenly everyone concentrated on the fact that I was rapidly losing too much blood and the plasma was running out. I recognized the voice of my cousin, Tavo Mendez, in the confusion.

Probably I was often unconscious. When not, my main concern was attempting to determine whether I was alive. The voices around me were debating the same problem. I don't know how much time elapsed before a decision was reached. When it was, I made a bumpy but otherwise somewhat formal transfer to the operating theatre. I thought my two brothers were pretending to guide the trolley amidst a number of doctors and nurses, and wondered if they would soon be doing the same at my funeral.

I heard some familiar-sounding sobs and a variety of whimpers, some flash bulbs exploding, and the voice of a lawyer friend who sometimes shouted in English. The fact that I could discern the two different languages for some reason convinced me that definitely I was not dead. To my wandering mind the use of English loomed as a landmark of quite extraordinary significance in the reduced proportions of my existence.

The operating theatre seemed to have only one door and reminded me of 'the last mile' in some North American novels. The face of Dr Octavio Vallarino, whom I had known for many years, came into view. He remarked that I had been lucky; it was his definite opinion that only one of the bullets, somewhere in the back of my neck, signified an immediate cause for concern.

A nurse approached nearby behind me. She said she was Gloria, the sister of my secretary, Marlene Worthington, whom I could hear just outside the door. At that time I was gripped by a disquieting emotion. Gloria must have been very competent; it seems that she realized before I did that the sensation which I could not recognize was fear. It was caused by my difficulty in breathing and she quickly explained I should breathe through my mouth.

Dr Crespo was the specialist on respiratory tracts. He asked whether I knew what a tracheotomy was and said he thought it should be performed without delay. I could still speak a little at that time and told him to go ahead. I was thinking of Elizabeth Taylor's tracheotomy operation at the London Clinic when she almost died, and I had some idea of what was involved. Dr Crespo proceeded.

Just before he started, Archbishop McGrath, who is an unusually tall man and an unusually young Archbishop, was looking down on me dressed in alarmingly full regalia. He asked me, 'Do you believe in God?' and although my reply was not totally satisfactory he speeded through the last rites. Some vestiges of my legal training, combined with my habitual contrariness, had made me reply, 'I have decided not to decide.' Crespo admonished me for using my diminishing strength in speech.

The room was gloomy and I could distinguish a scruffy policeman standing near by. I tried to ask him where I was but found it impossible to speak, so he rather helpfully went out of sight and apparently informed the staff nurse. With the curious resilience of human nature I became aware of the possibilities for communication inherent in the movement of my eyebrows. Although I could not speak, the human mind, being what it is, recalled that some primitive tribes even negotiate treaties and other contracts through sign language. I did not yet realize that the signs a paralytic can make are extremely limited, but I did make a mental note of the importance in analogous circumstances of watching the patient's face carefully. Meanwhile I deduced that I was in the post-operative room.

There was no way to know how much time passed before my mind unclouded again. The extreme discomfort and horror of my position alerted my instinct for survival. I was lying face downwards on a narrow board which reached up to the breast bone, and my head was supported by straps across the chin and forehead. My right arm, with the elbow bent at a right angle, was encased in plaster to the fingers. The tracheo-tube inserted in a hole at the front of my neck was the only means of breathing, and I was in serious jeopardy if the nurse did not adjust it correctly in the dim light under the bed. Without being able to move my head an inch I could nevertheless make out some tubes dangling and draped about, presumably connected to my body in various unspecified places.

The sense of self-preservation cleared my brain and set it ticking. I discovered that the contraption on which

I was lying was on a swivel, and after half an hour face down I was turned over like a chicken on a spit to lie for two hours on my back. I was horrified to realize that no one knew exactly how to work the thing, as it had been sent over brand new from another institution and its cardboard packings were still lying about the room. It was called a Stryker bed. The principle consisted of two boards, like a waffle iron, turned over from time to time and the top board removed. The purpose was to aid circulation and avoid continuous pressure on the back leading to bedsores. Stryker beds are not designed to take into account an arm in a plaster cast. It was necessary to swivel the machine quickly otherwise my head fell to one side, but someone had to move my arm just as quickly. If they failed, it was nearly wrenched out of its socket. Sometimes the nurse leading the turn got her hand trapped in the mechanism, but fortunately there were no lamentable accidents.

About the second or third time I found myself face down my brother Modi came and lay on the floor under the bed to be sure everything was in place and to talk to me. I saw two ladies' shoes that were recognizable and then Marlene, my secretary, got down on her hands and knees to tell me something. But before she could get the message through, two more shoes and a familiar pair of trousered legs appeared on the scene. It was my Uncle Arnulfo, who had just flown down from his coffee plantation in Boquete. The hypnotic, positive and optimistic attitude of Uncle Arnulfo was most helpful. He used to practice medicine a quarter of a century earlier and was still treated as a professional by Dr Octavio Vallarino and by my neurosurgeon, Dr Antonio Gonzalez-Revilla. Uncle Arnulfo is more than accustomed to the rough and tumble of Panamanian political life, having been four times elected President and three times overthrown. In spite of fifteen years of exile from the capital he still had by far the biggest following in the country, and I had run as a member of his political party. To cheer me up he told me that the election result gave me the highest number of votes of any Deputy in the history of Panama.

On 8 June, three weeks after my birthday, I was in Bath, the west of England city where Yehudi Menuhin held an annual music festival. Rudolf and I went through the stage rehearsal of a new pas de deux created for the festival opening, accompanied by Yehudi playing on stage as we danced. After dining at a restaurant we arrived back at the hotel near midnight. Yehudi's wife, Diana, herself an ex-ballet dancer, was at the door of our taxi almost before I could get out, saying quickly and without any preamble, 'Margot, it's all right, don't worry. Tito has been shot but it is not serious, he is alive and in the hospital.'

The dreaded thing had happened and I was thrown completely out of gear, not knowing how to think. As so often happens in life, the event when it occurs is not at all as anticipated. I realized for the first time that I had held at the back of my mind a constant fear of Tito being shot and killed. Our one-storey house by the sea was the particularly dangerous scene in which I expected it to happen, for anyone could easily have fired in through the bedroom window. As soon as Diana told me he was alive I revised my mental picture of the situation and saw him sitting up in bed smiling. At the same time, I could visualize no details to fill in the picture. Who had shot him? Where had it happened? Where was the injury? Was it more serious than I thought? But the last idea was not to be entertained.

Kenneth MacMillan, the choreographer of our new dance, sat with me in my hotel room while Joan Thring, who was there to look after Rudolf and me, tried to cope with the telephone calls. They came chiefly from the press, with conflicting stories from Panama. Nothing was clear, and I foolishly and vainly drank two or three brandies to steady myself. English country hotels being notoriously short of telephones, the only one was in some other part of the building. Joan came in and I guessed from her manner of prefacing what she had to say that the news was going to be disagreeable. Unable to endure the thought that Tito might, after all, die, I found myself rushing impulsively down a long corridor and hiding in an empty, unlit banquet hall. There Rudolf found me crying in an old-fashioned plush armchair. 'There is telephone call from Tito's brother for you,' he said.

At that time the radio link with Panama was exasperating. An intermittent connection deprived the listener of about two words in every six, causing endless repetition in the endeavour to get a complete answer.

'Margot? I'm ... ... hospital.'

'How's Tito?' I shouted.

'All right ... very serious ... ... out ... ... operating theatre.'

'Is he all right now?'

'Fine, he was ... ... wiggling his toes now.'

'What?'

'He's wiggling his toes ... ... all right.'

'What should I do?' I asked, shouting my loudest. 'I am supposed to have a première here tomorrow. Should I leave now for Panama or immediately after the première?'

'He's OK now.'

'Are you sure he's out of danger? Is it really all right for me to leave after the show?'

'... ... out of danger.'

'Right, I will be there Wednesday night. Tell Tito...' And the connection broke off altogether.

So Tito was out of danger. I imagined he had been hit perhaps in the leg and was sitting up with one of those big cages holding the weight of bedclothes off the wound. I forgot Panama is too hot for bedclothes, and unluckily I had mistaken which brother I was speaking to. If I had realized it was the overoptimistic one I might have tempered my relief. But at that point, and for a long time to come, my mind refused to conceive the possibility of permanent, serious injury.

'Wiggling his toes?' Whatever did he mean? But I dismissed the words as incomprehensible.

My stepson, Roberto, who was sixteen and at school not far from Bath, travelled with me on the plane. At my first glimpse of the newspaper headlines I saw the word 'Paralyzed'. After a moment's shock, I hastily put the papers down out of Roberto's reach, not wanting him to be anxious and upset all the long journey. I was confident I knew better than the journalists after my conversation with Tito's brother. 'Out of danger', I reassured myself. Roberto later told me that he had already seen the papers at the airport and was hoping to hide them from me, as he did not want me to be anxious and upset the whole long journey. So the papers remained unopened under my feet and neither of us mentioned what we had read.

Grave family faces met us in Panama and drove us straight to the hospital. Quite a crowd of people stood outside by the bulletin board. They had been there for two days, keeping a vigil, ever since the radio appeal for blood donors had gone out and met a response from hundreds of volunteers. Even before that, as news travels fast in Panama City, within half an hour of the shooting people had rushed to the hospital, the old ladies crying, the men grim-faced to wait around for news.

Roberto and I clutched each other's arm as we walked along the corridor, spearheading a jostling group. Someone said, 'We expected you yesterday.' I felt reproved, but nothing anyone said could have prepared me for the sight in store.

We entered an enormous, empty, half-darkened ward. It was about eight o'clock at night. There were ten empty beds and on the left as we went in Tito was lying flat on his back without pyjamas or pillows on some kind of a narrow table, like an ironing board. A small draw sheet was his only covering. His right arm, in a plaster cast, was suspended from a stand that bore its weight. More stands near his feet held bottles to feed him intravenously. As I approached, I saw the tube through which he breathed, coming out of a hole in his neck. I was appalled, shocked beyond measure. At last I understood that he was more than desperately ill, and that I should not risk tiring him even by my presence. I went closer and whispered very gently in his ear, 'Darling, I am here.' He opened his eyes and turned them towards me without moving his head. Their expression indicated that he recognized me and understood my words. He even tried the very faintest of smiles. I repeated in his ear, 'I'm here now, darling. I won't tire you any more. I will come back in the morning.' Roberto spoke to him very quietly, too, and he seemed pleased.

The surgeon told me that the paralysis might be merely temporary, the result of swelling caused by the removal of a bullet lodged against his spine. In three days the swelling would subside, and he would know more.

Dr Gonzalez-Revilla came each morning with a little hammer and a pin to test Tito's reactions. His chest and upper arms felt the pinpricks, but the rest of his body stayed inert. On the third morning I saw bad news on the surgeon's face, and suddenly my heart seemed to fall over itself and land in a heap somewhere in my tummy. It was a few minutes before my natural optimism returned. I just could not believe that Tito wouldn't somehow manage to recover. Nevertheless, I guessed that he must be prey to some agonizing thoughts and, later in the day, I whispered to him that I had been considering all that our future might bring, the best and the worst, and that I was not afraid of anything.

Uncle Arnulfo, full of confidence, swept in each morning very early, saying, 'Tito is doing well. I see a great improvement.' Arnulfo is a tallish, very well-preserved man in his sixties, handsome, compact and giving the appearance of everything being well ordered and under control. He doesn't waste time or words but speaks briskly in clear-cut tones. He has undoubted magnetism and I find that I automatically stand up when he enters the room. He is very fond of Tito. He described to me how he had been shot and wounded in the throat many years before, in a political fracas. 'Being a doctor myself, I knew the dangers if the surgeon should make the slightest error and cut my vocal chords. I didn't want to take any chances, so I insisted that he remove the bullet without an anaesthetic. Like that I could keep talking and be sure he saw the cords vibrating as he operated.' What a splendid man! No wonder he is adored by his countrymen. He has the courage and manner of a great leader, and the common sense too.

Tito's condition improved daily. The lung drained and the tracheo-hole closed. He could speak perfectly and told me how his total resources had been centred on remaining alive in the first two days. Unable to speak, he had devised a way to attract attention by pursing his lips and making a sound such as headwaiters use in Italy to summon their minions.

After tremendous discussion about his safety, he was moved to a private room. It had two doors. One was locked and an armed guard was posted in front of the other. Beside him, a large notice declared visitors strictly prohibited, and this reduced them to manageable numbers. Tito's followers, including Clifford, the son of Milton Garvey, who had attended us on our first Bahamian cruise, did not trust the official guard one bit and organized their own roster to guard the guards. There was serious concern that someone would try to complete the job that Alfredo Jiminez had bungled. The police announced that they were searching for the attacker, but no one believed they were trying very hard. Tito was the only person unconcerned, and at no time have I ever heard him say a bitter word about Jiminez.

Dr Gonzalez-Revilla, who had undoubtedly saved Tito's life, thought he should be transferred as soon as possible to Stoke Mandeville Hospital in England for rehabilitation treatment. I believed this to mean he would learn again how to move after temporary paralysis. It did not occur to me that the condition was permanent. Or perhaps more accurately, my mechanism for self-protection does not allow my mind to admit any ideas that my system is not prepared to withstand. Until the time of Tito's injury I was always vaguely aware of some incalculable emotional abyss into which I might easily fall if pushed by circumstances or thoughts I was too weak to endure. Now that tragedy had arrived, it was a long time before I realized what everyone else knew perfectly well – that Tito was incapacitated and probably a quadraplegic for life.

When at last I understood what had happened, so many months had passed that I was able to accept the facts. Or, more likely, I had refused to understand until the passage of time prepared me to the point where I was *able* to accept. Curiously, over the last four or five years I have lost that constant dread of the abyss. I hope it means we have passed through our greatest trial and come out on the other side.

Four weeks after the shooting, Tito left Panama, still on his Stryker bed, to fly to England. With him went his brother Modi, a doctor, a nurse, his secretary, Marlene, and five Teddy bears, who travelled comfortably strewn about on first-class seats, nonchalant expressions on their furry faces. Tito had insisted on having them in his hospital room. They had been in our bedroom at home, and were part of the family.

I had left Panama two weeks earlier. Before leaving I consulted Dr Gonzalez-Revilla. 'I am supposed to be dancing in London at this time, Dr Gonzalez-Revilla,' I told him. 'Do you think it would be safe for me to go on ahead of Tito to fulfil my engagement there?' He replied, 'Your husband is getting on well so far, but I must warn you there is one danger in cases such as his. At any moment he could suffer a thrombosis.' 'In that case I would fly back immediately,' I said. He replied simply, 'You would be too late.'

I did not tell Tito of this disquieting conversation, and we had already discussed my departure. He appeared to be getting on well, his family was around him and he thought it made sense for me to get back to my dancing. With sadness, I arranged for our pretty little house to be sold, the contents stored, and I flew back to London.

There, through dancing too soon after a two-weeks' gap, I injured a calf muscle. Luckily, or perhaps unluckily, it healed in a few days and I was ready to leave for a short Continental tour the day after Tito reached England on 4 July.

I had time to see him safely at Stoke Mandeville, where, to my great relief, he was immediately parted from the alarming swivel bed (which I never saw again). I had to be on my way to Italy, to Spoleto, for the first performance of *Raymonda*, which is a ballet in three acts with plentiful dancing for me. I found it really hard work, and we were all exhausted at the end of each interminable day of rehearsal. I telephoned Tito morning and evening.

On the morning of 9 July, a month and a day after the shooting, I went to the theatre very early to put on my makeup for the final dress rehearsal. From the moment I awoke I had felt very unhappy. As I walked alone through the deserted streets of that melancholy mountainside town, I was thinking about Tito and remembering that his voice on the telephone had sounded unusually tired the night before. The loneliness of dancing and travelling, always away from the people one loves, overpowered me. Had Tito died four weeks earlier, I thought, I would be totally unable to continue living, let alone dancing. As I contemplated the idea I could feel only an infinite black void inside and out.

Half an hour later, as I sat in the dressing room completing my makeup, Joan Thring came in. She had been with me in Bath on the night when I heard of the shooting. I noticed that she looked quite pale, and as she spoke I found myself involuntarily rising from the chair and trying to run away from things I did not want to hear. But this time I listened. 'They telephoned from the hospital to say you must return at once. A plane leaves Rome at 2:30 this afternoon. I have ordered a car and Alitalia will have someone at the airport to see you on to the flight.' 'Whatever can have happened?' I asked helplessly. 'They said nothing; only that you must go at once.' Rudolf came into the room. The *Raymonda* production was very important to him — it was the first three-act ballet he had ever staged, and no one was standing by to replace me at the première next day. But, realizing the extreme gravity of the situation, he was unusually gentle and seemed dreadfully upset for me as he said, 'You must pack and leave right away. Don't think about the ballet. The drive takes two and a half hours, so you must leave in half an hour.' They took me back to the hotel, dazed. My mother was there, having arrived two days earlier for a holiday. She was already packed to return home. I hugged Joan and Rudolf, thankful for these real friends in a time of crisis, and climbed into the unpromising-looking taxi driven by an old Spoleto driver. He set off at a sedate pace, and my mother and I sat silent, trying not to become exasperated by his methodical slowness.

As we rattled along, steadily instead of swiftly, I knew my mother was praying. I didn't know exactly what I was doing. In total ignorance of what had happened to Tito I was, as it were, holding him constantly in a tight thought. There was no picture in my mind: just Tito, the idea of Tito, the existence of Tito, the necessity for Tito. Then suddenly, inexplicably, the thought was empty. I tried to find him, but he was no longer there. I simply ceased to feel anything at all. I carefully noted the time. At Stoke Mandeville, it would be just before midday.

I was completely numb for about an hour altogether. Then I became aware that we were in the suburbs of Rome, and I remembered that we should have taken the circular bypass to reach the airport on the far side of the city. Lunchtime traffic in Rome is impossible, and seeing St Peter's on the right, I became furious. I realized the driver didn't know his way at all. I invented some Italian words to shout at him to stop and to inquire the way. At a petrol station we picked up an eight-year-old boy who, for all his confidence, didn't know any more than the old driver. Absolutely desperate by now, and with only forty-five minutes left before the plane should take off, I leaped out of the car at some traffic lights, hysterically dragged my mother and the luggage out, and started yelling for a taxi. A stranger, whom I shall never forget to the end of my days, astounded by the wildness of my manner, realized my plight was urgent and, without asking any questions, fetched his own car and brought us to the airport with just eight minutes to spare.

At the Alitalia counter no one had heard of me, but I was so aggressive and uncontrolled by then that they hurriedly pushed us into the departing plane to be rid of me.

At London Airport Leonard Lindley, our kindly chauffeur for eight years, was waiting, grey with anxiety. I was prepared for the worst this time, and it was a relief to hear anything at all after the hours of helpless ignorance. 'He's still alive,' said Lindley. 'It was just announced on the radio a few minutes ago.' 'But what happened?' I asked. 'I don't know. The hospital won't give any further information.' One more grim hour brought me to Tito's bedside. Why was I again unprepared for what I saw? Why hadn't I realized that, if his life hung by only a thread, he would be in a coma? I don't know. I had thought that as he was still alive I would be able to whisper in his ear, 'I'm here now.' Instead, he was not dead, yet more than a million miles away. An ugly gadget protruded from his mouth. I suppose it was to prevent him from choking by swallowing his tongue. A new kind of despair enveloped me. It was Tito but not Tito, and there was nothing to do but watch and wait.

Dr Guttman came into the room. He is now Sir Ludwig Guttman, having been honoured for his extraordinary work of over twenty-two years in the treatment and research of spinal injuries. He had founded Stoke Mandeville in preparation for casualties of the 1944 Normandy invasion. Sir Ludwig is quite simply a genius. He is small, neat, precise and sometimes peppery, despite the kindly blue eyes behind his rimless spectacles. His dynamic presence and authority were instantly assuring as he came into the room with a quick light step. In spite of all his long years in England he retains a splendid German accent, which I know he would hate me to reproduce in print. His concisely delivered observations sound so much less effective in thin English, and his accented delivery was a definite factor in the superb discipline he maintained in his hospital. All the employees were conscious of what Dr Guttman would say if displeased with their work.

Dr Guttman said, 'Your husband is still alive – just. He suffered a convulsion and his heart and breathing stopped. He was dead, but we pulled him back from heaven by one foot.' As he spoke he reached up as though grabbing Tito's ascending leg before it vanished through the ceiling. He made it clear, however, that I should expect nothing. Apparently the long flight had tired Tito, and symptoms of the thrombosis, of which the doctor in Panama had warned me, had accumulated gradually in the days while I was in Italy. The previous night he had been delirious, and in the morning his fever went out of control, reaching 108°. An injection had restarted his heart, but he was now in a coma, and it was unlikely he would live.

I stayed beside Tito's bed, just watching. He barely breathed, and occasionally stopped altogether. I was terrified, and turned anxiously to Mr Pullen, the kindly nurse who was in constant attendance on Tito. Mr Pullen reassured me. 'It's all right,' he said. 'When that happens I just belt him like this. Don't worry.' With 'this' he pounded Tito's chest, and the breathing began again. I breathed a lot easier, too, after that. It seemed such a simple way of keeping a person alive. As I continued my vigil, watching the grisly object in Tito's mouth through which the scant breaths passed, I became convinced that his body knew, of its own accord, how to spare itself every slightest effort except those vital to survival. His motionless form appeared to me like a battlefield, within which an invisible war was waging between mysterious science-fiction forces. The fiercer the battle, the less his body moved. It was only by immobility that Tito could win.

Some consternation followed about the whereabouts of Tito's son, Roberto, who should have arrived from his school in mid-afternoon. The police were asked to look out for him along the route, but he had vanished. When he turned up, four hours late, he said he had reached the seaside and had to turn back towards London. I remembered my involuntary impulse to run away from bad news and questioned him closely. As I thought, he had seen the front-page headlines about his father as he bought his ticket at the station, but he said he was quite unconscious of boarding a train that was going in the wrong direction.

Roberto soon mastered all the charts – of temperature, blood pressure and so forth – that were entered up every fifteen minutes. I thought to ask him when the big crisis had occurred, and was not surprised to hear that it had been almost at noon, just when I had sensed it as we bumped along in the old taxi from Spoleto.

That night no one slept much. When daylight came at last, Tito was still living. Dr Guttman was the first in to see him. 'If he lives through this, it is a miracle,' he said. I thought these were unusual words for such a scientific man, and I began to feel great affection for him. In half an hour he was back again. 'In all my forty years as a doctor,' he exclaimed, 'I have never seen a man survive a fever of 108°. I could not believe it. I had to take the temperature myself.' But still he held out little hope.

In the afternoon Tito's breathing eased slightly. So did Dr Guttman's face. So did my heart. I ventured to ask a question: 'If Tito should come out of the coma, will he be as before?' Of course I wanted only one answer, and that was 'Yes.' But with Guttman's reply I felt suddenly sick – not only for myself but because I had been imbecilic enough to ask my question in Roberto's presence. 'As I have never known a man to live after such a fever, I cannot possibly tell what effects it might have.' The words were like a death sentence. Roberto bravely showed no emotion – or perhaps he was already aware of the danger. To me it was like a bottomless pit of unknown terrors opening at my feet. I quickly shut it from my mind, trying to forget.

That night I was talking to a young male nurse across the bed. He was a compassionate boy, working in the hospital during his vacation from a seminary. As we both looked down at Tito the boy said, 'It is tragic,' and shook his head from side to side. I was nettled by his remark, and said sharply. 'You don't think he will live, do you?' He didn't reply but went on gazing sadly at the unconscious figure. I decided that I just did not feel up to explaining that Tito had often managed to do the unexpected.

A second day went by. In the evening Tito's breathing was stronger, and the coma obviously lighter. Dr Guttman leaned over him and shouted loudly in his ear, 'Wake up, Arias! Wake up!' He slapped him lightly. The next evening this treatment had the desired effect. Tito stirred. I ran to him and spoke a few words. Some while later he managed to mumble something, which I felt sure was the nickname he used for me. The nightmare of the coma had lifted and I felt very happy. I didn't realize what worse anxieties were in store.

On the fifth day I left the hospital for the first time, just to dine locally with Jimmy Ortiz-Patino and some other friends who cared deeply about Tito. Towards the end of dinner I felt terribly uneasy, and noticed that the headwaiter had taken on a strong resemblance to Dr Walsh in the hospital. Hurrying back to the ward, we found the familiar signs of crisis. The bottles and tubes, the ice, and a fan blowing over Tito's uncovered torso. His temperature was rising again, but this time, thank God, it was soon under control.

The interminable hospital days were a period similar to the war, that I knew would eventually come to an end and be like another book on the shelf. There were pages of laughter and despair. As Tito came out of the coma his speech was almost incomprehensible. I tried to imagine one tiny part of his mind's agony at this new horrific setback, and begged kind Dr Melzack to give him a word of reassurance so that he might sleep. As I sat up late with him night after night, Dr Guttman ordered me to rest, fearing I would break down. But he underestimated the advantage, in times of stress, of a long ballet discipline.

A new worry now came into my life – finance. I took stock and realized that political assassinations, whether successful or not, usually catch the family concerned at the worst possible time. At the end of a political campaign everyone is cleaned out of cash. It was the holiday period and the next Covent Garden season was not till October. No performance, no pay. So, as soon as Tito was out of danger, I hurried back to Spoleto, just in time for the last day, and then on to Baalbek to dance *Raymonda,* in spite of the nine-day interruption to my training. The warm climate saved me from injury, but it was an anxious time and the telephone link to England was spasmodic.

Back at Stoke Mandeville, Tito was battling inch by inch. Yet even near to death he made a joke of everything. There was at first a very serious doubt about the condition of his brain. I thought the sentences he tried to pronounce were typical of the old Tito I knew, but it was hard to be sure I was not deceiving myself. When Dr Guttman held up his hand showing three fingers in front of Tito's face and asked, 'Arias! How many fingers have I?' Tito struggled to control his diaphragm, his larynx and his tongue and finally brought out the word 'Eleven.' There was a gleam of satisfaction in his eye. Sir Ludwig looked alarmed for a moment and then, recovering himself, gave him an affectionate pat and said, 'Ah, Arias. You have a sense of humour!'

On the other side of the coin, the plight in which Tito found himself called for superhuman courage. Every little word required an enormous effort, and he rarely slept more than three hours at night. Rehabilitation sessions and speech therapy left him grey and drawn with exhaustion. His anxiety about the chances of his mental and physical recovery was probably the worst torture of all. Not a day went by without his begging me to let him die. It was a matter I had to think over very seriously, because I knew that if, with the passage of time, he should still find living intolerable, there was no way he could end his own life: his arms and hands were useless. I concluded privately that, being his wife, I was the one who would have to help him. I further resolved to do it, if it became necessary. I did not fear what would happen to me, as I would not care once he was no longer there.

Other patients in the hospital, more advanced in their recovery, told me that for the first few months they, too, had wished to die. I kept this in mind and always replied to Tito, 'Please wait a bit longer. I don't think you should make a decision when you are still so weak and ill.'

The ward sister was the redoubtable Sister 'Mac', whose temper the entire hospital was aware of. I loved and respected her dearly because she was so like the early Ninette de Valois, intelligent, efficient and never admitting to a heart as soft as butter behind the alarming manner. One wintry Sunday I asked her if I could perhaps take Tito for a drive. And so it was that he saw the dry fields and leafless trees of Buckinghamshire in the weak rays of a November sun. It was a crisp afternoon, quite exhilarating, and that night Tito slept well for the first time. He had grown to believe he would never get out of the hospital. That set me to reflecting on a certain similarity between hospitals and schools – it is necessary to have holidays from both. So when Christmas came round, Tito spent four days at my mother's house. About that time my mother consulted a fortune teller, who said that 'an ill person close to her would be in England a whole year without leaving the country'. This turned out to be accurate, as it happened. When he went abroad it was to Sam Spiegel's yacht in the Mediterranean, and in the knowledge that life was supportable after all. The trip was another 'holiday', after which he returned to Stoke Mandeville, where he was to be a patient for one more year.

The Royal Ballet made another U.S. tour in the spring of 1965. Jacqueline Kennedy invited Rudolf and me to supper after a New York performance. I sat next to Bobby Kennedy, who said he was going to London at the weekend to unveil a bust of his late brother. After my second vodka I found the nerve to ask if he could possibly find time to visit Tito in hospital. I knew that it would do more for Tito's morale than anything in the world. He replied that he would go on the Saturday. By the end of dinner I felt so guilty for imposing on him that I said, 'Please don't go if it's a nuisance. I don't want to bother you, and probably you haven't time. I know you must have so much else to do.' He got thoroughly fed up with me, shutting me up with the words: 'I have said I will go and I will go. Now be quiet.' And there was a rare friend indeed!

I remember Bobby most for his amazing capacity to worry about hundreds of people at once, in detail and in general. Not one member of his extensive family was out of range of his thoughts; he knew where they all were, and he knew their problems. In addition, he cared a lot about his friends and worried about whole sections of humanity as well. Capable of hate as well as love, he wasn't a man for half-baked emotions or impractical theorizing.

In fact, I have rarely met a man of more genuine compassion. Moreover, he was quick, intelligent, human and, above all, a realist. What a senseless and irreplaceable loss to the world.

Mrs Rose Kennedy asked me to call on her some while after she had lost Bobby and after her husband had died. She still led a full life, starting with early morning Mass and spending a lot of time on the Kennedy Foundation project, which is committed to helping the cause of the mentally retarded. She showed no self-pity as she spoke of God taking three of her sons but giving her a retarded daughter. The power which her faith gives her, enabling her to cope with the deep tribulations of her life, was an impressive lesson. My short conversation with her influenced me profoundly, leaving a mark out of all proportion to the length of our meeting.

ELEVEN

Tito was in Stoke Mandeville for some two years, and then became an outpatient for about six months at the Ludwig Guttman Centre in Barcelona. Soon after that he at last returned to Panama. Meantime his secretary, Marlene Worthington, who is a very attractive Panamanian with an English name and a Chinese profile (and is a champion fencer for good measure), had kept him in close touch with events in Panama. There was not a twist in political manoeuvring there that escaped his knowledge, though he was five thousand miles away in a hospital bed. The hospital orderlies at Stoke Mandeville were all Spanish; there were so many jokes cracked in Tito's native tongue that he felt less of an exile; in fact, the austere little room was always a centre of laughter when I returned each evening from a long day of classes and rehearsals in London.

One evening they told me how Tito, lying on a plinth in the physiotherapy ward that afternoon, had been rolled over on to his left side. Simultaneously, the patient on the next plinth was rolled over on to his right side. There was a second of disbelief and then guffaws of laughter as the two recognized each other. Poor Assis de Châteaubriand, ex-Ambassador of Brazil, had suffered three severe strokes and, like Tito, could neither move nor speak. Even this did not deter Château then, any more than Tito now, from travelling the world and entertaining his friends. Château gave a party at the Embassy in London to celebrate his purchase of Aberdeen Angus cattle for Brazil. Dr Guttman was invited, and he accepted but told Château, his host and patient, that he was sorry he could not permit him to attend his own party. Château declined to hear and hired an ambulance, from which he emerged in London, sitting in his wheelchair, wearing a poncho and a gaucho's hat, to be carried up the Embassy steps to a round of applause from his guests. Till his death he never failed to write the daily article that was syndicated in his newspapers, nor did he lose his zest for living. 'I don't like countryside,' he said. 'I like asphalt and night clubs.'

In preparation for Tito's return to Panama, Miss Bromley, his physiotherapist, taught him to bang on the table with a special wooden gavel. This was to enable him to vote in the National Assembly. Many people were amazed that he should want to return, and one journalist asked incredulously, 'Surely, Dr Arias, you are not thinking of going back to Panama after what happened?' He got the offhand reply, 'Oh yes, I will go there, get shot again and come back to Stoke Mandeville.' It was not really such a joke.

For a long time he still hoped to regain his speech before facing his supporters. In the end, he went back, still physically incapacitated, and minus that most essential of politicians' weapons, speech.

It was the most moving and triumphant moment of our lives as Tito was lowered from the plane on a forklift at Tocumen Airport, in Panama, two and a half years after he had been flown out on the Stryker bed. A colossal crowd of well-wishers swarmed across the tarmac to greet him, and to follow in a two-mile motorcade to the city. Uncle Arnulfo took Tito in his own car, and a note of slapstick was introduced by an unscheduled rain storm in what was supposed to be the dry season. The open cars were halted while umbrellas were found, and the procession moved on at a more moderate speed. People along the route who came out to see the cause of excitement shouted greetings to Tito, who responded with a slight wave of his left arm, the most spectacular result of his rehabilitation struggle. And with his smile – the smile that is unchanged, and unembittered, and warms the hearts of all who receive it.

A few days later I was full of pride as I watched him raise his own hand to take the oath at his swearing-in ceremony in the Panamanian National Assembly.

The beneficent heat of his native climate helped mitigate Tito's anguish at finding himself captive in a wheelchair in the haunts he had roamed freely all his life. I, too, found it incredibly painful whenever I revisited places where Tito had been standing and walking the last time we were there. With the years these sufferings receded, together with Tito's nightmares of being shot and my dreams that he was restored to normal health.

Needless to say, dancing commitments soon took me away from Tito in Panama. He had formulated the dictum, 'Our separations are only geographical', putting into words our relationship, which my mother, who thinks more of such theories than I do, believes to date from an earlier incarnation. Without accepting the theory of the soul's rebirth, however, I can see no reason why we should not share some common ancestry that accounts for our affinity just as satisfactorily.

With the next political campaign coming up for Tito in little over a year, it was no time for me to retire. I now began to work harder than ever. I was lucky to have the chance to add Juliet to my repertoire of lovelorn females. Kenneth MacMillan created his own version of the ballet that had bowled me over when I saw Ulanova and the Bolshoi and, despite my usual misgivings about my age and ability, I grabbed the role enthusiastically. It was during Tito's first year at Stoke Mandeville, and to my joy he came to the opening night at Covent Garden.

Two years later, in 1967, Roland Petit was invited to create a ballet for Rudolf and me. He intended a completely English work but, by the time it came to the orchestral rehearsal, the composer-conductor, Marius Constant, addressed the orchestra in the following words: 'Gentlemen, I expect you have all heard of Milton's *Paradise Lost*?' 'Yes, yes,' murmured the sixty-odd musicians in the pit, with approval in their voices. 'Well, gentlemen,' Marius continued, 'I just want to tell you that this ballet has nothing whatever to do with Milton's *Paradise Lost*!'

It was a striking ballet for both of us. Rudolf, as Adam, made a spectacular dive through a huge pair of lips – the kind of thing that really only happens in French ballets. (Leonor Fini once wrote the scenario for a ballet in which Zizi Jeanmaire was bald, and chased after a wig that flew about the stage on a wire, while girls dressed as whipped cream meringues did fouetté turns in unison to signify Leonor Fini's gluttonous dreams. Fred Ashton choreographed the ballet, thus proving there is nothing the French could do that he couldn't do better, if he wished.) My own entrance in *Paradise Lost* was from a trapdoor in the middle of a ramp at the back of the set. To reach it I had to crawl on my hands and knees, under the steeply sloping rostrum, from the wings to centre stage, a distance of some thirty feet. Then I had to lie in a cramped position on the floor waiting for the trap to open. At the new Lincoln Center in New York that May I was crawling along one particular night and saying to myself, 'This is a hell of a way to spend your forty-eighth birthday!' Thinking it quite funny I told Rudolf about it after the performance, but instead of laughing he said wistfully, 'I wish I could think I am dancing still on forty-eighth birthday.'

I rather think it was that same night that the New York public inaugurated the custom of singing 'Happy Birthday' for me at the end of the evening. The last time it happened I was flattered and touched beyond words when the singing was led by Jack Lanchbery, our conductor, and the full orchestra. Few stars in the annals of the 'Met' can have enjoyed such a tribute. As my grandmother used to say, 'Little things please little minds.'

No doubt every silver lining has to have its cloud. We went on to Washington, where one night I had occasion to share a taxi with a stranger in my hurry to get to the theatre. The stranger sat in front beside the driver. Half turning towards me, he said, 'You greatly resemble Mrs Caffritz. Are you by any chance she?' I wasn't exactly complimented, because I had met Mrs Caffritz, and she would hardly mind my saying that her figure is not that of a ballerina. Grasping at a straw, I asked, 'Which Mrs Caffritz?' He said he meant the well-known hostess Mrs Gwen Caffritz. That was who I was afraid he meant. Thinking it nevertheless a funny joke against myself, I was cast down to find that the first person I related it to didn't think it funny at all. Obviously she saw the resemblance, too. Well, well!

Whenever possible I spent a few days in Panama, where Tito was thinking ahead to the next elections. Marlene and Tito's indispensable manservant, Buenaventura Medina, had between them mobilized Tito to travel to remote areas by whatever means were available. A long day's ride over almost impassable roads in a jeep would have exhausted the healthiest of men, but Tito thrived on it and I finally stopped worrying about him when I watched him lowered over the side of a launch in his wheelchair and rowed ashore in a dinghy to be landed on an island beach. My heart was in my mouth lest the little craft should overturn, but Tito said reassuringly, 'Don't worry about me. Paralyzed people always float. That's one of the advantages!' He was really happy campaigning, in spite of his infirmities. Faithful friends spoke at his rallies, while Tito presided silently but impressively in his chair.

Uncle Arnulfo was running for President for the fourth time in his life. Our young friend Louis Martinz, who had previously cared only for the arts, was developing a social conscience and involved himself deeply in Arnulfo's campaign. Arnulfo won and Tito regained his seat in the Assembly. Louis was appointed supervisor of protocol in the new Government.

On inauguration day we were at the Assembly building at eight-thirty in the morning. Louis was trying not to lose his cool in the face of an unexpected predicament. His predecessor in Protocol had spitefully removed all the copies of the diplomatic lists so that Louis could have no idea in what order of precedence he should seat the Ambassadors. He said to me, 'I don't know what to do. I think I will greet each Ambassador with a warm smile and say, "Your Excellency, I am sure you know where *your* seat is," as though they were all top of the list.'

The inauguration took place on 1 October 1968 amid some heated demonstrations in the street from opposition parties, who were very poor losers. However, it was not the opposition but the police who overthrew Uncle Arnulfo eleven days later, and he had to retreat to the Canal Zone, which is so handy on these occasions, with the border of the Zone right in the middle of town.

Tito reckoned it was not too wise to smuggle a paralyzed man past the police guards at three in the morning because they would see the car more easily than he could see them. So, with the resourceful Marlene and Buenaventura, he hid in a friend's house until a little after midday and then found a road on which the patrolmen had gone off for lunch, thus slipping into the protection of the Zone without incident. I would have been frightened to death had I known, but I was dancing in London at the time.

Also sheltering in the Canal Zone was Louis Martinz, so anxious to fight back that he embroiled himself in a courageous attempt to steal some U.S. Army equipment. At dead of night he raided a store and had just filled the boot of a car with guns and ammunition when American soldiers jumped out of the damp jungle undergrowth and surrounded him with torches and machine guns. 'Put your arms up,' ordered the Lieutenant. Louis obeyed promptly. 'Lie on your face on the ground,' was the next command. Louis had barely recovered from a bad cold, and it was the height of the rainy season. 'What?' he asked. 'Lie in the mud? You can't be serious.' But the Lieutenant was in deadly earnest, and Louis was in a filthy mess and very wet in no time at all.

With the coup in Panama our lives were once again thrown off course. Our household possessions, rather depleted after the police 'searched' our rented villa, were bundled back into storage minus the linen, half the china, various easily portable gewgaws and all the silver knives. A few forks and spoons remained, and Tito observed that the 'custodians' probably didn't know how to use those, and so had left them behind.

We now had no house of our own in any country. We were gypsies. Clearly this again was not the best moment for me to retire. In any case, my dancing was rather stronger now, through the necessity of keeping pace with a dynamic Tartar approaching his prime. In the following years I danced sporadically at Covent Garden, but also covered incalculable distances and met with amusing adventures on many tours, which often followed a crazily illogical geographical pattern.

Far from relinquishing the taxing classical ballets, I added *La Sylphide*, which dates from 1840 and is in a style of dancing particularly difficult to master late in life. Rudolf commented, 'I learn from you, keep pot burnished and boiling.' Of course, I received good and bad reviews for these many performances all over the world, but so long as my services remained in demand I thought it wiser not to read any of the notices and just get on with the show. Friends brought to my attention one critic who won my heart by writing, 'Margot Fonteyn, who has triumphed in many more exotic places, last night conquered Flatbush.' I seem to get more satisfaction out of such offbeat tributes than from the more solemn assessments of my art, which, frankly, I find too boring to read.

In Marseilles, where one is propositioned by almost everyone, I liked a stockily built stagehand who respectfully expressed a penchant for my thigh muscles. Wanting to wish me well for my fourth *Sleeping Beauty* performance in three days, he approached as I was exercising on the stage, and with great warmth, said, 'Merde!' This, in the French theatre, is the equivalent of 'Good luck'. But it also has another meaning altogether, which is expressed in English by a four-letter word. Lest I had not understood his amiable intention, he decided to translate for me and said, 'Sheeet!' with careful emphasis and with an endearingly friendly smile on his rough, handsome face. The attention of stagehands always pleases me, for they are in the theatre for a job, not for art, and I value their interest in my side of the business. There used to be a man at the old 'Met' in New York who nicknamed me 'Dimples', until one year when, as I returned for yet another season, he exclaimed, 'Oh, now I have to call you Dame Dimples!' Another stagehand in America wrote me a little note saying, 'You hold the stars in place with your dance.'

Another unusual compliment was paid in a Brazilian city by a representative of the Council, who begged me to please take tea with the Governor's wife at the Palace because, as he put it, 'If you accept the invitation of his wife, you can save the Governor from going to jail.' Of course I went, but had to leave town before hearing whether the visit was efficacious.

In Managua, Tito was with me, and we were invited after the ballet by the 'strong-man' of Nicaragua, General Anastasio Somoza, whose beautiful wife, Hope, had built the fine new theatre in which we had danced. Buenaventura usually lifts Tito into the front seat of limousines because the back seats are too far recessed to be reached. I sit between the driver and Tito, so as to hold him steady on the road. On this occasion General Somoza's son was seeing us off after the supper. As I got into the car he said curtly to the driver, 'Get that machine gun out of the front seat; there's a lady riding with you.' The driver replied, 'I need it in case of emergency.' Young Somoza said, 'If there is an emergency use your head.' To which the soldier replied, 'It is better to shoot first and use my head after.' By which time Buenaventura was laughing so much he could scarcely lift Tito into the car.

The performances there were such a success that we were booked to return a few months later, but by that time the lovely theatre was one of the very few buildings left standing. The public who might have filled it had lost their houses, and many had lost their lives, in a devastating earthquake.

In Costa Rica I was surprised to see myself billed in

huge letters, outside the exquisite little theatre, as 'The Memorial Ballerina of the World'. This perplexed the natives, too, until it was found to be a misprint for 'Memorable'. In Montevideo there was such a demand for tickets that three rows of seats were banked up in the wings, so that the stage was more like a boxing ring. In Argentina a very attractive lady was brought to my dressing room and refused absolutely to let me out of her sight until I was driven away in a car after the show. I thought she was an unusually nice 'fan', who declined my suggestions to watch the other dancers in the programme. Then I was enlightened. She was a police lady deputized to protect me from kidnappers.

At Omaha airport coffee shop I sat next to Jesse Owens, winner of four gold medals in the 1936 Berlin Olympics. We discussed music and athletics over breakfast, and I thought this wise, gentle man, 'the world's fastest human – one hundred yards in ten seconds', was also one of the world's great human beings.

I was congratulated and kissed after a performance in Canberra by the very attractive Mr Billie Sneddon, whereupon his wife burst into tears. Whether from emotion generated by the ballet or because of the kiss I never knew. I mistook President Figueres of Costa Rica for a security agent, which amused him immensely, and I met Mrs Gough Whitlam of Australia, who was absolutely charming but so tall that I had to stand on pointe to talk to her. In Chile Tito was congratulated on his very talented daughter – me!

Not all the adventures were in such a light vein. In San Francisco, during the year that hippies were new and untainted 'flower people', a tall biblical figure in the crowd as we left the stage door said, 'Would you like to come to a freak-out?' 'What is it? Some kind of a party?' I asked, very curious. 'Yes,' he replied. Rudolf and I were going to Trader Vic's for supper with a largish group of friends, but I took the address anyway.

On the way home I suggested we go to see what the party was like. Rudolf wasn't keen, but in the end we all went, 'just for twenty minutes'. The host, Paul, was Irish, bearded, wore sandals and looked as I imagine St John to have looked. When we arrived he told a girl to go out and buy a 'half lid'. Guessing it to be marijuana I said, 'For heaven's sake, don't get it for us; we don't smoke.' There was no coffee or wine or any of the usual things one finds at parties. I felt sure the Irish would have tea, but no luck. We were about to leave politely when the doorbell rang and the next thing I knew I had snatched up my white mink coat as we were swept up to the roof by these lethargic-looking people, who moved surprisingly quickly when something called the 'fuzz' was mentioned.

We spent a long time under the stars. I folded my coat inside out and kept it on my knees to keep it from getting dirty. An attempted departure via the fire escape was unsuccessful, and on our return to the roof some policemen met us and escorted us to the local station. An hour or two passed, then they decided to take all sixteen of us to jail. At this news I thought it correct to inform the Royal Ballet manager, the kind Vernon Clarke. I said, 'This is Margot speaking. I'm dreadfully sorry to wake you up at five in the morning, but Rudolf and I are being arrested.' 'Where are you?' he asked. I said, 'In Haight-Ashbury.' 'Haig-what?' asked Vernon, who seemed not to have heard of the famous hippie district which tourists were constantly being urged to visit. I thought it beautifully English of him.

We were driven to prison in a Black Maria, and I was put in the charge of a lady warder who took away my handbag and all its contents except the lipstick. 'That's not much good without a mirror,' I said. 'You are not allowed a mirror,' she replied. She searched me – I suppose for drugs. I started to laugh, and she asked severely what was funny. 'It strikes me as funny,' I said, 'because I have never smoked a cigarette of any kind in my life.' She looked down at my particulars on a card on her desk and said reprovingly, 'You are on a narcotics charge you know.' I said, 'I still think it's funny.'

The fingerprinting was incredibly thorough and took

fifteen minutes. I began to believe I had fifteen hands. Next I was shown through a door that really did have 'Mug Room' written over it. Therein was taken what I guess did not in any way resemble a Cecil Beaton portrait.

At about six in the morning, when these formalities were over, I asked if I could possibly telephone my husband, reverse charges, in Panama. I did not want him to get the story from a newswire before I gave it to him. The lady warder left discreetly while I spoke to Tito, who was as only Tito could be. He just said, 'Don't worry, darling. I don't mind.' 'But you are in the middle of an election; I am afraid it's very bad for you to have your wife arrested. I am terribly sorry.' 'I don't mind, darling,' he repeated. Much relieved, I put down the phone and, to my great surprise, the previously severe lady came back into the room saying, 'Don't tell me you are my idol? Are you really Margot Fonteyn?' And she turned out to be so friendly that I was really quite sorry to leave.

Vernon Clarke had just arrived to get us out, and I couldn't believe my eyes at the mob of pressmen and photographers who were right inside the building. 'This would never be allowed in an English jail,' I said to myself, with typical chauvinism. Rudolf took the diversion very well considering he had not wanted to go to the party in the first place. He never reproached me, and I decided I should heed my natural reluctance to go sightseeing in future. This had anyway been discouraged by a poster that greeted tourists on arrival in one particular Latin-American state. Beneath a picture of the Leader was the caption, 'Standing or dead, but never on your knees!' I hurried on to the next country.

The announcement that I would dance at the Nico Malan Opera House in Cape Town set off a barrage of complaints in the South African and British press, and brought a stack of letters advising me to cancel the engagement as a protest against apartheid restrictions banning nonwhites from the newly built theatre. The English letters were curiously similar, using the same phrases in a different order like school essays. But the most impressive letters were from within South Africa itself, as it was noticeable that they came anonymously or that the senders very simply put press cuttings into the envelope, without trace of their identity.

I cabled David Poole, director of the Capab Ballet Company: 'Am being severely harassed. Could authorities allow at least one Nico Malan performance for the non-white public?' But the hullaballoo in the press naturally made it difficult for the authorities to backtrack. David Poole replied that they had agreed to one of the performances being transferred to the Three Arts Theatre, where white people would be forbidden. I felt this would be an inadequate solution, and asked in addition for a special free matinée for nonwhite children from hospitals, homes and dancing schools. I hoped thus to give one performance that everyone could consider as nonpolitical.

It did not seem my duty to wave a tiny defiant fist at a foreign government. I decided that I had been invited as a dancer, and I should not let myself by pushed into making a political point. Those whose business it was could use me as the object of their protest if they wished, but I would stick to my own last. If the ballet wanted me, I would go.

Protesting placards greeted me outside the Covent Garden stage door. A letter arrived from the UN Committee on Apartheid, but by this time the contract had been signed.

In the event, a sizeable crowd with banners reading, 'Dame Margot dances Apartheid tune,' and so on, greeted me on arrival in South Africa. The long journey had impaired my limited brain power, and I handled the confrontation rather poorly. A banner-waver said, 'You have let us down. Why did you come?' Feeling that a vague reply, like 'I have come to dance,' did not quite suit the gravity of the occasion, I replied, 'Well, at least you are able to make your demonstration.' To this someone on the other side said, 'Then why don't you go back now?' This was such a valid point that I was quite floored, but actually my visit provided a punchbag for many demonstrations. This seemed to me the most helpful thing I could do. Some white people anonymously bought tickets for the boycotted performance, which caused the dancers to refuse to perform if the whites were allowed in, as it would constitute a privilege unthinkable in reverse. But David Poole wisely quieted the rebellion by saying firmly, 'It is not our business. We dance. It is not our concern who buys the tickets.' The result was a small integrated audience, of almost equal numbers, which of course was absolutely illegal.

Such are the contortions of apartheid in practice that Eartha Kitt, who had just completed twelve performances to a white-only public at the same Three Arts Theatre, had to transfer to another for the two performances which nonwhites were permitted to see.

Away from South Africa it is hard to believe such absurd manoeuvrings can actually take place, but there is nothing funny about it on the spot. All in all, I was glad I had not acceded to the pressures to cancel my visit. It is easy to do nothing and so achieve nothing. The price I paid by disillusioning many hundreds of people was justified when Eartha Kitt understood and approved my action. 'You like to fight. I knew you were my kind of woman,' she said, and the group of African housemaids she invited to lunch at her hotel – exclusive, elegant and for white people only (and which accommodated her as a rare exception) – wrote marvellous little notes thanking me. I was also deeply touched that the famous coloured poet Adam Small agreed to meet me even though he did not approve my decision.

Pursuing my policy of live and let live, or of dancing and letting others ride their pet hobbyhorses, I later accepted an invitation from the Generals who overthrew President Allende of Chile. So I got myself into hot water again with those who like to tell others their business. In this case I had little sympathy for my accusers, who were fanatics, and I don't believe fanatics make much effort to see all sides of the question in hand.

By chance, I went straight from Chile to dance with a Soviet Russian partner in another country; it was in the week that Solzhenitsyn was expelled from his homeland.

I really don't believe in muddling art and politics. People might want to turn to the first to get away from the second, and I think my duty is to any people who want to see me dance, wherever they may be.

Some of these last tours I made were the funniest and happiest, partly because I felt like a concert recitalist who has played the printed programme and reached the encores. So late in life, I thought no one would expect too much of my dancing, and I was able to enjoy the performances instead of dreading them.

Heinz Bosl, tall, distinguished and with an extraordinary jump, as though gravity was reversed, came from Munich for some dates in Florida. To start with I thought him a dandy and a hypochondriac. Perhaps it was his poor English that made him seem rather solemn. As we dashed from city to city on one-night stands there came one early morning at an airport when Heinz sat next to me in the cafeteria. I said automatically, 'How are you this morning?' He replied, 'I am very ill. I have a fever, and with me it goes very quickly high.' I thought, 'There goes the hypochondriac, but just wait, I'll fix him!' So I said sweetly, 'Oh, Heinz, I'm sorry. I've got a thermometer here. We had better take your temperature.' The thermometer came out of his mouth at 103°, and the next thing I knew I was saying, 'Good heavens! You really are ill. You can't possibly dance tonight. What are we going to do?' He said, 'Don't worry, I will be all right.' Sure enough he was.

How could anyone have guessed that little more than two years later, at the age of twenty-eight, this brilliant young dancer would die so tragically of cancer?

Heinz's English improved rapidly, and he turned out to be so amusing that I found him the most delightful and entertaining companion imaginable on our many tours together, even the last tour, when we both believed his frequent fevers and feelings of weakness to be merely the aftermath of a severe attack of flu. Even then, so shortly before his death, his dancing showed no signs of that fatal illness of which I hope and pray he was never aware.

From our first *Sleeping Beauty* in Berlin, with a minimum of rehearsal, to Heinz's last public performance in St John's, Newfoundland, he was an easy and inspiring partner whose love of dramatic and romantic roles matched exactly my own tastes in ballet. Offstage, his talent for impersonation and his sense of the absurd wove gloriously funny interpretations of the people we encountered and the natural phenomena – such as a typhoon in Hong Kong and an earthquake in Japan – into which our engagements led us. The stories were never unkind.

When Heinz and I danced with the Tokyo Tchaikovsky Memorial Ballet, we met there a very famous star from Russia, Vachtang Chaboukiani. Like most of the other dancers with whom I worked in their old age, I expected Chaboukiani, a once incredibly handsome Georgian with fiery eyes and astounding virtuosity, to be an intimidating teacher. He was instead as sweet as could be. How we laughed to find ourselves walking arm in arm down a Tokyo street. 'Who could ever have guessed we would meet *here*?' we said. He helped me a lot in rehearsal, and whenever I said, 'It's no good. I really can't dance any more,' he would say, 'I understand. I know everything.' And I knew that he had gone through the days of being an old dancer himself. He gave Heinz and me, for a present, a pas de deux of his own choreography to Schumann music. Sadly, we never had time to include it in our repertoire. What a dear man, still commandingly tall, not so handsome any more, but wise and philosophical.

I also danced a lot with Ivan Nagy (pronounced Yvon Nodge in Hungarian), who says 'fobulous' and 'octually'. As with Viktor Rona, my other Hungarian partner, we danced *Gayane* together. The pas de deux ends in what is called a 'po-po' lift, which is quite an odd pose to get into with a stranger at the first rehearsal, and in addition

I was always frightened of falling – though it was nice to be able to assure Ivan that he did the best po-po lift of anyone. I told him about the Turkish trade delegation brought to a ballet performance at Covent Garden. After watching a modern pas de deux for some minutes, one of the delegates turned to his British Council host and whispered, 'Are they married?' Ivan found the anecdote 'hilorious'.

Ivan has rare good manners, and I had to say, as we embarked on a seven-week tour of Australia for Michael Edgeley and Scottish Ballet, 'Ivan, it's all right to be very polite for two or three days, but it doesn't make sense for seven weeks.' He had been so well brought up in Budapest that his manners held for all the tour. He called me 'My Lady', so I called him 'Sir' – the more so after he said it had an unfortunate meaning in Hungarian.

With Attilio Labis I was stranded in a broken-down car at Chillicothe, Ohio, one freezing night. We urgently had to reach Huntington to catch a plane to New York and there connect to Europe. Incredibly, the garage attendant telephoned his girlfriend at two in the morning, and she came for us in her car with her father. The two of them drove us for four hours through snow and ice to Huntington – never have I known such kindness from absolute strangers, and for no reason except that they were marvellous people.

While I was in Darwin with the Australian Ballet, a message came from Mrs Imelda Romualdez Marcos, wife of President Marcos of the Philippines, inviting me to stay with them during our performances in Manila. The cable said that there would be accommodation for my maid and hairdresser. This last bit made me nervous, as my entourage was nonexistent. However, Dame Peggy van Praagh, the director of the Australian Ballet, had thoughtfully put Carole, her press assistant, at my disposal for the tour. I told Carole I didn't dare stay at the Palace unless she came as my secretary. On arrival at Manila airport we stepped straight from the plane into waiting cars to be driven to Malacañang Palace. This made it uncommonly difficult for Carole to leave the country after my departure, because as far as immigration was concerned she had never arrived. The cabled invitation had explained that the First Lady would be away when I arrived, and that Mrs Cojuangco and Mrs Oledan would escort me to the Palace. As we passed by the new theatre where we were to dance, I, of course, wanted to go in. A Russian variety performance was in progress, and I decided to wait and see two Bolshoi dancers who were to appear late in the programme. By the time we got out of the theatre, the palace aide had a message to say that President Marcos had been waiting up for my arrival but had now retired to bed. 'Oh, dear,' I thought, 'that's hardly the best way to start off my visit.' I did not then know what an absolutely charming and attractive man is the President, or what an unusual woman is his wife.

The First Lady received me the next day and, in response to my expression of delight with the lavish rooms I occupied, she said, 'Yes? You see that is called Suite 1. It is reserved for people of Prime Ministerial rank. But I said, "It is only reasonable that there should be Prime Ministers in the arts as well as in politics, and Dame Margot is a Prime Minister in the arts, so she is entitled to Suite 1."'

Mrs Marcos is one of those people who looks always calm and unharassed, who moves with unhurried grace and who crams into one day more achievement than most of us could manage in a month. If one compliments her, she replies modestly, 'I have very good helpers.' Her voice is warm and languorous; she is very beautiful and perfectly groomed. Her face bears no line or wrinkle and, what is more, looks as though it never will. There is something so composed about her that there seems to be no reason why she should ever look a day older. Her apparent lack of exertion is deceptive. As she talked to me in a leisurely way, I noticed that an intense preoccupation with her welfare projects kept breaking through, or rather showed through, her tranquil exterior. I understood that I was with a person of high philanthropic ideals, laced with a dose of good common sense. She passionately loves the arts, for which she has built a fine and practical Cultural Centre. It is worth pointing out that this, and the excellent theatre in Managua, were born of the wills of two beautiful and exceptional women, Mrs Hope Somoza of Nicaragua and Mrs Imelda Marcos of the Philippines, to bring art to their countrymen. They are not the products of urban or federal committees. The First Lady explained that she had raised the money to build ten villages, and that her eleventh project had been the Cultural Centre because material necessities alone do not bring human happiness. She had also thought to build in an endowment for running costs, instead of spending the full amount on the edifice alone.

I was determined that Tito should see what was being achieved in the Philippines because of its similarity, in climate and economic problems, to Panama. When I returned with him three years later, the First Lady's various projects had reached remarkable proportions. The Nutrition Programme, for example, includes a basic daily nutriment for three million children up to the age of six years, to help reduce the risk of mental retardation after birth, and there are innumerable welfare schemes based on teaching people to help themselves. Ex-prisoners are rehabilitated by working on civic amenities such as the Central Park and new Folk Art Theatre. She took us with her to visit the construction site, at two in the morning, as is her habit, to cheer the workers along.

On my first visit Mrs Marcos talked to me about my writing my autobiography. She was quite insistent and added, 'You know that I am very determined when I believe that something should be done.' That was the impulse for this book's existence. It is my way of expressing respect to a woman of great courage and imagination who cares about people.

To get back to ballet business, the year 1975 brought me an astonishing number and variety of surprises, and two sad losses that hurt very deeply. One was Vera Volkova, the teacher I had known since I was a child in Shanghai, an alert and amusing woman who died, as did my recent partner, the young Heinz Bosl, of cancer. Both were highly intelligent artists, the one contemplating retirement, the other still rising towards the height of a brilliant career.

The surprises the year brought me were a small spate of new roles and ballets, all of them coming unexpectedly at quite short notice and gathering momentum as the months passed.

The sequence began in February with a Gala Performance at Covent Garden, at which I danced with Rudolf in an excerpt from John Neumeier's *Don Juan*. Anthony Dowell, who is better known for the perfection of his dancing, designed a beautiful costume for me. Neumeier's insistence on the emotional content of his choreography made the experience of working with him very enjoyable.

Had Heinz Bosl lived, we would have danced the ironically titled *Death and the Maiden* with Chicago Ballet, but we never got beyond one rehearsal in the middle of a taxing North American tour in the spring. Instead, Ivan Nagy took his place, and we did Ben Stevenson's *Elegie*. The Chicago performances brought me together with Valery and Galina Panov, and we immediately became warm friends.

Meanwhile, I was also rehearsing with Martha Graham for her ballet *Lucifer*, especially created for Rudolf. Of course, Graham's dance style is very different from the classical ballet I have done all my life. She had an interesting way of leaving the rehearsal room when I was a few minutes into learning my part. At first, I thought she wanted to spare me the embarrassment of her observation, as I repeated over and over some movements that I could not get quite right. I assured her that I did not at all mind making a fool of myself. Later, however, I thought that she preferred to leave me alone with her young principal dancers to see what ideas they would produce while she was not looking. When she returned to follow our progress, she added her finishing touches to the choreography with a master's instinct for line and effect.

I understood why she has been for so long the leader of modern dance; she has authority, intelligence, individuality and style – in short, she is a star, and the Martha Graham Gala in New York on 19 June was certainly a star occasion. Tickets for the performance went on sale from $10,000 down to $50, and at least six were sold at the top price. Fans wore 'Martha, Margot, Rudi' buttons.

Among other things, the Gala may have been a sort of official celebration of the marriage between classical ballet and modern dance. The two had been quietly living together for some time, with leading choreographers of the modern school mounting works for major ballet companies, and some classically trained dancers preferring to work with contemporary groups, or alternating between the two. This was a very different state of affairs from the old days when 'ballet' and 'modern' were not on speaking terms at all. Martha laughingly told me that she formerly used the flexed foot in her choreography because she hated everything the pointed toe stood for. She added, 'I have grown more tolerant now. After all, one cannot turn one's back on three hundred years of tradition.'

She said so many other interesting things, such as, 'I never think a dancer is alone on stage because there is always the relationship to surrounding space.' My imagination had not run to the possibility of space as a partner. What a comfort that might have been.

Exquisitely and dramatically dressed, Martha dominated her Gala from a Chinese chair beside the proscenium arch, where she announced each ballet. The First Lady, Mrs Gerald Ford, set her own seal of prestige on the evening; Halston made the *Lucifer* costumes as a generous donation to the Martha Graham Foundation; and the headdress I wore, consisting of platinum mesh and real diamonds, was another contribution. One or two diamonds came loose at the rehearsal and fell to the floor in the wings. My dresser naturally thought they were the usual rhinestones and was amazed to see me hysterically scrambling around on my knees to retrieve them. My biggest problem was what to wear on my feet. One imagines that ballet pointe shoes are not ideal, but bare feet are no better. They present their own disadvantages, but the other dancers sympathetically helped me to overcome them. It was quite a new world, and I felt privileged to be received so warmly by the company.

Simultaneously with the Chicago Ballet tour and the Graham rehearsals, I also managed to learn *The Moor's Pavane* in preparation for a season with Rudolf at the Kennedy Center in Washington, D.C., in July; but before that, I was able to squeeze in six Royal Ballet performances, dancing with Desmond Kelly, at the ancient Herod Atticus Theatre in Athens. There, by chance, we met a Panamanian friend of Tito's, whom I had always supposed to be half-Chinese. Tito told me this was not the case; the man had been in Japan as a child, and in the great earthquake he suffered injuries which necessitated plastic surgery. Not surprisingly, the face the Japanese doctors gave him had an oriental aspect.

The various travels and activities of these months left me less than a week in London for Frederick Ashton to choreograph all the dances David Wall and I would do in *Amazon Forest*, a completely new ballet being prepared in Rio de Janeiro to open on 6 August. As always, Fred was early for the first rehearsal. He lit a cigarette and stood up nervously, saying, 'I don't know what we are going to do. I haven't an idea in my head.' Less than one hour and a half later, David and I had a dreamy new love pas de deux, which I find an unbelievable bonus at this stage of my ballet life.

Fred, who hates to travel, came to Brazil and even enjoyed most of the wild confusion of the month-long tour. Each performance ended with a Grand Finale for thirty-six corps de ballet, eight principals and two parrots. The parrots, in a cage hanging near the backdrop, delighted everyone with their vivid additions to the orchestration. (I was telling Sir Steven Runciman, the British historian, about them, and he said that in the nineteenth century a parrot held the Chair of Cornish Language at London University. Apparently, he belonged to an old lady who was one of the last people to speak Cornish, and when she died, only her parrot could speak it, so he was made a professor.)

From among those days in Brazil, dancing to an incredible one hundred and seven thousand exuberantly enthusiastic people, one special day stands out. It goes back to my father's childhood, to the prologue of this book and that mysterious Indian name, Imbituba.

It was seventy-five years, perhaps to the very day, after my father arrived there by rickety coastal boat – my grandmother dreadfully seasick and distressed by the cockroaches – that I landed by light plane (also a rough journey) in a field outside Imbituba, fully expecting all traces of that remote seaside paradise to be obliterated by concrete promenades and neon-lit hamburger haunts. I could hardly believe it true that the dirt roads, the deserted beaches, the little painted cottages, the single-track railway and the old engine sheds were exactly as I had always imagined them. The town is extended, of course, and now has a fine church, but with every step I took, I was sure my father had trodden the same dust and gravel while the soft breeze ruffled his boyish hair. It was a strange sensation, like finding myself in a place visited often in a recurring dream. One old, old inhabitant could recall riding donkeys by the seashore with the English children; the house they had occupied was gone and the site overgrown.

If the glorious *Amazon Forest* ballet had been my last new work, I would have ended my story right there in Imbituba, or perhaps in Panama, where I expect to end my days; but October of this busy year brought another exciting and totally different ballet, *Scarlet Pastorale*, choreographed by Peter Darrell on a slightly depraved plot, with stunning costumes and setting. The opening night in Edinburgh also brought me two more handsome and gallant young men to dance with: Graham Bart of the Scottish Ballet, and the South African Augustus van

Heerden. Someone suggested that all these partners could not possibly be as charming, good-looking and nice as I claim, but they really are.

Of course, I am aware that many people think I should have stopped dancing by now, and I agree with them; on the other hand, there are also many who seem glad that I continue, and they have no need to say so if they don't mean it.

That mundane factor, the discontinued manufacture of pure silk tights, threatened to force a retirement decision – although everyone in the world except me can manage to wear nylon – until the most generous and lovable of ballerinas, Svetlana Beriosova, gave me her own tights when she stopped dancing classical roles. Even so, I would probably give up except that the enticing invitations keep coming in, and it would be silly to retire just before an opportunity to return to Japan or Santo Domingo, or to dance in Guatemala, and, after all, who could ever resist a week in Mauritius?

So I just go from day to day, not worrying too much and remembering one of my mother's sayings when I was very small. 'What's for dinner today, Mummy?' I would ask, and she would reply enigmatically. 'Wait and see when the time comes.'

EPILOGUE

Everything of importance about my life is somewhere in this book. I have tried to write of people and events as they affected me at the time and to present a mosaic of large and small pieces laid out for all to see and interpret as they will. I have not concealed anything. If there are omissions, they were simply superseded by stronger memories which crowded them out of the picture.

People sometimes like to know what happened to the main characters in a story. Sadly, the fate of some of the old ballerinas intensifies my own dread of outliving my friends and resources, to end up forlornly.

Princess Astafieva died a lonely old woman in her seventies a few months after I went to Sadler's Wells.

Olgo Preobrajenska lived on in Paris to the age of ninety-four. To support herself she taught until her very last years, when her wandering mind repeated and confused the exercises. She died in a home with none of her beloved birds to console her but still so physically strong that she stacked the bedroom furniture against her door to prevent strange nurses from invading her loneliness.

The last time I visited Mathilde Kschessinskaya in her villa at Passy, the garden was unkempt, there was dust on the tables in the house and dead plants in the pots. As a result of breaking her hip she walked with difficulty, supporting herself from one piece of furniture to the next. She told me, emotionally, of the death of the Grand Duke André and of his lying-in-state, attended by three thousand Parisian Russians; how she had received their condolences without allowing herself to shed one tear in their sight. An old retainer, an ex-officer of the Imperial Guard. tended the Princess as best he could till the end, which came when she was two months short of being a hundred years old.

Lubov Egorova lived to be ninety-two. She, too, died a widow, mainly dependent like the others on the charity of friends and ex-pupils.

And what of the rest of us? My mother at eighty is full of wisdom and understanding, young in spirit, an avid traveller and beloved by friends of all ages the world over. My father at eighty-five is sweet, patient, meticulous, alert and full of energy – I would say spry. My brother and I are closer than at any time previously – especially since I can now relax my necessarily total commitment to ballet and return to human form.

Dame Ninette de Valois, in retirement, is so approachable that I cannot believe I ever found her frightening.

She is stimulating and amusing with her quicksilver mind never lagging behind current events in life or theatre, and her compassionate heart remaining always with the young dancers. The one thing she seems unable to comprehend is her own greatness.

Sir Frederick Ashton is more lovable than ever. His ear for music, his eye for movement and his perception of human nature make him to ballet as Shakespeare is to drama. His choreography shows us the heart of the matter as no one else has ever done.

Sir Robert Helpmann is always the complete man of the theatre, one of the world's greatest entertainers; it is his life. He has mellowed, like all of us, but his wit is unimpaired and adroitly catches the person and the situation with just the quip to remind us of life's absurdity. The secret of living is to laugh.

These people, together with Michael Somes and Leslie Edwards, are the ones who did most to guide, push, support, comfort and make me into whatever I was, when Tito rescued the human heart trapped inside the ballerina.

Pamela May, widowed so young, remarried after the war. Her husband, Charles Gordon, was another of Tito's close friends at Cambridge, so the 'Triptych' of long ago have come, all three, to live happily forever more.

Rudolf Nureyev brought me a second career, like an Indian summer, and is thus a latecomer to the list of people I am bound to by inextricable ties of life and dancing and the love of dancing. Intelligent, quick, his sense of humour in full bloom, he is now an assured man of the world; working, learning and living with undiminished zest – a phenomenon of dance.

Tito went back to Panama two years after Uncle Arnulfo was overthrown. It was impossible to know how the new government would receive him, but I think the element of danger made the return more tempting to him and, when he found himself left in peace, he decided to stay. We took an apartment right on the sea. The splendid Buenaventura, whose name means 'Good Adventure', was major-domo. The cook, by chance, was called 'Welcome' in Spanish. Sombra, or 'Shadow', was the handyman: too handy sometimes, as Tito told me he was head of the Burglars' Union of Panama. He had been a bodyguard in the political campaign, and he is a resourceful fellow – useful to have on one's side for advice about the best type of lock to buy for the front door.

When I danced with Alfred Novochenok of Leningrad at a college hall in Panama, Sombra mastered a new trick. Standing unofficially at the entrance, using all his considerable gap-toothed charm, he ushered couples through to the vacant chairs; but having retained one of their two tickets, he would deftly resell it at the door. By curtain time there was chaos inside the hall and out. Driving me home afterwards in his truck, with his attractive wife and masses of flowers, Sombra said to me with glee, 'Madam Margott, the theatre was absolutely full to see you dance. Ooh! Do you know, plenty people who came with tickets couldn't even get in at all!'

The Government kept watch on our flat day and night, imagining that Tito still held revolutionary ambitions; but he had thrown them out long ago, after Fidel Castro used his triumph for communist ends. I thought it must be comforting, all the same, for a quadraplegic to know that a military regime considered him potentially dangerous.

In fact, he is a man whose life will not be fulfilled until he has the opportunity to make some significant contribution to the well-being of his countrymen. In this connection, his meeting with President Marcos of the Philippines was the most stimulating experience of many years. The President quickly appreciated Tito's thorough comprehension of his objectives and methods, for, in spite of his handicaps, Tito manages to be remarkably well-informed on world affairs. He is not ambitious for personal power; he is an imaginative thinker and planner; and, in his own words, 'Being paralyzed gives me more time to think.' He is the most clear-thinking, humane, unprejudiced man, with the highest integrity and a wilful sense of humour that combine to make him totally irresistible.

As for myself, I need to have a purpose in life and for that I might sacrifice some of the luxuries that I enjoy; fortunately I am fairly adaptable. I try to be aware, flexible and unbiased in my thinking. If I have learnt anything, it is that life forms no logical patterns. It is haphazard and full of beauties which I try to catch as they fly by, for who knows whether any of them will ever return?